Daemo[n]
server t[o]
message,

mail message with improperly formed Internet address

sender

daemon lurking out of sight, waiting for something to do

daemon
page 47

encrypted message

!@#$&}{&*@()#)#
@!&#*$^@$$"@:>>
!*@&*#   ^$%@!#
#&$&^!   %%$*()
@#":<>   @)#($
$!)%(^**   ^"??>^$
%*#&@($&*#^$%@!
#&$&^!%%$*()@+}#"

data encryption key

decrypted message

Hi Steve
I'm sending you this message so you can test the data encryption key we are going to use for our secret communication.
--Dave

decrypt
page 49

username@address

finger
page 70

flame
page 71

FOR EVERY COMPUTER QUESTION, THERE IS A SYBEX BOOK THAT HAS THE ANSWER

Each computer user learns in a different way. Some need thorough, methodical explanations, while others are too busy for details. At Sybex we bring nearly 20 years of experience to developing the book that's right for you. Whatever your needs, we can help you get the most from your software and hardware, at a pace that's comfortable for you.

We start beginners out right. You will learn by seeing and doing with our **Quick & Easy** series: friendly, colorful guidebooks with screen-by-screen illustrations. For hardware novices, the **Your First** series offers valuable purchasing advice and installation support.

Often recognized for excellence in national book reviews, our **Mastering** and **Understanding** titles are designed for the intermediate to advanced user, without leaving the beginner behind. A **Mastering** or **Understanding** book provides the most detailed reference available. Add one of our pocket-sized **Instant Reference** titles for a complete guidance system. Programmers will find that the new **Developer's Handbook** series provides a higher-end user's perspective on developing innovative and original code.

With the breathtaking advances common in computing today comes an ever increasing demand to remain technologically up-to-date. In many of our books, we provide the added value of software, on disks or CDs. Sybex remains your source for information on software development, operating systems, networking, and every kind of desktop application. We even have books for kids. Sybex can help smooth your travels on the **Internet** and provide **Strategies and Secrets** to your favorite computer games.

As you read this book, take note of its quality. Sybex publishes books written by experts—authors chosen for their extensive topical knowledge. In fact, many are professionals working in the computer software field. In addition, each manuscript is thoroughly reviewed by our technical, editorial, and production personnel for accuracy and ease-of-use before you ever see it—our guarantee that you'll buy a quality Sybex book every time.

To manage your hardware headaches and optimize your software potential, ask for a Sybex book.

FOR MORE INFORMATION, PLEASE CONTACT:

Sybex Inc.
2021 Challenger Drive
Alameda, CA 94501
Tel: (510) 523-8233 • (800) 227-2346
Fax: (510) 523-2373

SYBEX

Sybex is committed to using natural resources wisely to preserve and improve our environment. As a leader in the computer books publishing industry, we are aware that over 40% of America's solid waste is paper. This is why we have been printing our books on recycled paper since 1982.

This year our use of recycled paper will result in the saving of more than 153,000 trees. We will lower air pollution effluents by 54,000 pounds, save 6,300,000 gallons of water, and reduce landfill by 27,000 cubic yards.

In choosing a Sybex book you are not only making a choice for the best in skills and information, you are also choosing to enhance the quality of life for all of us.

The Internet Dictionary

CHRISTIAN CRUMLISH

SYBEX® San Francisco ◆ Paris ◆ Düsseldorf ◆ Soest

Developmental Editors:
   Steve Lipson, Brenda Kienan

Editor: Valerie Potter

Technical Editor: Samuel Faulkner

Book Designer and Desktop Publisher:
   Seventeenth Street Studios

Production Coordinator: Sarah Lemas

Illustrator: Seventeenth Street Studios (Lily Alnev)

Cover Designer: Joanna Gladden

to Briggs

Acknowledgments

I'D LIKE TO THANK Richard Frankel for unflagging technical advice and support, and my family and friends for tolerating my occasional disappearances from the face of the planet when work overwhelms me.

At Sybex, I'd like to thank Guy Hart-Davis for suggesting that the glossary from my previous title, *A Guided Tour of the Internet*, might make a good starting point for an Internet dictionary, and R.S. Langer for approving the idea. My original developmental editor, Steve Lipson, is responsible for some of the rigor in the technical areas of the book, especially those regarding traditional LAN networking. The current developmental editor, Brenda Kienan, helped keep the project on track, and Val Potter, the book's editor, has been a very good cop indeed, along with shaping up a chaotic and somewhat inconsistent manuscript into the coherent, well-organized, and thoroughly cross-referenced edition you hold in your hands.

Sam Faulkner, my technical editor, often suggested complementary definitions that helped clarify mine, and offered some worthy additions to the entries. The book's designer and desktop publisher, Lorrie Fink, deserves special thanks for the crisp, attractive design that I think you'll find easy to use without the sternness of a traditional dictionary page. Artist Lily Alnev took my crude, sometimes stick-figure examples and turned them into charming illustrations. And Sarah Lemas, the production coordinator, managed to proofread the book, keep track of the many editorial changes, and hold the production schedule together all at the same time.

Introduction

S SOON AS YOU GET access to the Internet and start poking around a little, you run into terminology that sounds completely strange. Some words you can figure out from context, but most you can't. You can ask people that you encounter, and most people are very helpful, but some will tell you to **RTFAQ**, or even worse, to **RTFM**. (Boldfaced words are separate entries in this book.)

So that's where there this book comes in. This book is not a technical manual. It won't help you work out how to configure a network. It's a huge list of the most common Internet terms, explained in plain English. There are many cross-references in the definitions, so you won't get lost in a maze of unfamiliar words.

■ Types of Words in This Book

The words in this book are drawn from several interrelated categories. First, there are technical terms, from the broad world of computers, from **LAN**s and networking in general, and from the Internet in particular. Some terms have a slightly different meaning when used in reference to the Internet than when used in reference to LANs. When that's the case, I've given the Internet definition first and tried to make the distinction clear.

Next, there's jargon—terms that describe or are used with the various services available through the Internet, such as **Usenet**, **IRC**, **FTP**, **gopher**, the **Web**, and so on. Included in this category are the names of applications that perform Internet services. Finally, there's the slang that has arisen out of the writing-oriented culture of **mailing list**s, **newsgroup**s, IRC **channel**s, **MUD**s, and so on. These are some of the sillier sounding words, such as **spam**, **troll**, and **flame**.

In addition to words, there are quite a few acronyms and abbreviations. Some of these are shorthand for conversational expressions, such as **btw** and **fyi**. Others are the initials of standards organizations or other official bodies, such as **ISO**, **ANSI**, and **CCITT**.

Finally, there are the names of companies that provide access to the Internet. Their entries are marked with the words [**service provider**] or [**online service**] and they generally include an e-mail contact address and a telephone number.

No matter where the words come from, the object is the same. If you hear, or see, an unfamiliar term, look in the book and you'll find a simple, straightforward definition.

■ Long Internet Addresses

Many of the definitions include references to Internet resources where more information can be found. Addresses such as these need to be typed the same way, letter for letter, or the connection will fail. Some of these addresses (particularly **URLs**—Web addresses) are too long to fit on a single line of text and lack any acceptable place to break. When that happens, we've instructed our typesetters to break the address after a dot (.) or a slash (/) without inserting a hyphen. When typing in such an address, copy it character for character, without pressing Enter where the break occurs. For example, the address of *Enterzone*, a magazine I publish on the **World Wide Web**, is http://enterzone.berkeley.edu/ enterzone.html; do not press enter after *edu/* when you type it.

■ Numbers and Symbols

Numerals and words that start with or otherwise contain numerals are alphabetized as if the number were spelled out. So, for example, you'll find **10base2** in the Ts and **802.x** in the Es.

There's a special section for symbols (punctuation and other computer-keyboard characters) at the beginning of the dictionary, and, like the numbers, the symbols are alphabetized as if their standard name were spelled out.

■ Changes and Corrections

The Internet is evolving so rapidly that a book such as this can only aspire to be a snapshot of the current state of things. Still, a large portion of the vocabulary of the Net is fairly well established and won't be changing soon. Inevitably, new Internet services will arise and will bring their own jargon with them, and addresses for some sites will cease to function.

Therefore, if you discover anything in this book that does not work as described, or if you notice an omission of some term that really belongs here, feel free to send me some e-mail and straighten me out. My address is xian@netcom.com. Please put the word Dictionary in the Subject line of your e-mail. You can find my **home page** on the Web at http://enterzone.berkeley. edu/homies/xian.html.

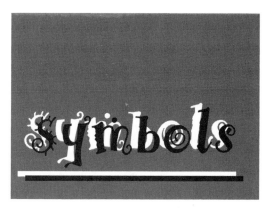

■ **&** *Ampersand.* In **HTML (Web)** documents, used with special codes to indicate special characters (the HTML code for an ampersand itself is *&*).

■ **< >** *Angle brackets,* or *brokets.* 1. They surround address **return path**s in e-mail **header**s; 2. In **IRC, MUD**s, and some e-mail and **Usenet post**s, brackets surround descriptions of actions or expressions, for example, <looking over my left shoulder> or <groan>. Similarly, some use <grin> or <g>.

See also **>>** (double right angle bracket), **>** (right angle bracket).

■ **@** *At.* In Internet **e-mail address**es, it separates the **username** from the **domain**.

■ **** *Backslash,* or *backslant.* 1. In **DOS path**s, it separates directories and subdirectories;

2. In **UNIX**, it precedes **switch**es (command line arguments).

■ **^** *Caret,* or *hat.* 1. Indicates an exponent (for example, x^2 means x^2, that is, x *squared*); 2. Sometimes used in e-mail and **Usenet post**s to underscore and emphasize text on the preceding line, as shown at the bottom of the page.

■ **^]** Escape is sometimes represented by this pair of characters. If you're seeing it, some application is misinterpreting something.

■ **:** *Colon.* In **URL**s, a colon appears after the **protocol** name. In e-mail and **Usenet post**s, sometimes indicates included text.

■ **,** *Comma.* In **Usenet newsreader**s, you can often **cross-post** your **article** to several **newsgroup**s by simply listing them one after another, separated by commas. Likewise, in most **mail program**s, you may list several e-mail recipients the same way, separated by commas.

■ **.** *Dot.* The separator character for **domain name**s, **newsgroup name**s, and other **UNIX**-oriented files.

■ **..** *Double dot.* In **UNIX** (as in **DOS**), the abbreviation for a **parent directory**.

```
pc-lover@online.com wrote:
>DOS is a snap once you figure out config.sys.
                                  ^^^^^^^^^^
But that's the problem with PC-compatibles in a nutshell!
They make you deal with such awkwardly named setup files.
```

■ **——** *Double hyphen.* Many **mail programs** and **newsreaders** automatically include a line containing just two hyphens before **append**ing a signature. Many **anonymous remailer**s strip off any part of a message following such a line to make sure that **sig blocks** are not included by mistake.

■ **"** *Double quotation mark.* They surround **URLs** in **Web HTML** documents.

■ **>>** *Double right angle brackets.* In **UNIX**, they **append** the redirected output of a command to the end of a file.

■ **//** *Double slash.* In **URLs**, the separator between the **protocol** and the **site** name. For example, in the URL http://enterzone. berkeley.edu/enterzone.html, *http* is the protocol, *enterzone.berkeley.edu* is the address of the **Web server**, and *enterzone.html* is the file name of the **home page**.

■ **!** *Exclamation point,* or *bang.* 1. It precedes each **site** in a **UUCP bang path**; 2. In some **UNIX** programs, it enables the user to **shell out**; 3. Overuse of exclamation marks to punctuate **Usenet post**s is one of the hallmarks of a **newbie** or a **B1FF**.

■ **#** *Number sign, pound sign, hash,* or *octothorp.* 1. In the **UNIX ftp** program, if the command **hash** is given, one hash mark appears on the screen for every kilobyte of data transferred; 2. In **Web** references, # indicates the start of an **anchor** within a specified **HTML** document.

■ **( )** *Parentheses.* They surround users' **real name**s after their **e-mail address**es in mail and **post**s.

■ **%** *Percent.* In **UNIX**, job numbers are preceded by %.

■ **|** *Pipe, bar,* or *vertical bar.* 1. In **UNIX**, used to redirect the output of one program into another. For example, the UNIX command *ls|more* creates a short listing of files in the current directory and displays them one screenful at a time (using the **paging program** *more*); 2. In e-mail and **Usenet post**s, sometimes indicates included text.

■ **?** *Question mark,* or *query.* A **wildcard** character in **UNIX** (and hence in many Internet applications), it stands for any single character.

See also * (star).

■ **>** *Right angle bracket.* 1. In **UNIX**, it redirects the output of a command into a file; 2. In e-mail and **Usenet post**s, this character commonly indicates included (quoted) text.

■ **;** *Semicolon.* In **Web** documents, special characters are preceded by an ampersand (&) and followed by a semicolon. For example, the less than sign is indicated by < (because the plain < indicates the beginning of a tag).

■ **/** *Slash, forward slash, solidus,* or *virgule.* In **UNIX** (and hence in **gopher** addresses and **URLs**), the separator character between directory levels. For example, my home directory where I have my Internet account is /u39/xian.

■ **:-)** The basic *smiley* **emoticon** (tilt your head to the left and you'll see it). Often used as a disclaimer, as in "just kidding."

- ∗ *Star*. 1. A **wildcard** character in **UNIX** (and hence in many Internet applications), it stands for any number of characters; 2. In e-mail, and especially on **Usenet**, where **plain ASCII** text is the norm, writers place stars before and after words to emphasize them, like so: "That's what *you* think."

- ∗.∗ *Star-dot-star*. The **DOS wildcard** for any file name. In **UNIX**, just * will suffice.

- ~ A *tilde*, used in the **UNIX mail** program to issue commands (instead of inserting text).

- **$0.02** *Two cents*. Appended to a **Usenet post**, this means "I'm just putting my two cents in."

- _ *Underscore*, or *underline*. 1. Used to separate names in some **e-mail addresses**; 2. Used in place of spaces in the names of files transferred from Macintoshes to other platforms; 3. In e-mail and on **Usenet**, where **plain ASCII** text is the norm, writers place underscores before and after titles to suggest underlining or italics, like so: "The origin of fnord is explained in _Illuminati!_"

- **;-)** *Winkey*, a winking **smiley** (tilt your head to the left and you'll see it). A more ambiguous sort of disclaimer than

    :-)

■ **a** The command to add a **bookmark** in the UNIX programs **gopher** and **lynx**.

■ **AARNet** (*are-net*) [Australian **service provider**] aarnet@aarnet.edu.au.

■ **ABE** (rhymes with *babe*) A DOS **binary**-to-**ASCII** conversion program for sending files via **e-mail**.

See also **BinHex**, **MIME**, **uuencode**.

■ **ABEND** (*ab-end*, n) A computer **crash** (from "abnormal end" **error message**).

■ **abstract syntax** A **syntax** (set of rules for properly formed commands) not limited to a single **application** or **platform**.

■ **Abstract Syntax Notation One (ASN.1)** An OSI language used to

encode **Simple Network Management Protocol packet**s, part of the infrastructure of the Internet.

■ **Acadiana Free-Net** [service provider] bobbrant@delphi.com, (318) 837-9374.

See also **free-net**.

■ **acceptable use** Internet service providers require that all their users agree to some guidelines of acceptable use of Internet and Usenet resources. Acceptable use policies vary from provider to provider.

■ **access** (n) 1. A connection to the Internet; 2. A type of Internet connection (network access, **dial-up** access, etc.); 3. The ability to perform certain activities or read privileged information.

(v) 1. To connect to the Internet; 2. To connect to a **site**; 3. To open a file.

■ **Access Control List (ACL)** A **site**'s table of **services** and **hosts** authorized to use those services.

■ **access privileges** Authorization for a specific level of access.

access privileges

■ **access provider** An institution providing Internet access, such as a commercial **service provider**, university, or employer.

See also **free-net, online service.**

■ **account** (n) A form of access to a computer or network for a specific **username** and **password**, usually with a **home directory**, an **e-mail inbox**, and a set of **access privileges**.

■ **ACK** (rhymes with *pack*) 1. Acknowledgment from a computer that a **packet** of data has been received and verified; 2. The **mnemonic** for ASCII 6.

■ **ACL**

See Access Control List.

■ **ACM**

See Association for Computing Machinery.

■ **active star** A network design (a way of arranging the **devices** themselves in a network) in which a central **hub** retransmits all network traffic (see illustration).

See also **passive star, token ring.**

■ **AD** (*ay-dee*)

See Administrative Domain.

■ **Addicted to Noise** A music magazine, featuring sound clips, on the **Web** at http://www.addict.com/ATN/.

■ **Add/Strip** A Macintosh **shareware** program that inserts or deletes **carriage returns** (**ASCII** 13) at the end of each line of a **text file**, for conversion between **Macintosh** and **UNIX** systems.

See also **newline.**

■ **address** (n) 1. A unique identifier for a computer or **site** on the Internet—this can be a numerical **IP address** (**logical** address) or a textual **domain name address** (**physical** address); 2. A fully specified **e-mail address** (of the form *username@host.domain*).

■ **address book** In some programs, a list of abbreviations for **e-mail address**es.

See also **alias.**

■ **address command** A UUCP extension that provides additional routing and confirmation options to the basic file-copying transaction that underlies UUCP.

■ **Address Mapping Table (AMT)** A table used to resolve **physical** addresses into **logical** addresses.

■ **address mask** The portion of an **IP** address that identifies the **network** and subnet.

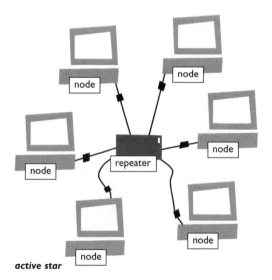

active star

- **address resolution** Conversion of a physical address into a logical address.

- **Address Resolution Protocol (ARP)** A TCP/IP protocol for converting physical addresses to logical addresses.

- **ADJ** (rhymes with *badge*) [**Boolean operator**] *Adjacent to.* A text search with ADJ between two words matches only documents in which those words are adjacent.

- **admin** Administrator, as in *sysadmin*.

- **Administrative Domain (AD)** The portion of a network overseen by a single administrator.

- **administrator** 1. A system administrator (someone who runs a network); 2. Someone who maintains the addresses and handles the administrative chores for a mailing list or other Internet discussion group.

- **administrivia** Information regarding the administration of a mailing list or moderated newsgroup, such as the announcement of a new moderator, posted to the list or group.

- **Advanced Interactive Executive (AIX)** IBM's UNIX clone.

- **Advanced Networks and Services (ANS)** [service provider] maloff@nis.ans.net, (703) 758-7700, (800) 456-8267.

- **Advanced Program-to-Program Communications (APPC)** An IBM peer-to-peer network protocol.

- **Advanced Research Projects Agency (ARPA)** A U.S. Department of Defense agency that, along with universities and research facilities, created ARPAnet, the precursor of the Internet.

- **advTHANKSance** *Thanks in advance.*

- **AFS** *See* Andrew File System.

- **agent** 1. The process in client/server communication that handles negotiation between the client and the server (see illustration); 2. A Simple Network Management Protocol program that monitors network traffic; 3. A program that performs some action on the behalf of a user without the direct oversight of the user. *See also* intelligent agent.

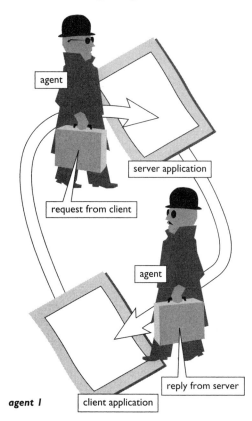

agent
server application
request from client
agent
reply from server

agent I   client application

- **Agora** [service provider]
  info@agora.rain.com, (503) 293-1772.

- **AI**
  See Artificial Intelligence.

- **AIR NFS** A Windows version of NFS
  (Network File System).

- **AIX** *Advanced Interactive Executive*, IBM's
  UNIX clone.

- **Akron Regional Free-Net** [service
  provider] r1asm@vm1.cc.uakron.edu,
  (216) 972-6352.
  See also free-net.

- **Alachua Free-Net** [service provider]
  76314.352@compuserve.com,
  (904) 372-8401.
  See also free-net.

- **alias** (n) 1. An abbreviation for an **e-mail
  address** stored in a **mail program**, allowing
  the user to type or select the shorter alias
  instead of the full address; 2. An alternate
  name for an Internet address.

- **ALL-IN-1** A VAX e-mail and conference
  program.

- **Almont Expression** [service provider]
  gpratt@aol.com, (313) 798-8171.

- **The Aloha Free-Net Project** [service
  provider] mathews@gold.chem.hawaii.edu,
  (808) 533-3969.
  See also free-net.

- **alt.** A hierarchy of **newsgroup**s in the
  Usenet mold but outside of Usenet proper,
  devoted to "alternative" topics. It is easier to
  create alt. groups than to create standard
  Usenet groups, and it's effectively impossible to remove them.

- **alt.config** A newsgroup for the discussion
  of new newsgroup formation in the **alternative newsgroup hierarchy**. Although the
  alt. hierarchy was created in part to sidestep
  the consensus rules of **Usenet**, there is still
  a range of views about what new alt. newsgroups should be created, how they should
  be named, and whether they will be accepted and propagated by **system administrator**s all over the Net.

- **alternative newsgroup hierarchy**
  1. Any **hierarchy** of **newsgroup**s in the
  Usenet mold but not, strictly speaking, part
  of Usenet; 2. The **alt.** hierarchy in particular.

- **alt.fan group** A newsgroup devoted to a
  real-world or **Net** celebrity or villain.

- **alt.plastic.utensil.spork.spork.spork**
  One of several spork **newsgroup**s (a *spork* is
  a cross between a spoon and a fork). An
  example of improper use of a **dot** instead of
  a **hyphen** (plastic.utensil) and of a popular
  silly group ending.

- **alt.swedish.chef.bork.bork.bork**
  The original **silly group** with a *gag.gag.gag*
  ending.

- **AlterNet** [service provider]
  info@alter.net, (800) 488-6383.

- **America Online (AOL)** [online service]
  info@aol.com, (800) 827-6364. America
  Online added full Internet access in 1994.
  The resulting flood of new users, especially
  on **Usenet**, was greeted with dismay by
  many longtime users.

- **American National Standards Institute (ANSI)** U.S. organization that develops and promotes voluntary standards in a wide range of academic and research fields.

  See also **Open Systems Interconnection**.

- **Amiga** A line of desktop PCs, famous for their handling of graphics and the evangelical zeal of their users. Many Amiga users include an **ASCII graphic** double check mark in their **sig block**s.

- **Amoeba** A silly name for **Amiga**.

- **ampersand (&)** In **HTML** (**Web**) documents, used with special codes to indicate special characters (the HTML code for an ampersand itself is *&*).

- **AMT**

  See **Address Mapping Table**.

- **analog** (adj) Representing values as physical states and changes in values as changes in physical states. In a stereo, for example, a CD player converts the **digital** information encoded on the CD into an analog signal sent to the amplifier.

- **Anarchie** (*anarchy*) A **Macintosh** program that combines the functions of **archie** and **FTP**.

- **anchor** (n) An **HTML** tag that indicates a **hypertext link** or the destination of such a link.

- **AnchorNet** [service provider] pegt@muskox.alaska.edu, (907) 261-2891.

- **AND** [Boolean operator] *And*. A text search with AND between two words matches only documents containing both words.

- **Andrew File System (AFS)** A set of network **protocol**s that makes remote files accessible as if they were local (as contrasted with being available via **FTP**).

- **angle brackets** They surround return addresses in **e-mail header**s. In **IRC** channels, **MUD**s, and some e-mail and **Usenet post**s, angle brackets surround descriptions of actions or expressions: for example, <looking over my left shoulder> or <groan>. Similarly, some use <grin> or <g>.

  In e-mail and Usenet posts, a right angle bracket (>) commonly precedes included (quoted) text.

  In **UNIX**, a right angle bracket redirects the output of a command into a file. A double right angle bracket (>>) **append**s the redirected output of a command to the end of a file.

- **annoybot** (n) An **IRC** 'bot that pesters real users.

annoybot

■ **Anomaly—Rhode Island's Gateway to the Internet** [service provider] info@anomaly.sbs.risc.net, (401) 273-4669.

■ **anon.penet.fi** The best known **anonymous remailer** service, info@anon.penet.fi.

■ **anonymous FTP** The most common use of **FTP**, the Internet file transfer protocol (see illustration below). FTP sites that allow anonymous FTP don't require a **password** for access—you only have to log in as *anonymous* and enter your **e-mail address** as a password (for their records).

■ **anonymous remailer** A service that provides anonymity to users on the Net who wish to send mail and **Usenet post**s without their actual e-mail address and real name attached. Instead of sending mail or posting articles directly, users send them to the anonymous remailer, with special **header** lines indicating the ultimate destination and the pen name of the user (if any). The remailer strips off any identifying information and sends the message or post on its way.

■ **ANS**

See **Advanced Networks and Services**.

■ **ANSI** (*antsy*) **American National Standards Institute**, or various standards promulgated by them.

■ ***.answers** Moderated Usenet news-groups dedicated to the posting of **FAQs** (frequently asked questions) and their answers.

■ **Anterior Technology** [service provider] info@radiomail.net, (415) 328-5615.

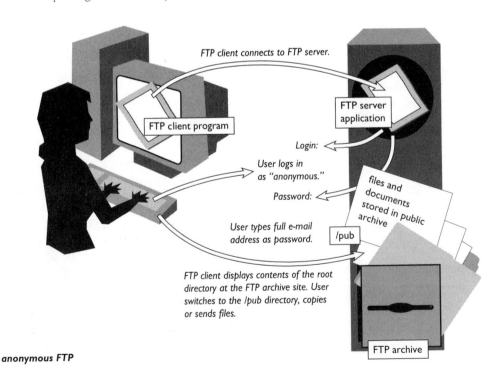

FTP client connects to FTP server.

FTP client program

FTP server application

Login:

User logs in as "anonymous."

Password:

User types full e-mail address as password.

files and documents stored in public archive

/pub

FTP client displays contents of the root directory at the FTP archive site. User switches to the /pub directory, copies or sends files.

FTP archive

anonymous FTP

- **any key** Some programs prompt you to continue by telling you to press any key. This means that any key you press will suffice to continue the process. There is no specific "Any" key.

- **AOL** The standard abbreviation for America Online, from aol.com, the subdomain and domain for that online service.

- **API** (*ay-pee-eye*)
  See Application Programming Interface.

- **APK—Public Access UNI* Site** [service provider] zbig@wariat.org, (216) 481-9436.

- **app** *Application*, program.

- **APPC**
  See Advanced Program-to-Program Communications.

- **append** To attach a file to the end of another.

- **Apple** A computer company based in Cupertino, California, that makes the Macintosh computer.

- **Apple Attachment Unit Interface** Apple's Ethernet interface.

- **AppleLink** Apple's online service for employees, developers, and industry people, @applelink.apple.com; being phased out in favor of eWorld.

- **AppleTalk** Apple's built-in LAN software.

- **application** A computer program that performs a specific function for the user, as contrasted on one hand with a document (which is a file created by an application) and on the other with a shell, environment, or operating system (all of which handle communication between the user and the computer itself).

- **application layer** The top (seventh) layer of the OSI Model.

- **Application Programming Interface (API)** Software that controls communication between a program and a computer environment.

- **April Fool's jokes** Beware strange news or e-mail posted on April 1st.
  See also kremvax.

- **.arc** A DOS file extension that indicates a compressed archive file.

- **archie** A client/server application that gives users access to databases (also called *indexes*) that keep track of the contents of anonymous FTP *archives*—hence the name (see illustration on the following page).

- **archie client** The archie program you run to get information from an archie server.

- **Archie for the Macintosh** A Macintosh archie client.

- **Archie for Nextstep** An archie client for the Nextstep operating system.

- **archie server** The archie program that houses a database listing the contents of anonymous FTP sites, in a searchable form, accessible to archie clients.

- **archie site** A computer with an archie server running on it.

- **archive file** A file that has been compressed or that contains a number of related files.

A
B
C
D
E
F
G
H
I
J
K
L
M
N
O
P
Q
R
S
T
U
V
W
X
Y
Z

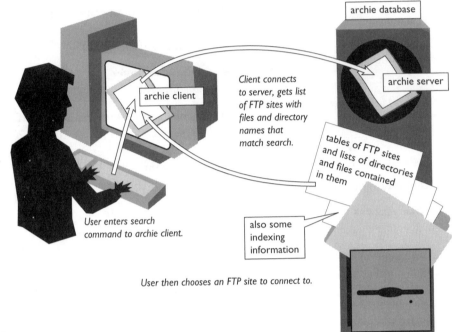

Client connects to server, gets list of FTP sites with files and directory names that match search.

archie database

archie server

tables of FTP sites and lists of directories and files contained in them

archie client

User enters search command to archie client.

also some indexing information

User then chooses an FTP site to connect to.

archie

■ **archive site**   1. An **FTP site**, a computer on the Internet that stores files; 2. Any repository of information accessible via the Net.

■ **Are you on the Net?**   This question usually means, "Do you have an **e-mail address** that can be reached from the Internet?"

■ **argument**   An additional statement (or subcommand) added to a command to modify how it works or what it works on. For example, to copy a file on most **operating system**s, you type a copy command, followed by several arguments—the name of the file to be copied and the name of the file to copy it to.

■ **ARMM**   Dick Depew's Usenet **robot** (ARMM stood for *Automated Retroactive*

Minimal Moderation) intended to retroactively cancel anonymous **posts** and post **follow-up**s. It spun out of control instantly during its first run on March 31, 1993, posting follow-ups to its own follow-ups, **spam**ming several **newsgroup**s, and **crash**ing systems all over the Net. For more on this, see the Net.Legends.FAQ at gopher://dixie.aiss.uiuc.edu:6969/11/urban.legends/Net.Legends.FAQ.

See also **despew**.

■ **ARP**

See **Address Resolution Protocol**.

■ **ARPA**

See **Advanced Research Projects Agency**.

■ **ARPAnet**   (*are-pah-net*) The predecessor to the **Internet**, established in the 1970s by

ARPA, which demonstrated the utility of the TCP/IP protocols. It no longer exists, having been superseded by the Internet.

■ **article**   A Usenet newsgroup post, that is, a message posted publicly and available for reading by every subscriber to the newsgroup(s) it's been posted to.

■ **Artificial Intelligence (AI)**   A field of computer science research aimed at understanding how the human mind thinks and creating intelligent machines that can learn from their experiences.

■ **AS**

See Autonomous System.

■ **asbestos**   Usenet or e-mail posters expecting flames often speak of donning asbestos overalls or other protective gear.

■ **ASCII**   (*askee*) *American standard code for information interchange*. ASCII is a standard character set that's been adopted by most computer systems around the world (usually extended for foreign alphabets and diacriticals).

■ **ASCIIbetical order**   A sorting order based on the ASCII character set that corresponds to English alphabetical order but sorts symbols and numbers before letters and uppercase letters before lowercase letters.

■ **ASCII file**   A file containing text only. ASCII files are easier and quicker to transfer than binary files.

■ **ASCII file transfer**   A method of file transfer by which an ASCII file is sent as a sequence of characters (letters, numbers, and symbols) instead of as a sequence of binary data (1s and 0s). When necessary, newline characters are changed by the file-transfer program.

See also binary file transfer.

■ **ASCII font**   A "font" created out of plain ASCII characters, usually found in sig blocks, often spelling out the writer's name.

A fairly conservative ASCII font is shown at the bottom of the page.

See also BUAF.

■ **ASCII graphic**   A drawing composed of ASCII characters, such as an enormous medieval sword, an attempt to limn Bart Simpson, or a map of Australia.

An eagle (by Yao-Song Ng) is shown on the following page.

■ **AskERIC**   An educational information service of the **Educational Resources Information Center (ERIC)**, askeric@ricir.syr.edu.

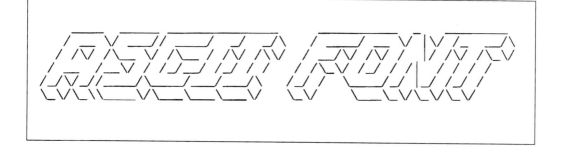

ASCII graphic

■ **ASN.1**

See Abstract Syntax Notation One.

■ **aspect ratio** The proportion of height to width. Most computer displays have a 3 to 4 aspect ratio.

■ **assigned numbers** Standard numbers for **ports**, **sockets**, and so on, established by the Internet Assigned Numbers Authority.

■ **Association for Computing Machinery (ACM)** An association of computer researchers and developers that serves as both a source of technical information and an umbrella group for numerous SIGs (**Special Interest Groups**).

■ **asynchronous** (adj) Not happening at the same time. The word is used both for data transmission and for human communication (**e-mail** is asynchronous, as opposed to IRC, which is **synchronous**).

■ **Asynchronous Transfer Mode (ATM)** A standard for handling heavy network traffic at high speeds. Also called *fast packet*.

■ **asynchronous transmission** A transmission method that uses **start bits** and **stop bits** to regulate the flow of data, as opposed to **synchronous transmission**, which uses a clock signal.

■ **AT commands** (*ay-tee commands*) Hayes-compatible modem commands, most of which begin with *AT* (for "attention"), such as *ATZ*, which resets a modem's factory initialization (the basic settings for the modem when it was created).

■ **aTdHvAaNnKcSe** *Thanks in advance.*

■ **Athene** An online fiction magazine available at ftp://quartz.rutgers.edu/.

■ **ATM**

See Asynchronous Transfer Mode.

■ **atob** (*ay-to-bee*) A UNIX program that converts ASCII files to binary files.

■ **attach** To send a document along with an e-mail message.

■ **attached file** A file sent with an e-mail message.

■ **attachment** A file sent with an e-mail message (see figure below).

■ **Attachment Unit Interface (AUI)** A universal **Ethernet** device that connects to a transceiver.

```
I'm sending you this note icon to use on your Windows desktop.
        --xian


--Press any key to go on.--

This message contains raw digital data, which can either be viewed as text
or written to a file.

What do you want to do with the raw data?
1 -- See it as text
2 -- Write it to a file
3 -- Just skip it

1█
```

attachment

■ **attribute** (n) A setting associated with a file that indicates whether the file is a *system file* (a protected file created by the operating system and not to be tampered with), a *hidden file* (one that won't show up in normal file listings), or an *archive file* (one that has been grouped out of many and/or compressed) and who can read it.

■ **attribution** The portion of a **Usenet** **follow-up post** that identifies the author of quoted text (from previous posts). Be very careful to attribute a quotation to the correct author, or face the ire of whomever you are misquoting. (When **America Online** first made Usenet available to its members, its **newsreader** software contained a **bug** that seemed to attribute the text of a follow-up to the author of the preceding post, which annoyed **oldbies** to no end.)

■ **a2i communications** [service provider] info@rahul.net, (408) 293-8078.

■ **AUI**

See **Attachment Unit Interface**.

■ **Austin Free-Net** [service provider] jeff_evans@capmac.org, (512) 288-5691.

See also **free-net**.

■ **authentication** Verification of the identity of the sender of a message.

■ **automagically** (adv) Happening automatically and so smoothly that the process appears to be magic.

■ **Autonomous System (AS)** A set of **routers** overseen by a common administrator, using the same **protocol**.

■ **autoselect** (v) In **Usenet kill files**, to select automatically—the opposite of to **kill** (to mark as already having been read). A kill file comprises instructions to search for certain key words and then either kill or autoselect the articles containing those words.

■ **A/UX** Apple's **UNIX** clone for the Macintosh.

■ **awk** (rhymes with *gawk*) A **UNIX**-based programming language for manipulating text.

■ **AzTeC Computing** [service provider] joe.askins@asu.edu, (602) 965-5985.

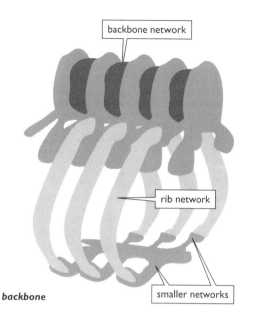

backbone

- **b** The shortcut for **back** in many UNIX programs.

- **back** The command in **paging programs**, **gopher clients**, **newsreaders**, and **Web browsers** to back up one screenful or return to the previous **menu** choice or **link**.

- **backbone** A large, fast network connecting other networks (see illustration, above right). The **National Science Foundation** maintains one of the largest backbones in the United States, **NSFnet**.

- **backbone cabal** A now-defunct group of large-site administrators who set in place most of the procedures for **Usenet newsgroup** creation and orchestrated the **Great Renaming** of the Usenet **hierarchy**.

- **back door** A security loophole that allows a **programmer** to evade restrictions and enter an otherwise secure system. If a back door remains after the software is released, it becomes a security risk.

- **background** In a **multitasking** computer environment, any processes that take place out of sight or with lower priority than the main process are said to take place in the background.

  See also **foreground**.

- **backslash** The \ character, often found above the Enter key on keyboards. In **DOS**

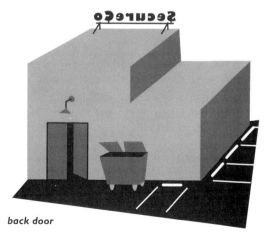

back door

paths, it separates directories and subdirectories; in **UNIX**, it precedes **switch**es (command-line **argument**s).

See also **directory**, **subdirectory**.

■ **backspace** (v) To use the **Backspace key** to move a cursor to the left and in the process delete characters on a computer screen.

■ **Backspace key** A key found directly above the Enter key on most computer keyboards, often used to erase characters to the left of the cursor. (On some systems the Delete key plays this role.)

Use of the Backspace key in **terminal emulation**s that don't support it sometimes leaves the original text on-screen, followed by one ^H character for every time Backspace is pressed. This results in the digital equivalent of an unzipped fly.

■ **Bad Thing** Something generally or widely accepted to be bad. Racism is a Bad Thing. So is **spamming** **Usenet**.

See also **Good Thing**.

■ **balanced line** A cable containing electrically equal wires, such as a **twisted-pair cable**.

■ **balun** (*bal-un*, n) An impedance-matching device that connects a **balanced line** (containing electrically equal wires), such as a **twisted-pair cable**, to an **unbalanced line** (containing electrically unequal wires), such as a **coaxial cable**.

■ **bandwidth** (n) Literally, the speed at which data can be transmitted across a

medium. Also used colloquially throughout the Internet to refer to the speed or capacity of a network connection (which can be described as *low bandwidth* or *high bandwidth*) or network resources in general, something almost everyone at some time or another is accused of wasting.

If you post a **uuencode**d **binary file** containing a 9×12 24-bit image to a talk **newsgroup**, you're definitely wasting bandwidth. But even if you have a **sig block** of over four lines, if you include too much quoted text in your **follow-up post**, or if you continue a **flame war**, you too may be accused of wasting bandwidth.

■ **bandwidth hog** A user or process that consumes more than his, her, or its fair share of **bandwidth**.

■ **bang** (n) An **exclamation point**. It precedes each **site** in a **UUCP** mail path. In some UNIX programs, it enables the user to **shell out**.

See also **bang path**.

■ **bang path** A UUCP *mail path* that specifies every **site** along the way from the sender to the receiver. Although it is rarely necessary any longer to specify the route your mail will take (there are many interchangeable routes on the Internet), mail **header**s still sometimes include the entire bang path back to the sender.

■ **bar** A popular **dummy variable** used by **programmer**s in place of specific terms, such as the dummy mail address foo@bar.baz.

■ **barfic** (n) An ugly ASCII graphic. For example:

■ **barney** 1. A dummy variable used by programmers in examples in combination with **fred** (alluding to characters from *The Flintstones* television show); 2. A large, purple, talking dinosaur (star of the children's television show of the same name) who is praised and excoriated in various **Usenet newsgroups**.

■ **BARRNet** (*bar-net*) [service provider] info@nic.barrnet.net, (415) 723-7520.

■ **Bart Simpson** A popular subject of ASCII graphics in big, ugly **sig blocks**. I hope Matt Groening (cartoonist and creator of Bart) doesn't mind, but here's an example:

■ **baseband** (adj) Signal transmission that uses the entire **bandwidth** of the **medium**, the method used by most **LANs**.

See also **broadband**.

■ **BASIC** A programming language invented at Dartmouth College in the 1960s as a teaching language. (It stands for *Beginner's All-purpose Symbolic Instruction Code*.) Many feel it teaches bad programming habits.

■ **Basic Encoding Rules (BER)** A technique for **encoding** data (preparing data for transmission) defined in ASN.1 (**Abstract Syntax Notation One**).

■ **Basic Rate Interface (BRI)** An ISDN (Integrated Services Digital Network) service that connects **LANs** (local area networks) via 64 **kps** data channels.

■ **batch** (adj) 1. Noninteractive, handled without interaction, as in *batch mode*; 2. All at once, or in a bunch, as in *batch printing*.

■ **Baton Rouge Free-Net** [service provider] anniemac@acm.org, (504) 346-0707.

See also **free-net**.

■ **baud** (*bawd*) Usually confused with **bits per second** (bps), baud is technically the number of times per second that your **modem** changes the signal it sends through the phone lines.

■ **baz** A popular **dummy variable** used by programmers in examples in place of specific terms, such as the dummy mail address foo@bar.baz.

■ **bboard** A BBS. **Newbies** often refer to **Usenet newsgroups** as bboards.

■ **BBS** A *bulletin board system*, communications software that runs on a PC and enables users to log in via **modem**, check messages, communicate in topic groups, engage in **real time chat**s, and (sometimes) access the Internet.

BBS

■ **bcc:** *Blind carbon copy.* Borrowed from the world of paper memos, the blind carbon copy list is a list of additional recipients of an e-mail message whose names and addresses will not appear in the header. Not all e-mail systems support bcc:, so it is not a perfectly safe way of keeping a recipient's identity secret.

See also **cc:**.

■ **BCnet** [Canadian **service provider**] BCnet@ubc.ca, (604) 291-5209.

■ **beam** (v) 1. To transfer a file to someone (from *Star Trek* and other science fiction); 2. To wish someone well via e-mail.

beam I

(n) An expression of support sent electronically.

■ **Because It's Time Network** *See* BITNET.

■ **beige toaster** A derogatory term for a Macintosh.

beige toaster

■ **BER** (rhymes with *fur*) *See* **Basic Encoding Rules**.

■ **Berkeley Internet Name Domain (BIND)** UNIX **name server** software developed and distributed by the University of California at Berkeley.

■ **Berkeley Software Distribution (BSD)** A version of **UNIX** developed and

distributed by the University of California at Berkeley.

- **beta** (*bay-ta*) Prerelease software made available to a small group of testers (often called *beta testers*) in the "real world" to put it through its paces and identify any **bug**s or design flaws that did not show up when it was tested by the **developer**s before being shipped commercially.

- **BGP**

  See **Border Gateway Protocol**.

- **Big Blue** Slang term for **IBM** (from the corporate logo).

- **B1FF** Also called *BIFF*. A prototypical **newbie** on **Usenet**, looking for k00l warez (*k00l* is B1FF-speak for *cool*; *warez*—pronounced *wares*, from *software*—means pirated game software). He **post**s in all caps, substitutes numbers for letters, uses **exclamation mark**s liberally, and has a huge **sig block**—all of which are marks of a **BBS** culture of the 1980s populated mainly by teenage boys.

BIFF

- **Big Country Free-Net** [service provider] davidb@alcon.acu.edu, (915) 674-6964.

  See also **free-net**.

big red switch

- **Big Dummy's Guide to the Internet** The former name of the **Electronic Frontier Foundation**'s excellent free Internet guide, now named *EFF's Guide to the Internet*.

- **big-endian** (adj) 1. A storage format in which the most significant **byte** has the lowest **address**, as opposed to **little-endian**; 2. The way Internet addresses are written in the United Kingdom, starting with **domain**, then **subdomain**, then **site** (the opposite of the standard order on the rest of the Internet).

- **bigot** Someone who believes beyond all rational discussion that one particular type of computer is the best (or the worst).

- **big red switch** Sometimes abbreviated *BRS*, the on/off switch on a computer or any crucial **toggle** switch that, when switched off, will shut down the system. (See illustration, above.)

- **big seven** The seven top-level **Usenet** hierarchies (also known as *traditional newsgroup hierarchies*): **comp.**, **misc.**, **news.**, **rec.**, **sci.**, **soc.**, and **talk.**

A B C D E F G H I J K L M N O P Q R S T U V W X Y Z

■ **Big Sky Telegraph** [service provider] jrobin@CSN.org, (800) 982-6668 (in Montana only), (406) 683-7338.

■ **binaries newsgroup** A Usenet newsgroup dedicated to the posting of uuencoded binary files, often .gif or .jpg image files. Some sites won't carry binaries newsgroups because their uuencoded binaries consume so much bandwidth (and storage space on the news site computers).

■ **binary** 1. Base 2, a numerical system using two digits: *0* and *1* (compare with *decimal*—base 10, a numerical system using 10 digits: *0* through *9*); 2. A binary file.

■ **binary data** Computer information stored in the form of *0*s and *1*s (most program files and image files, as well as some documents, are stored as binary data).

■ **binary file** A file that contains more than simple text, such as an image file, a sound file, or a program file (as opposed to an ASCII file, which contains text only). It must be copied literally, bit for bit, or it will be corrupted. Also called an *image file*.

■ **Binary Synchronous Control (Bisync)** An IBM protocol for controlling communications in synchronous environments.

■ **binary file transfer** A file transfer in which every bit of the file is copied exactly as is (as opposed to a text transfer, in which the text is transferred to whatever format the receiving machine prefers).

■ **BIND** *See* Berkeley Internet Name Domain.

■ **BinHex** A Macintosh program that converts binary files to ASCII files so that they may be transmitted via e-mail. *See also* uuencode.

■ **BIOSIS/FS** A database of biological and biomedical research available through the OCLC (Online Computer Learning Center).

■ **Birds of a Feather (BOF)** An ad hoc discussion group on a conference program.

■ **bis** In modem standards, an enhancement to the standard, but not a completely new standard. V.32bis is an improvement on V.32, for example.

■ **Bisync** (*bye-sink*) *See* Binary Synchronous Control.

■ **bisynchronous** (adj) Communication in which the sending and receiving takes place at the same time.

■ **bit** A binary digit, the smallest unit of computer information, transmitted as a single *on* or *off* pulse symbolized by *1* or *0*.

■ **bit bucket** 1. An imaginary place where extra bits land when they "fall off a register" —the computer equivalent of forgetting to "carry the 1" during addition (see illustration, opposite page); 2. The computer equivalent of the circular file, or the place where all lost socks and pencils go.

■ **bitnet.** A hierarchy in the Usenet mold populated by newsgroups gated to BITNET listserv mailing lists.

■ **BITNET** *Because It's Time Network*, a huge network distinct from the Internet but fully connected to it, used largely for e-mail and listserv mailing lists.

■ **bits per second (bps)** A measurement of the speed of a **medium**, meaning the number of **bits** that can pass through the medium in one second.

See also **kilobits per second**.

■ **bitty box** A derogatory term for a personal computer, from the **workstation** or **mainframe** point of view.

■ **BIX** [online service] *BYTE Information Exchange,* an online service created by *BYTE* magazine. TJL@mhis.bix.com, (800) 695-4775, (617) 354-4137.

■ **biz.** A **hierarchy** in the **Usenet** mold dedicated to commercial and business communication. Advertising is explicitly permitted in the biz. hierarchy.

■ **The Black Box** [service provider] info@blkbox.com, mknewman@blkbox.com, (713) 480-2684.

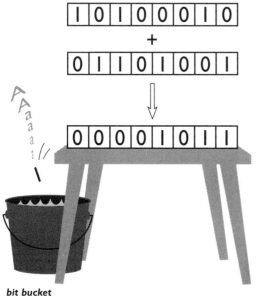

bit bucket

■ **black hole** The place where missing e-mail messages or **Usenet post**s are said to have disappeared to.

See also **bit bucket**.

■ **blind carbon copy**

See **bcc:**.

■ **block** (n) A standard unit of data (the size varies from system to system) measured in terms of storage or transmission.

■ **Blue Ridge Free-Net** [service provider] obrist@leo.vsla.edu, (703) 981-1424.

See also **free-net**.

■ **board** (n) 1. A **BBS**; 2. A computer **circuit** board.

■ **BOF**

See Birds of a Feather.

■ **bogometer** (*boe-gom-i-ter*) A mythical device that measures **bogosity** or **bogon** flux.

See also **bogon, bogus**.

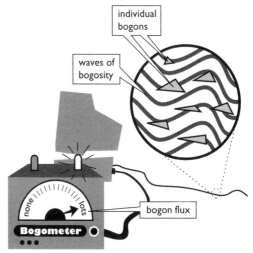

bogometer

- **bogon** (*boe-gon*, n) A mythical basic particle of **bogosity**.

  See also **bogus**.

- **bogon filter** A mythical device that can limit the flow of **bogons**.

- **bogon flux** A mythical measurement of the strength of a field of **bogons**.

- **bogosity** (*boe-goss-i-ty*) The extent to which something is **bogus**.

- **bogus** (adj) 1. Lame, stupid, false, useless; 2. Fake.

- **bogus newsgroups** Silly or joke-named **Usenet**-style **newsgroups** created by pranksters with the necessary **access** privileges.

- **boink** (n) A party at which participants of a **Usenet newsgroup** meet in the flesh.

- **bomb** (v) To **crash**, to suffer from an unrecoverable error.

  See also **letterbomb**, **mailbomb**.

- **bookmark** In gopher clients and Web browsers, a reference to a **menu** or **page** to which you might want to return later. In gopher clients, bookmarks appear together on a gopher menu. In Web browsers, they appear on **hotlists**.

bookmark

- **Boolean operator** One of several conjunctions used to limit or specify a **search criterion** (from George Boole, nineteenth-century English mathematician).

Operator	What it specifies
ADJ	The terms on either side of the operator must appear adjacent to each other in the source text.
AND	The terms on either side of the operator must both appear in the source text.
NAND	The term before the operator must appear in the source text, and the term that appears after the operator must not.
NOT	The term appearing after the operator must not appear in the source text.
OR	One of the terms on either side of the operator must appear in the source text.
XOR	Only one, but not both, of the terms on either side of the operator must appear in the source text.

Boolean operators may be combined with parentheses if necessary to clarify the order of application.

See also **Boolean search**.

- **Boolean search** A method of searching a **database** or text in which **Boolean** operators are used to limit and specify the search criterion.

■ **boot** (v) To start or restart a computer, or, technically, to load and start the **operating system**. The term comes from the expression "lifting oneself by one's bootstraps," because the computer **kernel** must write the remainder of the **startup code** itself each time the computer is booted.

See also **power cycling, reboot.**

■ **BOOTP**

See Bootstrap Protocol.

■ **Bootstrap Protocol (BOOTP)** A protocol for booting diskless **nodes** on a network.

■ **Border Gateway Protocol (BGP)** An exterior **gateway protocol** based on the External Gateway Protocol used by NSFnet.

■ **'bot** A robotic entity on the Net that automatically performs some function that people usually do. Many **IRC channels** are kept open by semipermanent 'bots that stay connected just as real users might. In the past, people have **spam**med **Usenet** by employing 'bots to automatically **post** (**robopost**) reams of redundant text.

■ **bounce** (v) E-mail that fails to reach its destination and returns to the sender is said to have bounced.

■ **bounce message** A message from a mailer **daemon** indicating that it cannot find the recipient of an e-mail message and is returning it to the sender.

■ **Bourne shell** A common **flavor** of UNIX shells.

■ **box** (n) A computer, as in a UNIX box.

■ **bozo** (*boe-zoe*, n) A fool, a kook, a crank, a luser.

■ **bozo filter** A kill file. It allows you to filter out the bozos whose **Usenet posts** you don't wish to see.

■ **bozotic** (*boe-zot-ic*, adj) Having the qualities of a **bozo**.

■ **bps**

See **bits per second.**

■ **brain dump** (n) An undifferentiated mass of information, often in response to a simple question (by analogy from **core dump**, **screen dump**, etc.).

■ **brain-dead** (adj) 1. Completely broken, nonfunctional, usually said of hardware or software; 2. Ridiculously inappropriate, said of an approach to a problem.

■ **branch** (n) 1. An intermediate part of a **logical tree**, somewhere between the **root** and a **leaf**; 2. A participant in a **tape tree** who receives copies of a tape from her parent and makes copies for her children (who may themselves be branches or leaves).

See also **child directory, parent directory, vine.**

■ **BRB** (written only) *[I'll] be right back.*

■ **BRI**

See Basic Rate Interface.

■ **bridge** A device that connects two network components (such as **zones**) that use the same **protocols** (see illustration on the next page).

See also **brouter, router.**

A
B
C
D
E
F
G
H
I
J
K
L
M
N
O
P
Q
R
S
T
U
V
W
X
Y
Z

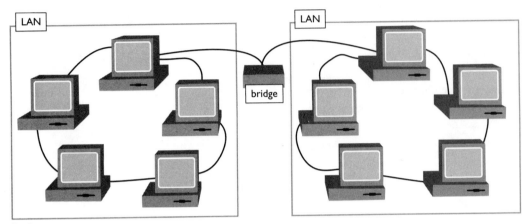

bridge

■ **brief** (adj) An operating mode for some systems and applications in which the prompts and reports of activities are abbreviated or skipped altogether.

See also **verbose**.

■ **broadband** (adj) **Signal** transmission that can carry multiple signals at once, each on separate **channel**s, each taking up a portion of the **bandwidth**.

See also **baseband**.

■ **broadcast** (n) A transmission sent to all **host**s or **client**s at once, such as "System going down in 10 minutes. Please finish up."

■ **broadcast storm** The confusion and possible network breakdown that occurs when a faulty **packet** is broadcast, generating multiple incorrect packets in response, ad infinitum.

■ **broket** (*broe-ket*) An **angle bracket**: < or >.

■ **brouter** (*brow-ter*) A device that combines the functions of a **bridge** and a **router**, controlling transmission from one network component to another (as a bridge) and from the network to the Internet (as a router). (See illustration.)

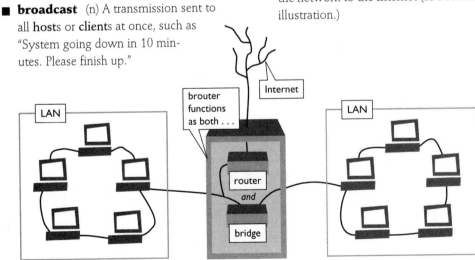

brouter

■ **browse** To skim an information resource on the Net, such as **Usenet**, **gopherspace**, or the **Web**.

■ **browser** A **client** program used to view **Web** documents.

■ **BSD**

See Berkeley Software Distribution.

■ **btoa** (*bee-to-ay*) A **UNIX** program that converts **binary files** to **ASCII files**.

■ **btw** (written only, also *BTW*) *By the way.*

■ **BUAF** (*bee-you-ay-eff*) *Big, ugly ASCII font.* Character sets made from ASCII characters, often generated by special programs and often used to spell out names in **sig block**s.

Here's a charming example:

```
              iiu.
          x@$$R$$N.
     :$$#`     '$$E  @$:           @$~
    W$$`        `$E  $$>       :$$"
   4$$          '$E  '$$L    :$$~
   ~$&          9$!     R$WW$F
   R$k        .$$      `$$~
    #$$L.u$$$~        9$
     `#$$$R~         :$F
                    8$>
                    #F
```

■ **BUAG** (*bee-you-ay-gee*) *Big, ugly ASCII graphic.* Large, often crude drawing composed of ASCII characters, such as a map of

Australia, a medieval sword, the *U.S.S. Enterprise* (from the TV show *Star Trek*), etc., often appearing in a **sig block**.

At the bottom of the page is one of the less elaborate *Enterprise*s.

■ **Buffalo Free-Net** [service provider] finamore@ubvms.cc.buffalo.edu, (716) 877-8800 ext. 451.

See also **free-net**.

■ **buffer** (n) A **memory** location that stores a certain amount of data or text until it can be processed or displayed. A screen's *display buffer* is the amount of text you can scroll back to review (see illustration on the next page). If your computer or connection freezes and you type repeatedly until each keypress results in a beep, then you have overflowed your *keyboard buffer*.

■ **bug** (n) A flaw in a program (from the expression "working the bugs out"). Also, jokingly defined as an undocumented feature.

■ **buggy** (adj) Said of software, unstable, unreliable, full of **bug**s.

■ **bulletin board system**

See **BBS**.

■ **bundle** (v) To group **packet**s of data into a single **cell** for transmission over a **cell-switching** network.

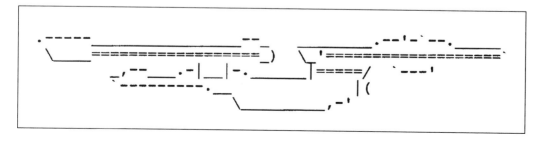

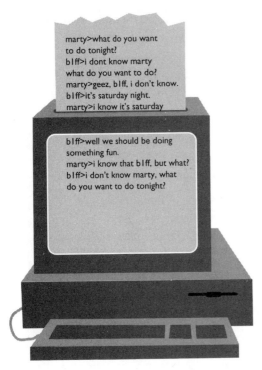

```
marty>what do you want
to do tonight?
blff>i dont know marty
what do you want to do?
marty>geez, blff, i don't know.
blff>it's saturday night.
marty>i know it's saturday

blff>well we should be doing
something fun.
marty>i know that blff, but what?
blff>i don't know marty, what
do you want to do tonight?
```

buffer

- **Bunyip** The company formed by the people who invented **archie**.

- **burble** (v) To **flame** at a very low level of competence or clarity.

- **bus** (n) An electronic pathway or connector.

- **bus topology** Also *daisy chain*, a network architecture in which all **node**s are connected to a single **cable** (see illustration, opposite).

  See also **ring topology**, **star topology**.

- **buzz word** Also *stop word*, a word so common that it is useless to search for it (such as *and*, *address*, *record*, and so on). Most searchable **databases** have lists of buzz words and **filter** them out during searches.

- **by hand** (adv) Executed step-by-step by a human being, instead of automatically by a computer process.

- **byte** A binary "word" (unit of meaning), usually consisting of eight **bits**.

- **BYTE Information Exchange (BIX)** *See* **BIX**.

- ***bzzzzt*, wrong** A rejoinder to an incorrect **Usenet post**, alluding to radio and TV quiz shows in which a timer buzzes when a contestant answers incorrectly.

bus topology

■ **c** The **catch up** command in some **UNIX** newsreaders.

■ **C** A programming language developed at Bell Labs that has become a standard for scientific and commercial applications. C++ is an **object-oriented** successor version of C.

■ **cable** A sheathed length of wires used to transmit signals from device to device.

See also **coaxial cable**, **fiber-optic cable**, **twisted-pair cable**.

■ **California Online Resources for Education** [service provider] kvogt@eis.calstate.edu, (800) 272-8743.

■ **Call for Votes (CFV)** A stage in the **Usenet newsgroup** creation process, after the **Request for Discussion** (RFD).

■ **Campus-Wide Information Server (CWIS)** The information system for a college or university, usually including schedules, announcements, job listings, bulletin boards, calendars, and so on.

■ **cancel** On **Usenet**, to delete an **article** after you've **posted** it. It takes a while for the article to vanish everywhere, as the cancel message has to catch up with the propagating article (see illustration below).

■ **canonical** 1. Deriving from an official source. In *Star Trek* **newsgroup**s, facts that come from any of the television series or movies is considered canonical; 2. Prototypical, to **progammer**s. For instance,

```
10 GOTO 10
```

and

```
Do x=x+1 until x>x+1
```

are canonical **infinite loop**s.

cancel

```
pc-lover@online.com wrote:
>DOS is a snap once you figure out config.sys.
              ^^^^^^^^^^

But that's the problem with PC-compatibles in a nutshell!
They make you deal with such awkwardly named setup files.
```

■ **Canton Regional Free-Net** [service provider] mkilcullen@ksuvxm.kent.edu, (216) 499-9600 ext. 322.

See also **free-net**.

■ **CAPCON** [service provider]

See **Capon Connect**.

■ **Cape Girardeau Free-Net** [service provider] lloos@delphi.com, (314) 334-9322.

See also **free-net**.

■ **Capitol Region Information Service** [service provider] nkurland@albnyvms. bitnet, (518) 442-3728.

■ **Capitol City Free-Net** [service provider] whit@jcn.com, (517) 321-4972.

See also **free-net**.

■ **Capon Connect** [service provider] jhagermn@capcon.net, (202) 466-7057.

■ **capture** (v) To save text as it **scrolls** across the screen. Captured text can be read while **offline**.

■ **carbon copy**

See **cc:**.

■ **card** A printed **circuit board**, added to a computer to enable it to control an additional **device**.

■ **caret** The ^ character. Indicates an exponent (for example, x^2 means x^2, that is, x *squared*).

The caret is also used in e-mail and **Usenet posts** to underscore and emphasize text on the preceding line, as shown in the example at the top of the page.

■ **careware** A form of **shareware** in which the creator of the software requests that payment be made to a charity.

■ **CARL**

See **Colorado Alliance of Research Libraries**.

■ **carpetbagger** Someone who comes to the Internet looking to make a quick profit

carpetbagger

in what they consider to be a ripe, undeveloped territory (borrowed from the American Reconstruction period's pejorative term for Northerners looking to make a quick buck off the war-torn South).

■ **carriage return** A character that moves the cursor back to the beginning of a line (ASCII 13), usually starting a new line in combination with a **line feed** character.

See also **newline**.

■ **carrier** A **signal** constantly transmitted by a **modem** over a phone line as a reference for the modem on the other end of the line. When a line is disconnected, some modems will report "no carrier."

■ **carrier detect** The notice that a **modem** has identified the **carrier signal** from another modem over a phone connection.

■ **Carrier Sense Multiple Access (CSMA)** A **protocol** that enables multiple devices to transmit on the same **channel**, by "listening" for the sounds of other devices and only transmitting when the line is clear.

■ **Carrier Sense Multiple Access with Collision Avoidance (CSMA/CA)** A version of CSMA in which devices can detect impending **collision**s and avoid them.

■ **Carrier Sense Multiple Access with Collision Detection (CSMA/CD)** A version of CSMA in which devices can detect **collision**s as they occur and resend the **corrupted signal**.

■ **cascade** A series of one-line **follow-up post**s, each a play on the previous one. Each post contains all of the previous ones leading up to the latest change, usually in ever-shortening lines, due to the rows of >'s (or sometimes other characters) automatically inserted by **newsreader post**ing commands to indicate an inclusion from a previous post. For example:

```
>>>>>I'm tired and I'm going to bed.
>>>>I'm wired and I'm holding my head.
>>>I've expired and I'm lacking bread.
>>I'm hired! I'm in the red.
>Inspired, I'll quickly wed.
I'm mired in this boring thread.
```

■ **case-insensitive** Not distinguishing between upper- and lowercase characters. In a case-insensitive search, *Internet*, *internet*, and *INTERNET* all match the same **key word**.

The DOS and Macintosh operating systems are case-insensitive, as are e-mail addresses. UNIX, on the other hand, is **case-sensitive**.

■ **case-sensitive** Distinguishing between upper- and lowercase characters. To a case-sensitive program, *Peter*, *PETER*, *peter*, and *PeTeR* all mean different things.

UNIX is case-sensitive; DOS and Macintoshes are not. E-mail addresses are not case-sensitive.

■ **cat** A UNIX command (short for *'catenate*, from *concatenate*) that can **pour** the contents of one file into another or **dump** the contents onto the screen.

A
B
C
D
E
F
G
H
I
J
K
L
M
N
O
P
Q
R
S
T
U
V
W
X
Y
Z

■ **catch up** When reading **news**, to mark all the **article**s in a **newsgroup** as read, to clean the slate.

■ **cc:** A list of additional recipients for an **e-mail** message in the header of the message (from *carbon copy*, a carryover from office-memo shorthand). Most e-mail programs enable the sender to add addresses to the cc: list.

■ **CCIRN**

See **Coordinating Committee for Intercontinental Research Networks**.

■ **CCITT** *Comite Consultatif International de Telegraphique et Telephonique* (International Telegraph and Telephone Consultative Committee), an international standards organization comprising telecommunications companies, part of the United Nations' International Telecommunications Union, creator of the **X.25**, **X.400**, and **X.500** standards.

■ **CCL**

See **Connection Control Language**.

■ **cd** A UNIX and DOS command meaning *change directory*.

■ **cdev**

See **Control Panel Device**.

■ **CD-ROM** *Compact Disc/Read-Only Memory*, a format for storing data on compact discs. Some CD-ROMs contain vast amounts of **shareware** that can be downloaded for free from the Net.

See also **shovelware**.

■ **CedarNet** [service provider] muffoletto@uni.edu, (319) 273-6282.

■ **cell** A packet with a fixed length (in bytes).

■ **cell-switching** A variation on **X.25** packet-switching protocol in which data is **bundled** into equal-sized **cells**.

See also **Asynchronous Transfer Mode**.

■ **Cello** An integrated **Web browser** and general Internet tool (**gopher, WAIS, Usenet, mail**) for Windows. Available by anonymous **FTP** from ftp.law.cornell.edu.

■ **censorship** The public spaces of the Internet (such as **Usenet newsgroup**s, **IRC**, and so on) are largely free from censorship and can be noisy and childish at times. **Online service**s, however, take more responsibility for the contents of their networks and may therefore place some restrictions on what can be written in public or even in private.

■ **central processing unit (CPU)** The heart of a computer, the part that does the "thinking."

■ **Central Virginia's Free-Net** [service provider] kguyre@cabell.vcu.edu, (804) 828-6650.

See also **free-net**.

■ **Cerf, Vinton** Codesigner of the TCP/IP protocols.

■ **CERFnet (DIAL n' CERF)** *(surf-net)* [service provider] help@cerf.net, (800) 876-2373, (619) 455-3900.

■ **CERN European Particle Physics Laboratory** *(surn)* (The acronym CERN comes from an earlier French title of the Lab: *Conseil Européen pour la Recherche Nucleaire*) The creators of the **World Wide**

Web and the first (text-based) **Web brows-er**, **www**. You can reach CERN on the Web at http://www.cern.ch/.

■ **CERT** *See* Computer Emergency Response Team.

■ **CFV**

See Call for Votes.

■ **Chameleon NFS** Socket, TCP/IP, and Internet tools software for Windows, made by NetManage. Information is available on the **Web** at http://www.netmanage.com/.

■ **Chameleon Sampler** A free collection of **socket**, TCP/IP, and **Internet tools** available via **FTP** from ftp.netmanage.com, in the /pub/demos/sampler directory, in a **self-extracting archive** file called sampler.exe.

■ **channel** (n) 1. The **path** along which one **device** sends a **signal** to another, meaning a physical **cable** or **wire** or an assigned frequency of a physical channel; 2. An **IRC** topic area.

■ **channel hopping** On IRC, jumping around from **channel** (definition 2) to channel.

■ **Channel 1** [service provider] whitehrn@channel1.com, (617) 864-0100.

■ **channel op** A privileged user of an **IRC** channel, able to **kick** antisocial participants.

■ **chanop** (*chan-op*)

See channel op.

■ **character** A letter, number, space, punctuation mark, or symbol—any piece of information that can be stored in one **byte**.

■ **character-based** Said of a computer, **operating system**, **environment**, or terminal emulation, displaying screens composed entirely of characters (as opposed to graphical images) and accepting input only in the form of characters (as opposed to mouse clicks).

■ **character-based interface** A computer **front end** which displays only characters on the screen—no graphics, no icons, no mouse pointer, etc. Many **dial-up** Internet connections are to **UNIX box**es with character-based interfaces.

■ **character length** A terminal emulation setting that determines the number of **bit**s in a **character** (usually seven or eight). **ASCII** characters require seven bits per **byte** (one byte per character); **binary** transfers may require eight bits per character.

■ **character string** A **string** of characters that must be handled as text, not as numeric data.

■ **Charlotte's Web** [service provider] shsnow@vnet.net, (704) 358-5245.

■ **charter** The founding document of a **Usenet newsgroup**, it defines what constitutes on-topic and off-topic discussion, and establishes whether the newsgroup is **moderated** or not (see illustration, next page).

■ **chat** (n) 1. **Synchronous** (happening in real time, like a phone conversation, unlike an e-mail exchange), line-by-line communication with another user over a network; 2. The chat program itself, now largely superseded by the **IRC** program.

(v) To engage in a chat.

A
B
C
D
E
F
G
H
I
J
K
L
M
N
O
P
Q
R
S
T
U
V
W
X
Y
Z

It is hereby agreed that the newsgroup named rec.arts.yams.moderated shall be a moderated newsgroup for the purposes of discussing artistic uses for yams.

charter

■ **cheapernet** Slang for the "thin" **Ethernet** specification, generally used in offices.

See also **10baseT**, **10base2**.

■ **checksum** An error-checking method in which the sending and receiving **modems** both sum up the **bytes** in a data **packet** and compare the totals.

See also **cyclic redundancy check**.

■ **Chester County Free-Net** [service provider] jseidel@locke.ccil.org, (215) 430-6621.

See also **free-net**.

■ **child directory** A subdirectory.

See also **directory**, **parent directory**.

■ **Chippewa Valley Free-Net** [service provider] smarquar@uwec.edu, (715) 836-3715.

See also **free-net**.

■ **chmod** (*see-aitch-mode*) The **UNIX** command for changing the read-write **permissions** of a file (from *change mode*).

■ **choad** (n) Slang for penis, popularized by the denizens of alt.tasteless.

■ **Church of the SubGenius** A half-serious antireligion founded by the Rev. Ivan Stang and blending the principles of **Discordianism** with '50s advertising clip-art images and mindnumbing homilies. SubGenii can be found in the **Usenet newsgroup** alt.slack and elsewhere on the Net, often talking about the deity Bob (sometimes BoB).

■ **CI$**

See **Compu$erve**.

■ **CIA World Factbook** A source of basic information on every country in the world, reachable by **WAIS** at world-factbook.src; also, one of the books made available for free by **Project Gutenberg**.

■ **CICnet** [service provider] info@cic.net, (313) 998-6703, (800) 947-4754.

■ **CIE**

See **Commercial Internet Exchange**.

■ **CIM** (*sim*)

See **CompuServe Information Manager**.

■ **cipher** (n) A code that involves **character**-for-character substitution (as contrasted with word-for-word substitution or other schemes), a simple example of which is rot13.

■ **circuit** A **channel** carrying an electrical current between two **devices**.

■ **circuit board** A computer **card** holding printed circuits.

■ **circuit-switched network** A network arrangement in which each **node** is connected to the next via a **dedicated line**.

See also packet-switched network.

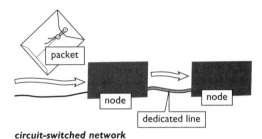

circuit-switched network

■ **CIS** *(see-eye-ess)*

See CompuServe.

■ **CIX**

See Commercial Internet Exchange.

■ **clari.** The Usenet-style **newsgroup** hierarchy dedicated to ClariNet news items.

■ **ClariNet** An online news service analogous to newspaper wire services. If your service provider gets a ClariNet **newsfeed**, then the news is part of your overhead cost. Otherwise, you can get ClariNet news by direct subscription. For information, send e-mail to info@clarinet.com.

■ **Clark County Free-Net** [service provider] tryan@netcom.com, (206) 696-6846.

See also free-net.

■ **Clark Internet Services (ClarkNet)** [service provider] info@clark.net, (800) 735-2258, then dial (410) 730-9764 (MD Relay Service).

See also free-net.

■ **ClarkNet**

See Clark Internet Services.

■ **CLASS**

See Cooperative Library Agency for Systems and Services.

■ **clear channel** A 64 kps **channel** with its entire **bandwidth** available for transmission.

■ **Clearinghouse for Networked Information Discovery and Retrieval (CNIDR)** An organization supporting research and cooperation relating to information resources on the Internet (such as WAIS, gopher, archie, and the Web) and ways to search and retrieve information from them. They distribute **free-WAIS**, a free version of WAIS. CNIDR can be reached on the Web at http://cnidr.org/welcome.html.

■ **Cleveland Free-Net** [service provider] jag@po.cwru.edu, (216) 368-2982.

See also free-net.

■ **client** An application or computer that communicates with and requests information from a **server**. In conventional networking, client usually refers to a computer; for Internet **client/server** applications, client usually refers to a program.

■ **client/server** 1. A method of distributing information or files in which a central **server** application archives (stores) the files and makes them available to requests from **client** applications; 2. A **LAN** architecture, in which files and other resources are kept on a central server computer and individuals interact with the network through client computers (see illustration, next page).

See also peer-to-peer.

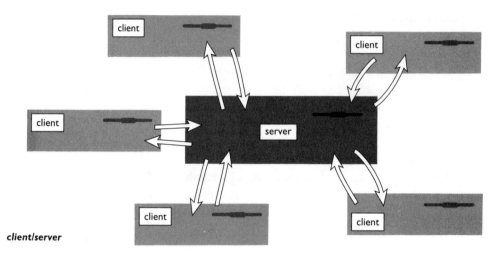

client/server

- **client/server application** A network application that functions with a central **server** as a repository of information and **client**s that communicate with the server and request information on behalf of individual users.

- **clip art** Generic pictures and icons, distributed as **image file**s (or in the days before personal computers, in huge books).

- **Clipper Chip** A U.S. government-sponsored **encryption standard** that telecommunications industries will be encouraged to adopt when it becomes final, according to pending proposals. The Clipper Chip includes a **back door** that would allow government agencies to eavesdrop on communication encrypted with the chip. (The government would need a court order to use the **decryption key**s, otherwise kept in escrow.)

  Opponents of the Clipper Chip are suspicious of the government following its own rules and believe that any individual or company should have access to the best encryption technology available, not just government-approved encryption.

- **clobber** Kill, delete, erase.

- **close** (v) To hang up a **telnet**, **FTP**, or other remote connection.

- **Cloud 9 Internet** [service provider] info@cloud9.net, (914) 682-0626.

- **clueless newbie** A derogatory term for a beginner who POSTS IN ALL CAPS or betrays some ignorance of the Net. We were all clueless newbies once.

  See also **netiquette**, **shouting**.

- **CMS**

  See **Conversational Monitor System**.

- **CNI**

  See **Coalition for Networked Information**.

- **CNIDR**

  See **Clearinghouse for Networked Information Discovery and Retrieval**.

- **CNS**

  See **Community News Service**.

■ **Coalition for Networked Information (CNI)** A coalition of libraries and research organizations dedicated to the sharing of information over computer networks.

■ **coax** (*co-ax*) Slang for **coaxial cable**.

■ **coaxial cable** (*co-axial*) Cable containing two **conductors**, one inside the other, used for **broadband** and **baseband** networks, as well as for cable TV (see illustration).

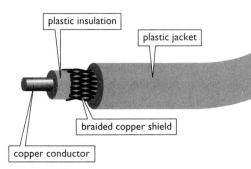

coaxial cable

■ **code** (n) Computer program contents.

(v) To write or edit a computer program.

See also **encode**.

■ **cognitive dissident** The vocation, coined by **Electronic Frontier Foundation** cofounder John Barlow, for those who challenge the status quo in **cyberspace**.

■ **COIN**

See Columbia Online Information Network.

■ **Coke machine** At one time or another, there have been many soda machines on the Internet. This usually means that some device monitors the machine, keeping track of how many cans of soda are in each slot and possibly how long they've been there (i.e., how cold they are). This device then updates an information file that can usually be **finger**ed from anywhere on the Internet. To see such a readout for yourself, try fingering drink@drink.csh.rit.edu.

■ **cold boot** (v) To start a computer that's completely off.

See also **warm boot**.

■ **collision** What happens when two devices try to use the same **channel** at the same time (see illustration, below).

■ **colon** In URLs, a colon (:) appears after the **protocol** name. In e-mail and **Usenet post**s, colons sometimes indicate included text.

■ **Colorado Alliance of Research Libraries (CARL)** An alliance of seven libraries that contribute to a database containing abstracts of thousands of journals. For more information, send e-mail to help@carl.org.

■ **Colorado SuperNet (CSN)** [service provider] info@csn.org, (303) 273-3471.

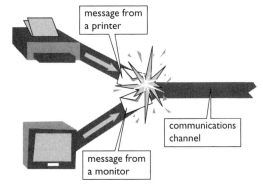

collision

■ **Columbia Online Information Network (COIN)** [service provider] ebarrett@bigcat.missouri.edu, (314) 443-3161 (ext. 350 for voice mail).

■ **com**

See comm.

■ **.com** The Internet domain dedicated to commercial entities, generally in the United States.

■ **comm** Communications (sometimes spelled *com*), usually in the context of communications software, a communications port on a computer, and so on.

■ **comma** In Usenet newsreaders, you can often cross-post your article to several newsgroups simply by listing them one after another, separated by commas (,). Likewise, in most mail programs, you may list several e-mail recipients the same way, separated by commas.

■ **command line** A single line of text, with a prompt, often at the bottom of the screen, where the user may enter commands directly. DOS and UNIX are command-line operating systems; Macintosh, Windows, and X Window are graphical environments that do not automatically make a command line available.

■ **command-line interface** A front end that allows or forces the user to memorize and type commands at a prompt, as opposed to one that allows or forces the user to click graphical elements and select commands from pull-down menus.

■ **command mode** A program mode in which you can enter commands. In vi, the UNIX text editor, users start off in com-

mand mode and will be frustrated if they try to start typing text. First, they must switch to insert mode.

■ **commercial access provider** A service provider that charges for access to the Internet, as opposed to employers, universities, and free-nets, which provide access for free.

■ **Commercial Internet Exchange (CIE or CIX)** An organization of service providers that represents the interest in making commercial transactions acceptable and secure over the Internet. For more information, send e-mail to info@cix.org.

■ **comm program**

See communications program.

■ **Communications Accessibles Montreal** [Canadian service provider] info@CAM.ORG, (514) 931-0749.

■ **communications program** A program that operates a modem and provides terminal emulation so that the user can log in to and communicate with a remote computer (see illustration, opposite page).

■ **Communications Terminal Protocol (CTERM)** Part of DECnet's virtual terminal service (protocols that allow a user to emulate a different terminal type) specifications.

■ **Communications Toolbox (CTB)** A Macintosh tool that allows a communications program to take advantage of existing communications links.

■ **Community News Service (CNS)** [service provider] info@cscns.com, (800) 748-1200, (719) 592-1240.

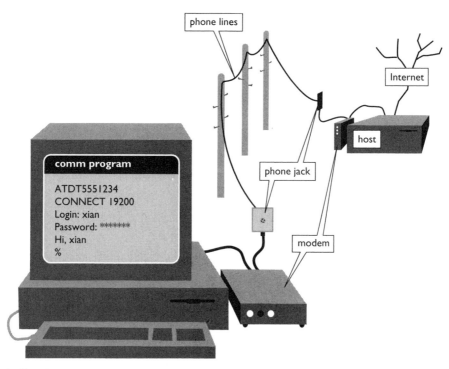

communications program

- **Community Service Network** [service provider] david_boan@martha.washcoll. edu, (410) 822-4132.

- **comp.** A Usenet hierarchy devoted to computers.

- **Compact Pro** A Macintosh shareware compression program. Files compressed with Compact Pro have a *.cpt* extension.

- **COM port** The communications port on a computer. On PCs, it's a serial port.

- **compress** (v) To squish a file in order to save disk storage space.

  (n) A UNIX compression program.

- **Compressed SLIP**

  See CSLIP.

- **compression** A method of squishing a file in order to save disk storage space or the amount of squishing.

- **Compu$erve (CI$)** A mildly derogatory name for CompuServe that refers to its expensive connect time fees.

- **CompuServe** [online service] Short for *CompuServe Information System* (CIS), an online service with partial Internet access. CompuServe has a long-established presence and provides a large number of services to its nearly two million subscribers. Once only linked via e-mail to the Internet, CompuServe is now in the process of adding new Internet features, most recently Usenet newsgroup access.

A
B
C
D
E
F
G
H
I
J
K
L
M
N
O
P
Q
R
S
T
U
V
W
X
Y
Z

For information, contact postmaster@ csi.compuserve.com, (800) 848-8990, (614) 457-0802.

See also service provider.

■ **CompuServe Information Manager (CIM)** A program that provides a graphical interface (or **front end**) for Compu-Serve, available for both Macintosh and Windows.

■ **CompuServe Information System (CIS)** *See* CompuServe.

■ **Computer Emergency Response Team (CERT)** A network-security task force available round-the-clock to assist Internet users with security problems. For more information, send e-mail to cert@cert.org or call their 24-hour hotline, (412) 268-7090.

■ **computer geek** Someone who enjoys messing around with a computer, not necessarily as a **programmer** or at the same level of sophistication as a **hacker**. This is not necessarily a derogatory term. It depends on the context and the company.

■ **computer-mediated communication** Any form of communication aided and abetted by computers, including, but not limited to, **e-mail**, **chat**, and **conferencing**.

■ **Computer Professionals for Social Responsibility (CPSR)** An organization of computer professionals concerned with the impacts computers might have on society. Originally formed to discuss the connections between computer research and the nuclear arms race, it now also addresses such issues as privacy, the role of the computer in the workplace, and research priorities in the coming century.

■ **Computer + Science Network (CSNET)** A computer-science research network that merged with **BITNET** to create the **Corporation for Research and Educational Networking (CREN)**.

■ **Computing Services Office** *See* CSO.

■ **CONCERT** [service provider] info@ concert.net, jrr@concert.net, (919) 248-1404, (919) 248-1999.

■ **conductor** A particular type of wire, such as copper.

■ **conferencing** (adj) Said of software that enables many users to engage in a more or less public, written conversation, either in

VP

VP: I guess you're wondering why I called you all here.

Sales: We assumed the quarterly reports are in.

Marketing: Is it good news or bad?

VP: A little of both.

Sales: Tell us the good first.

Marketing

Sales

conferencing

real time (as on an IRC channel) or not (as in a Usenet newsgroup).

■ **Connecticut Internet Exchange** [service provider] info@connix.com.

■ **connection** There are different types, or levels, of connection to the Internet, ranging from a direct network connection, through SLIP or PPP dial-up access, to character-based shell-account dial-up access, and simple e-mail gateways to the Net.

■ **Connection** [service provider] info@cnct.com, (201) 435-4414.

■ **Connection closed by foreign host** A message during a telnet or other remote login session that tells you that the host you've logged in to has closed the connection.

■ **Connection Control Language (CCL)** An AppleTalk scripting language for controlling modem functions.

■ **connectionless communication** A form of communication between applications in which data can be requested and supplied during intermittent connections.

■ **connection-oriented communication** A form of communication between applications in which all data is exchanged during a single connection.

■ **connect time** The amount of time you spend connected to your service provider. Many providers charge a fee based on your connect time. Others are flat-rate providers.

■ **Consortium for School Networking (CoSN)** A nonprofit organization that studies the uses of networking in K–12 schooling. For more information, send e-mail to cosn@bitnic.bitnet.

■ **conspiracy** The Internet is home to many conspiracy theorists and provides an excellent means for the sharing of theories, rumors, and evidence. Don't try to keep all the conspiracies straight or you'll lose your mind. Some of them deal with the creation and "control" of the Internet itself.

■ **contention** The situation when two devices both try to use the same channel. Every network must have some protocol in place to deal with issues of contention.

■ **control bus** The channel within a computer along which control signals (signals that control a device or routine) are carried. *See also* bus.

■ **control character** A special character, usually nonprinting, that starts or stops a computer function.

■ **Control key** The key marked *Ctrl* on most computer keyboards (the closest Macintosh analogy is the Command key). In combination with other keys, the Control key can send control characters to the computer. It is sometimes symbolized by ^, so Control-C might be written ^C or Ctrl-C.

■ **Conversational Monitor System (CMS)** The command-line interface of IBM's VM operating system.

■ **cookie** A fortune cookie program that spits out a different fortune every time you

cookie

run it. Some systems run cookie as part of their **startup** or **login** procedure.

See also **qotd**.

- **Cooperative Library Agency for Systems and Services (CLASS)**
[service provider] A **service provider** for member libraries: class@class.org, (800) 488-4559.

- **Coordinating Committee for Intercontinental Research Networks (CCIRN)**   A committee that coordinates research networks in North America and Europe.

- **copyleft**   The General Public License carried by **Free Software Foundation** software (such as **GNU**). It grants reuse and reproduction rights to anyone and everyone.

See also **emacs**.

- **copyright**   People debate how standing copyright law applies to articles **post**ed to **Usenet** or to texts in general made available on the Internet. This is thus far not settled law. Some people attach copyright notices to their Usenet posts.

- **core**   (n) 1. **RAM**, on UNIX and some IBM machines; 2. The name of a file that appears in your UNIX directory after a **core dump**. This file contains everything that was in **memory** at the time of the dump.

- **core dump**   (n) 1. A copy of the contents of **memory**, dumped into a file when an unrecoverable error occurs; 2. A **brain dump**.

- **Corporation for Research and Educational Networking (CREN)**
An organization formed by the merger of **BITNET** and **CSNET**. CREN can be reached via **gopher** at info.educom.edu.

- **corrupted**   (adj) Said of a file, block of data, or other communication, damaged in transmission.

- **CoSN**
See **Consortium for School Networking**.

- **cp**   The UNIX *copy file* command.

- **CPBI—Free-Net**   [service provider] steela@csusys.ctstateu.edu, (203) 278-5310 ext. 1230.

See also **free-net**.

- **cpio**   A UNIX command that makes whole directories into a single file, for easy transportation.

- **CP/M**   A PC **operating system** that preceded **DOS**. If someone mentions CP/M, they're bragging about how long they've been working with **microcomputer**s.

- **CPSR**
See **Computer Professionals for Social Responsibility**.

- **.cpt**   The extension of a file compressed with **Compact Pro**, a Macintosh program.

- **CPU**   *Central processing unit*, the heart of a computer, the part that does the "thinking."

- **cracker**   One who breaks into computer systems. What many people in the **real world** call a **hacker** (see illustration, opposite page).

- **cracking** The act of breaking into a computer system.

- **crack root** (v) To break into the **root** account of a **UNIX** machine and, most likely, use the root **privileges** to break into other accounts.

- **Craig Shergold**

  See Shergold, Craig.

- **crash** (n) An unrecoverable failure of a computer system, requiring **reboot**ing as a minimum response.

  (v) To suffer from a crash.

- **CRC**

  See **cyclic redundancy check**.

- **CREN**

  See **Corporation for Research and Education Networking**.

- **crippleware** **Shareware** that lacks a useful or even crucial functionality, in order to entice you into registering as an owner to obtain the uncrippled version of the program.

cracker

- **CRIS** [service provider] (800) 877-5045.

- **CRL (CR Laboratories Dialup Internet Access)** [service provider] info@crl.com, (415) 381-2800.

- **crlf** A combination of two characters (**carriage return** and **line feed**) that on some computer systems consitutes a **newline**.

- **crosspost** (n) A Usenet article posted simultaneously to more than one **newsgroup**. Most **newsreader**s will show you crossposted articles only the first time you encounter them.

- **cross-post** (v) To **post** a Usenet article to several **newsgroup**s at once. This takes up less disk space than posting it separately and repeatedly.

- **crosstalk** Interference between two wires in a cable.

- **CrossTalk** A communications and **terminal emulation program** for DOS and Windows.

- **cryptography** The study of codes and **cipher**s and other security issues.

- **C shell** A common **flavor** of UNIX **shell**s.

- **.cshrc** A startup **file** for the UNIX C shell.

- **CSLIP** *Compressed Serial Line Internet Protocol*, a faster version of **SLIP** in which Internet address information is compressed.

  See also **Point-to-Point Protocol**.

- **CSMA**

  See **Carrier Sense Multiple Access**.

A B C D E F G H I J K L M N O P Q R S T U V W X Y Z

- **CSMA/CA**

  See Carrier Sense Multiple Access with Collision Avoidance.

- **CSMA/CD**

  See Carrier Sense Multiple Access with Collision Detection.

- **CSN**

  See Colorado SuperNet.

- **CSNET**

  See Computer + Science Network.

- **CSO** *Computing Services Office*, a system for searching campus telephone and address listings, reachable by **gopher**.

- **CSO name server** A searchable **white pages** listing of **real names** and associated e-mail addresses, usually reached via gopher.

- **CTERM**

  See Communications Terminal Protocol.

- **CTSNET (CTS Network Services)** [service provider] info@crash.cts.com (server), support@crash.cts.com (human), (619) 637-3637.

- ***The Cuckoo's Egg*** A book by Clifford Stoll describing how he tracked East German **crackers** breaking into a system at Lawrence Berkeley Labs at the University of California at Berkeley.

- **CUSeeMe** *(see-you-see-me)* A new Internet **protocol** for **synchronous** video and sound communication.

- **CWIS**

  See Campus-Wide Information Server.

- **c-ya** (written only) *See you [later]*.

- **cyber-** A prefix overused to indicate a connection to computers, networks, technology, or futurism.

cyber-

- **cyberchat**

  See IRC.

- **cyberdelics** 1. Mind-altering effects brought about by computer technology (as opposed to hallucinogenic drugs); 2. Eye-bending screen savers.

- **CyberGate, Inc.** [service provider] info@gate.net or sales@gate.net, (305) 428-GATE.

- **cybernaut** A traveler in **cyberspace**, someone who uses their Internet connection to explore the furthest realms of cyberspace.

- **cyberpunk** 1. A largely hype-driven category of popular culture at the crossroads of computer technology, science fiction, and youth culture; 2. A genre of science fiction that appeared in the mid-to-late '80s and combined a bleak, noirish view of the future with a fetishization of technology and human-computer interaction.

■ **cyberspace** A term, popularized by author William Gibson, for the shared imaginary reality of computer networks. Some people use cyberspace as a synonym for the Internet. Others hold out for the more complete physical-seeming con-sensual reality of Gibson's novels.

■ **The Cyberspace Station** [service provider] help@cyber.net, (619) 944-9498 ext. 626.

■ **cycle power** (v) To turn a computer off and then on again.

■ **cyclic redundancy check (CRC)** An error-detection technique used during file transfers and other forms of data transmission. Both the sending and receiving **modem**s perform calculations on the data and then the two results are compared.

See also **checksum**.

■ **cypherpunk** An activist interested in the political potentials of universal Internet access and cheap, foolproof privacy.

A
B
C
D
E
F
G
H
I
J
K
L
M
N
O
P
Q
R
S
T
U
V
W
X
Y
Z

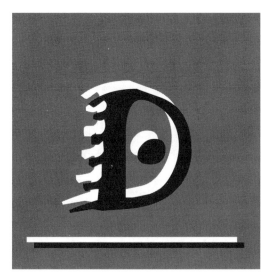

■ **daemon** (*day-min*) In **UNIX** and other operating systems, a program that runs all the time, in the **background,** waiting for things to do (possibly from **Maxwell's Demon**). When you **post** an **article** to a *.test **newsgroup,** daemons all over the world send you e-mail confirmations when they receive your post.

See also **demon.**

■ **daisy chain** A network architecture, also called *bus topology*, in which all **nodes** are connected to a single **cable** (see illustration).

daisy chain

■ **Dakota Internet Services** [service provider] dtarrel@dakota.net, (605) 371-1962.

■ **Danbury Area Free-Net** [service provider] waldgreen@bix.com, (203) 797-4512.

See also **free-net.**

■ **DAP**

See **Directory Access Protocol.**

■ **dark fiber** Unused cable in the fiber-optic network.

See also **fiber-optic cable.**

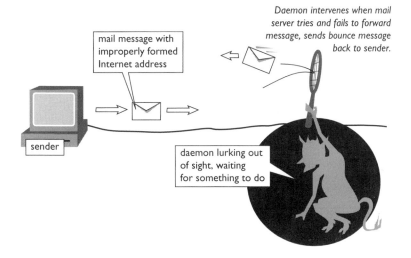

daemon

Daemon intervenes when mail server tries and fails to forward message, sends bounce message back to sender.

mail message with improperly formed Internet address

sender

daemon lurking out of sight, waiting for something to do

- **DARPA** *Defense Advanced Research Projects Agency*, the official name of **ARPA** during the 1980s and early 1990s.

- **DASNET** [service provider] postmaster@das.net, (408) 559-7434.

- **data** Information of any type, usually information stored, transmitted, or processed by computers.

- **database** A repository of information stored on a computer and accessible to searches.

- **Data Basix** [service provider] info@ Data.Basix.com (automated), sales@Data. Basix.com (human), (602) 721-1988.

- **data bits** In **asynchronous** data transmission, the **bit**s between a **start bit** (and sometimes a **parity bit**) and a **stop bit**, the only bits actually carrying data. There are usually seven or eight data bits, depending on the size of a **character**, or **byte**.

  Data bits is therefore one of the settings you have to specify on your **modem** to make a connection. Usually 7 or 8, it depends on the modem you're calling.

  See also **parity**.

- **data block** A unit of data sent from one device to another.

- **data bus** The **channel** within a computer along which communication signals are carried.

  See also **bus**.

- **data channel** Any **channel** over which **data** is sent in the form of a **signal**.

- **data communications equipment (DCE)** Devices such as **modem**s that

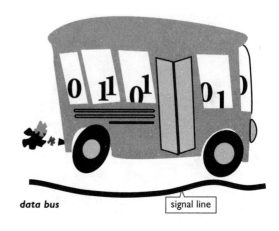

data bus   signal line

connect to a **serial port** and control data communications.

- **data encryption key (DEK)** An element of **key encryption** that is used to encrypt and decrypt data.

  See also **encryption**.

- **data encryption standard (DES)** A security **protocol** defined by the U.S. government.

  See also **encryption**.

- **data/fax modem** A modem that can transmit raw data or a **fax** image.

- **datagram** The basic unit of data transmission across a network, containing a **header**

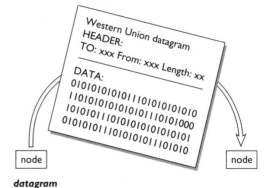

Western Union datagram
HEADER:
TO: xxx From: xxx Length: xx

DATA:
0l0l0l0l0l0l||0l0l0l0l0l0
||0l0l0l0l0l0l0l||0l0l0l0l0
l0l0l0l||0l0l0l0l0l||0l0l000
l0l0l0l||0l0l0l0l0l0l0l0l0l
0l0l0l0l||0l0l0l0l0l||l0l0l0

node   node

datagram

and the data itself. The header describes the data, its destination, and its relationship to other datagrams.

■ **Datagram Delivery Protocol (DDP)** An **AppleTalk protocol** that handles the routing of **datagram**s over an AppleTalk network.

■ **data link** 1. The device that enables data transmission; 2. An active connection for data transmission.

■ **data link layer** The second layer of the **OSI Model** that deals with transmission of data **frame**s from **node** to node.

■ **data stream** A series of **data block**s sent from one device to another.

■ **data terminal equipment (DTE)** A device at one end or the other of a data transmission. This usually means a PC or terminal.

■ **Davis Community Network** [service provider] acmansker@ucdavis.edu, (916) 752-7764.

■ **Dayton Free-Net** [service provider] pvendt@desire.wright.edu, (513) 873-4035.

■ **DCE**
See data communications equipment or Distributed Computing Environment.

■ **.dd** The **extension** of a file **compress**ed with DiskDoubler on the Macintosh.

■ **DDCMP**
See Digital Data Communications Message Protocol.

■ **DDN**
See Defense Data Network.

■ **DDN NIC** *See* Defense Data Network Network Information Center.

■ **DDP**
See Datagram Delivery Protocol.

■ **DEC** *(deck)* *Digital Equipment Corporation*, manufacturer of **VAX** (and before that PDP-11) **box**es and the **VMS** operating system.

■ **DEChead** *(deck-head)* 1. An employee of **Digital Equipment Corporation**; 2. A Deadhead (Grateful Dead fan) employee of DEC.

■ **DECnet** *(deck-net)* Network **protocol**s designed for **VAX** and PDP-11 computers, used by **Digital Equipment Corporation** operating systems instead of **TCP/IP**.

■ **DECnet/DNA** DEC's implementation of DNA (**Digital Network Architecture**).

■ **DECnet tunnel** A **protocol** for packaging **AppleTalk datagram**s within **DECnet packet**s.

■ **decrypt** To remove the **encryption** from a file or e-mail message and make it readable (see illustration on the following page).
See also **decryption key, encryption**.

■ **decryption key** In key encryption, a **key** used to decipher an **encrypt**ed message and make it readable.
See also **private key, public key**.

■ **dedicated** (adj) Assigned to a single task or able to perform only a single task.

■ **dedicated line** A telephone line dedicated to telecommunications.

decrypt

■ **deep hack** The extreme state of concentration, bordering on a trance, that **hackers** enter after long hours of hacking.

deep hack

■ **default** (n) A setting, state, instruction, or selection that a program uses unless you explicitly change it.

■ **default route** An entry in a **routing table** indicating where to route **packets** intended for destinations not otherwise listed in the table.

■ **Defense Data Network (DDN)** The network of networks used by the U.S. military, connecting with the Internet in some places and not in others.

■ **Defense Data Network Network Information Center (DDN NIC)** The Network Information Center for the DDN, a source of information as well as an administrative authority over the DDN.

■ **Defense Information Systems Agency (DISA)** The U.S. government agency that oversees the **Defense Data Network**.

■ **DEK**

   See data encryption key.

■ **delete** (v) To erase a character, file, or directory.

■ **Delete key** A key used in most environments to erase the character that the cursor or insertion point is on or just before. On some systems, Delete erases the character just typed or to the left of the cursor.

■ **delimiter** A character or symbol that indicates a break between two pieces of information, items in a table, or fields in a database.

■ **Delphi Information Service** [online service] An online service with full Internet access; walthowe@delphi.com, (800) 544-4005, (800) 695-4005, (617) 491-3393.

See also **service provider**.

■ **delurk** (*dee-lurk*, v) To **post** to a **list** or **newsgroup** for the first time.

(n) A first post to a newsgroup or list after the writer has **lurk**ed for a while.

■ **demon** A routine in a program that waits until it is needed (possibly from **Maxwell's Demon**).

See also **daemon**.

■ **Demon Internet Services** [U.K. service provider] internet@demon.co.uk, 081-371-1234.

■ **Denver Free-Net** [service provider] drew@freenet.hsc.colorado.edu, (303) 270-4300.

See also **free-net**.

■ **Department of Defense**

See **U.S. Department of Defense**.

■ **Depew, Dick** The inventor of **ARMM**, a **roboposting** utility designed to retroactively cancel off-topic **Usenet posts**. Depew's 'bot had a serious flaw and followed up its own posts, eventually bringing down part of the Internet in **sorcerer's apprentice mode**.

See also **despew**.

■ **deprecated** (adj) Being phased out in favor of a new **standard**.

■ **DES**

See **data encryption standard**.

■ **despew** (v) From [Dick] **Depew**, to **robopost** reams of junk to the Net.

See also **ARMM**, **spam**.

■ **developer** A software publisher.

■ **device** Any piece of computer equipment, though the term is often used to specify **peripheral** devices.

■ **/dev/null** On **UNIX** boxes, the **null** device. Data **piped** to /dev/null disappears. People **posting** controversial articles to **Usenet** sometimes add the notice "flames to /dev/null."

■ **dial up** (v) To use a **modem** to call up another computer or network and **log in** to it.

■ **dial-up** (adj) Said of an Internet access that requires the user to connect via a **modem**.

■ **dial-up account** An Internet **account** on a **host** machine that you must **dial up** with your **modem** to use.

■ **DIALOG Information Retrieval Database** A commercial online database service with hundreds of databases and millions of records. To connect to DIALOG, **telnet** to dialog.com.

■ **dictionary flame** A **flame** that focuses on someone's use of a particular word or their vocabulary, a weak sort of flame that indicates that the flamer has nothing substantial to say against the flamee.

■ **digest** (n) A collection of **mailing list** posts, sent out as one message.

■ **digestified** (adj) Turned into a **digest**. Not all **mailing list**s are available in a digestified form.

■ **digital** (adj) Representing values as discrete **bits**. CD is a digital medium because the sound or other information is *digitized* (converted into bits) and then stored. A CD player converts the digital information encoded on the CD into an **analog** signal sent to the amplifier.

■ **Digital Data Communications Message Protocol (DDCMP)** A DECnet data link protocol that can handle both **synchronous** and **asynchronous** links.

■ **Digital Equipment Corporation (DEC)** Manufacturer of **VAX** (and before that PDP-11) boxes and the **VMS** operating system.

■ **Digital Network Architecture (DNA)** A set of **protocol**s for network architecture.

■ **DIP** *Dual in-line package*, the housing for an **integrated circuit**.

■ **DIP switch** A switch used to select the operating **mode** of a **device**.

■ **directed information** Information intended for a particular recipient, such as private e-mail.

See also **undirected information**.

■ **directory** An organizing structure for files. In most **operating system**s, directories can themselves be organized hierarchically into a "tree" of parent and children directories (see illustration below).

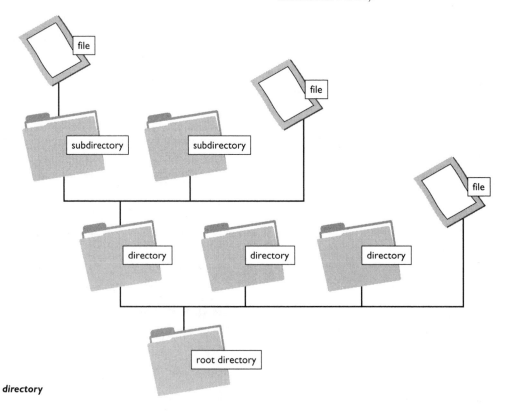

directory

■ **Directory Access Protocol (DAP)** An X.500 protocol governing communication between a Directory User Agent and a Directory System Agent.

■ **directory listing** A summary list of available files, possibly including file sizes, attributes, date and time of creation or last changes, and the owner, where appropriate.

■ **directory service** A database of sites and usernames that enables users to locate other users, hosts, and services.

■ **Directory System Agent (DSA)** X.500 software that serves directory information to Directory User Agents.

■ **Directory User Agent (DUA)** X.500 software that queries a Directory System Agent for directory information.

■ **DISA**

See Defense Information Systems Agency.

■ **disable** To temporarily disconnect or make nonfunctional (without necessarily shutting off).

■ **disclaimer** The line in some sig blocks asserting that the opinions of the writer are

>thus my 10 years of research culminate
>in these findings.

I agree!
 --jojo

--
jojo@yoyodyne.com
Joey Joe-Joe "Junior" Shabadoo

The opinions in this message are those
of Joey Joe-Joe Jr.'s and not those of
Yoyodyne, Inc., unless explicitly stated.

disclaimer

not necessarily those of the organization providing her Internet access.

■ **Discordianism** The principles of the Discordian Society, as set down in the *Principia Discordia* and other sacred (or profane) texts.

See also Church of the SubGenius, fnord.

■ **Discordian Society** Followers of the goddess Eris (or Discordia), a mostly farcical organization spawned from Robert Anton Wilson's *Illuminati!* trilogy.

See also Church of the SubGenius, fnord.

■ **discussion group** Any online group of likeminded people who may communicate via a mailing list, in a newsgroup, on an IRC channel, etc.

■ **disk** A medium for storing computer data, either built into the computer (a hard disk) or removable (a floppy disk).

■ **disk drive** The mechanism that spins, reads from, and writes to the disk itself.

■ **diskette** A 5¼" or 3½" removable floppy disk used for storing data.

■ **Disk Operating System**

See DOS.

■ **disk server** A network program that enables a computer to use a disk drive on another computer (or a partition of such a disk drive) as if it were a local disk drive.

■ **display buffer**

See buffer.

■ **Distinct TCP/IP Tools** A set of Internet tools for Windows sold by Distinct Corporation.

See also TCP/IP.

A
B
C
D
E
F
G
H
I
J
K
L
M
N
O
P
Q
R
S
T
U
V
W
X
Y
Z

■ **distributed computing** An approach to computing that allows applications to run the same way across different types of networks.

■ **Distributed Computing Environment (DCE)** A set of standards for servers, interfaces, and protocols promoted by the Open Software Foundation to enable distributed computing.

■ **distributed database** A repository of information stored on various hosts and accessible to searches as if stored in a single location.

■ **distributed server** Peer-to-peer network architecture, in which server functions are shared among the peer computers in the network, and disk drives, printers, and other devices are available to all.

■ **distribution** The geographic range that a Usenet post is distributed to. By default, most newsreaders will give posts *World* distribution.

■ **distribution list** A simple form of mailing list in which an alias is assigned to a list of e-mail addresses. Mail directed to the alias is sent to every address on the list.

■ **disusered** (adj) Denied access to the Net, having an account canceled.

■ **DIX** *Digital, Intel, and Xerox,* together the developers of the Ethernet protocol.

■ **DIX Ethernet**
See Ethernet.

■ **DNA**
See Digital Network Architecture.

■ **DNS**
See Domain Name System.

■ **doc** Slang for a document.

■ **documentation** Paper or online manuals that describe the functions of a computer system, often in incomprehensible terms.

■ **DoD**
See U.S. Department of Defense.

■ **dogpile** (v) To quickly follow up a Usenet post with a large volume of critical replies.

dogpile

■ **domain** The main subdivision of Internet addresses, the last part of an Internet address after the final dot. In the United States, the standard domains are as follows:

Domain	Meaning
.com	Commercial
.edu	Educational
.gov	Government
.mil	Military
.org	Non-profit organization
.net	Network

Outside the United States, the top-level domain is usually the country domain, such as *.ca* for Canada, *.de* for Germany (Deutschland), *.uk* for the United Kingdom, and so on.

See also domain name, locative domain name, subdomain.

■ **domain name** A complete description of an Internet site including a host name, subdomain, and domain, all separated by dots.

■ **domain name address** An Internet address expressed in terms of host, subdomain, and domain, as opposed to the numerical IP address. Also called a *fully qualified domain name*.

■ **domain name resolution** The process of converting domain names to numerical IP addresses, by consulting domain name servers.

■ **domain name server** An application that maintains a table of domain names and corresponding IP addresses in order to resolve the domain names of messages.

■ **Domain Name System (DNS)** A collection of distributed databases (domain name servers) that maintain the correlations between domain name addresses and numerical IP addresses, for example, the domain name address ruby.ora.com gets resolved into the numeric Internet address 134.65.87.3, and vice versa. DNS allows human beings to use the Internet without remembering long lists of numbers.

■ **d00dz** B1FFspeak for *dudes*, a term of address.

See also warez.

■ **DOS** *Disk Operating System*, the operating system developed for IBM PCs.

■ **dos2unix** A UNIX program that converts DOS text files to UNIX format (by stripping the carriage return character from the end of each line).

See also unix2dos.

■ **dot** The separator character for domain names, newsgroup names, and other UNIX-oriented files. Dots should only be used to separate hierarchical levels in newsgroup names, not to split compound names. So, for example, alt.fan.dave.barry would be improper, but alt.fan.dave-barry is fine.

■ **dot address** A 32-bit numerical IP address of the form *number-dot-number-dot-number-dot-number* (such as 192.100.81.101). Each of the four numbers can range from 0 to 255.

■ **dot file** A UNIX file whose name begins with a dot, such as .profile, .netrc, .cshrc, and so on. Dot files will not show up in a normal directory listing.

■ **dotted decimal notation**

See dot address.

■ **dotted quad**

See dot address.

■ **double dot** .., an abbreviation for the parent directory of the current directory in both UNIX and DOS.

■ **doubled sig** A sig block that appears twice at the end the of an e-mail message or Usenet post, a sign that the writer is a newbie or that the software is hiccupping. (See illustration, next page.)

■ **down** (adj) Said of a network or device that is not functioning.

A B C D E F G H I J K L M N O P Q R S T U V W X Y Z

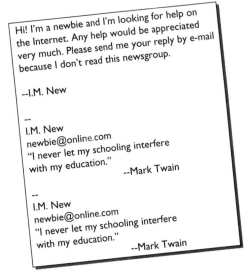

Hi! I'm a newbie and I'm looking for help on the Internet. Any help would be appreciated very much. Please send me your reply by e-mail because I don't read this newsgroup.

--I.M. New

--
I.M. New
newbie@online.com
"I never let my schooling interfere with my education."
                              --Mark Twain

--
I.M. New
newbie@online.com
"I never let my schooling interfere with my education."
                              --Mark Twain

doubled sig

- **download** To transfer a file over a **modem** from a remote computer to your desktop computer. (Technically, to transfer a file from a larger computer to a smaller computer.)

- **downstream** Where your **newsfeed** goes after it has reached your **host** and your host has sent it along to other **sites**.

  See also **upstream**.

- **DRECnet** A derogatory name for DECnet.

- **driver** Software that controls peripheral devices, such as monitors, printers, or keyboards.

- **drop-ins** Random characters that appear on the screen due to a faulty connection and/or **line noise**.

- **drop-outs** Characters that are missing from the screen or not passed on by the keyboard.

- **DSA**

  See **Directory System Agent**.

- **DS4** *Digital Signal Level 4* is 274.176 Mbps, a standard level of digital transmission service (also called **T4**).

- **DS1** *Digital Signal Level 1* is 1.544 Mbps, a standard level of digital transmission service (also called **T1**).

- **DS3** *Digital Signal Level 3* is 44.736 Mbps, a standard level of digital transmission service (also called **T3**).

- **DS2** *Digital Signal Level 2* is 6.312 Mbps, a standard level of digital transmission service (also called **T2**).

- **DS0** *Digital Signal Level 0* is 64 Kbps, a standard level of digital transmission service (also called *fractional* **T1**).

- **DTE**

  See **data terminal equipment**.

- **DUA**

  See **Directory User Agent**.

- **dual in-line package** The housing for an **integrated circuit**.

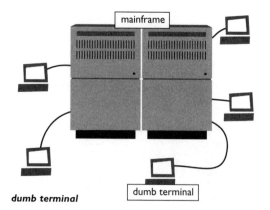

dumb terminal

■ **dumb terminal** A keyboard-and-monitor device that sends keystrokes to a computer and displays output on the screen (see illustration, previous page). If you **dial up** to a **UNIX shell**, then your **PC** is being used as a dumb terminal.

■ **dummy variable** A meaningless variable used in an example to demonstrate correct syntax, such as **foo**, **bar**, or **baz**.

■ **dump** (v) To send the contents of a file (or other data) to a **device** or another file, in order to print, display, or store the data.

■ **dup killer** (*doop killer*) FidoNet software that tries to detect and eliminate duplicate copies of the same message that may have arrived via different routes.

■ **duplex** Transmission of signals in two directions at once.

See also **full duplex, half duplex, simplex.**

■ **dup loop** (*doop loop*) A series of nearly identical messages that have eluded the dup killer.

■ **dynamic adaptive routing** A method of directing network traffic based on the current state of the network.

dup killer

■ **dynamic node addressing** A method of **address**ing used on **AppleTalk** networks in which **node**s are assigned network addresses as needed, but do not have stable consistent network addresses, as in an **IP** network.

■ **dynamic SLIP** A type of **SLIP** access to the Internet, in which the user is supplied with a new **IP address**, drawn from a pool of possibilities, every time she connects. This enables the **service provider** to assign fewer IP addresses to its SLIP customers, with the trade-off being that the users cannot function as a **host** without a consistent address. (See illustration below.)

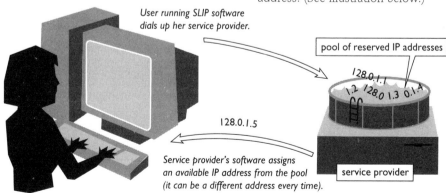

dynamic SLIP

A B C D E F G H I J K L M N O P Q R S T U V W X Y Z

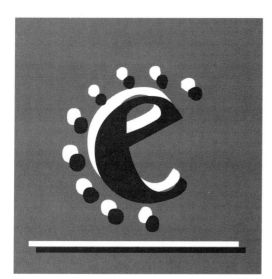

E&S Systems Public Access *Nix [service provider] steve@cg57.esnet.com, (619) 278-4641.

EARN

See European Academic and Research Network.

EarthLink Network [service provider] info@earthlink.net, (213) 644-9500.

EBCDIC (*eb-sa-dic* or *eb-see-dic*) *Extended Binary Coded Decimal Interchange Code*, a proprietary **IBM** character set that is not entirely compatible with **ASCII**.

echo (n) 1. A discussion group on FidoNet; 2. The method by which the characters you type are displayed on your screen, also known as *local echo*; 3. The method by which characters sent from a **remote** system are displayed on your screen, also known as *remote echo*. (See illustration to right.)

See also **forum**, **newsgroup**.

Echo Communications [service provider] horn@echonyc.com, (212) 255-3839.

EcoNet (*ee-coe-net*) A **BBS** dedicated to environmental issues. Its Internet **domain name** is igc.org.

ed (rhymes with *bed*) A **UNIX**, line-at-a-time **text editor**.

EDGAR *Electronic Data Gathering Archiving and Retrieval*, a database of corporate disclosure, transaction, and financial status data maintained by the United States Security Exchange Commission. For more information, see the **Web page** at http://town.hall.org/edgar/edgar.html.

Edge [service provider] edge.ercnet.com, (615) 726-8700.

editor 1. A **text editor**, a program used to edit simple text files; 2. Any program used

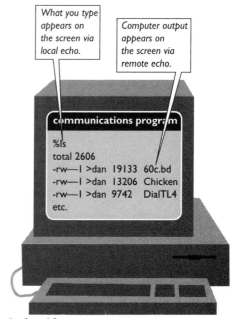

echo 2 and 3

to edit any type of file, such as a .WAV (Windows sound file) editor.

■ **EDLIS** *Exchange of Dylan Lyrics—Internet Service*, an underground organization whose agents respond to requests posted in rec.music.dylan and elsewhere on the Net.

■ **EDT** A text editor available on VMS machines and at Delphi Information Service.

■ **.edu** The Internet domain dedicated to educational institutions, generally in the United States.

■ **Education Central** [service provider] 374cylb@cmuvm.csu.cmich.edu, (517) 774-3975.

■ **Educational Resources Information Center (ERIC)** A service for schools providing online bibliography and journal abstracts, via gopher at ericir.syr.edu and via e-mail at askeric@ricir.syr.edu.

■ **EDUCOM** (*ed-you-com*) An organization dedicated to facilitating the use of computers in educational institutions. It is a supporter of the National Research and Education Network (NREN). Gopher: educom.com, e-mail: inquiry@bitnic. educom.com.

■ **ee** (*ee-ee*) A UNIX text editor.

■ **EFF** (*ee-eff-eff*) *See* Electronic Frontier Foundation.

■ ***EFF's Guide to the Internet*** Formerly *Big Dummy's Guide to the Internet*, the Electronic Frontier

Foundation's excellent free Internet guide, available via FTP, gopher, and the Web.

■ **EGP** *See* External Gateway Protocol.

■ **EIA** *See* Electronics Industries Association.

■ **EIA/TIA-568** A document coauthored by the American National Standards Institute, the Electronics Industry Association, and the Telecommunications Industry Association that specifies a wiring standard for buildings suitable for both LANs and telecommunications systems.

■ **8-bit clean** (adj) Said of a modem connection with 8 data bits and no corruption of the signal from line noise.
See also TIA (definition 2).

■ **802.x** A set of communications standards (802.1 through 802.5) for physical and electrical connections in LANs, defined by the Institute of Electrical and Electronic Engineers.

■ **80-character line length** The standard line length for an IBM or UNIX terminal, a recommended maximum line length for e-mail and Usenet posts (some prefer 75 characters to allow for quotation, since most e-mail and newsreader programs

> >Lines that are too long to fit on an 80-character screen will end up being wrapped unevenly
> >in many users' newsreaders and mail programs. Such lines are difficult to read and can
> >make the person who wrote the original post look clueless, even if it's really the fault of
> >incompatible software.
>
> I agree!

80-character line length

quote text by preceding it with a > or other character).

■ **e-journal** An *electronic journal*, an academic journal that circulates via an **e-mail mailing list**. One advantage e-journals have over print journals is that they are **searchable**.

■ **ELAP** (*ee-lap*) *See* EtherTalk Link Access Protocol.

■ **electronic bulletin board**

See BBS.

■ **Electronic Frontier Foundation**
A lobbying and advocacy organization, founded by Mitch Kapor and John Barlow, working for the preservation of freedom on the **cyberspace** frontier.

■ **electronic journal** Also called an *e-journal*, an academic journal that circulates via an **e-mail mailing list**. One advantage e-journals have over print journals is that they are **searchable**.

■ **electronic mail** Usually called **e-mail**, messages carried electronically from computer to computer.

■ **Electronics Industries Association (EIA)** A standards organization for the electronics industry, the coauthor of EIA/TIA-568.

■ **elm** (rhymes with *helm*) A full-screen UNIX e-mail program, easier to use than the basic, line-at-a-time **mail** but still more difficult than **pine**, which is much closer to modern word processors.

■ **.elmrc** A setup file for **elm**.

■ **emacs** (*ee-macs*) Also written *EMACS*, a UNIX text editor that doubles as an

operating environment, **mail program**, and **newsreader**.

■ **e-mail** (n) Also *email*, short for *electronic mail*, one of the most popular features of networks, **online services**, and the Internet in general, but you already knew that, didn't you? The term *e-mail* is used both for the overall process and for the messages carried electronically from computer to computer.

(v) To send e-mail.

■ **e-mail address** 1. An Internet mail **address** of the form *username@host.domain*; 2. The **username** portion of a mail **account** on a network.

■ **e me** Send me **e-mail**, please reply by e-mail.

■ **emoticon** A smiley or other sideways punctuation face such as these:

:-) :-(:-P %^) ;-) B-) :D

Emoticons can convey some insight into the writer's emotional state.

■ **emulation** For a computer, **operating system**, or **application**, the process of imitating the functions of another **environment**.

See also **terminal emulation**.

■ **encapsulate** To embed a higher-level **protocol** within a lower-level protocol to create a single **frame** for transportation over a network (see illustration, next page).

See also **protocol layer**, **tunneling**.

■ **Encapsulated PostScript (EPS)**
A device-independent file format for PostScript files. EPS files are portable and can be printed with any PostScript printer.

A
B
C
D
E
F
G
H
I
J
K
L
M
N
O
P
Q
R
S
T
U
V
W
X
Y
Z

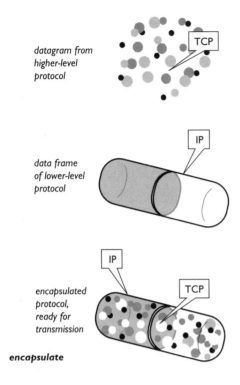

datagram from higher-level protocol

data frame of lower-level protocol

encapsulated protocol, ready for transmission

encapsulate

■ **encoding** The process of converting data to a coded format, generally to make it more easily transportable.

■ **encrypt** To scramble the contents of a file or e-mail message so that only those with the **key** can unscramble and read them. (See illustration to right.)

■ **encryption** A process of rendering a file or e-mail message unreadable to anyone lacking the **encryption key**.

■ **encryption key** A unique, secret data block used to **encrypt** e-mail. *See also* **decryption key**.

■ **end-to-end** (adj) Direct, said of a connection between two computers.

■ **end-user** (n) From a **programmer**'s perspective, the ultimate customer, the regular person using the program, **operating system**, or computer.

■ **Enter key** A large key on the right side of most keyboards (sometimes called the *Return key*) used to submit commands or insert hard returns (**newline**s) into text.

■ **enterprise computing** Corporate network computing, bridging a variety of **platform**s, **operating system**s, and networking **protocol**s.

■ **Enterzone** A hyperzine on the **World Wide Web** at http://enterzone.berkeley. edu/enterzone.html.

original message

Hi Steve
I'm sending you this message so you can test the data encryption key we are going to use for our secret communication.
--Dave

data encryption key

encrypted message

!@#$&}{&*@()#¡# $
@!&#*$^@$$"@:>>
!*@&*#   ^$%
#&$&^!   % $*()
@#":<>   ($
$!)%(^**   ^' >^$
%*#&@($&*#^$%
#&$&^!%%$*()@+}#"

encrypt

■ **environment** Also called *operating environment*, a **front end** for an **operating system**, a set of tools and a consistent look and feel that allow the user to interact with the computer. Windows is an environment that runs on top of the MS-DOS operating system.

■ **EOF** (*ee-oh-eff*) An *end-of-file* marker.

■ **.eps** The file extension for an Encapsulated PostScript file.

■ **ERIC**

See Educational Resources Information Center, AskERIC.

■ **Eris** The Goddess of Discord (from Greek mythology), worshipped by members of the **Discordian Society**.

See also **fnord**, *Illuminati!*

■ **error** An unexpected action or result, or incorrectly transmitted data. Any process that causes results which a computer cannot properly interpret.

■ **error control** Any method for verifying the correctness of transmitted data.

■ **error message** A message from the **operating system**, alerting a user that something has gone wrong. Error messages can be as cryptic as a random number or as informative as a complete explanation of the problem.

■ **escape character** 1. ASCII 26; 2. Any character which, when preceded by an escape (usually ASCII 26, the character that is transmitted when the Escape key is pressed), sends a command to a device, such as a terminal or printer. They are often represented on the screen as capital letters preceded by carets, such as ^E, ^X, etc.

■ **escape out** (v) 1. To substitute a special symbol for a character that would otherwise be misinterpreted (e.g., to escape out **slash** characters so they don't get interpreted as directory separators); 2. To run a temporary **shell** from within an application in order to send commands to the **operating system** (e.g., to escape out to **UNIX** to check your mail without exiting the **news-reader**).

See also **shell out**.

■ **escape sequence** A sequence of characters reserved for a special meaning by a computer's **operating system**; may be used to send commands (for example, to a printer).

■ **Eskimo North** [service provider] nanook@eskimo.com, (206) 367-7457.

■ **e-text** Written works made available electronically.

See also **Project Gutenberg**.

■ **Ethernet** A **LAN** network **protocol** and set of cabling specifications, originally developed by Digital, Intel, and Xerox, employing a **bus topology** and providing a transfer rate of up to 10 Mbps. Ethernet **node**s may be connected with **unshielded twisted-pair** wiring or thick or thin **coaxial cable**. Ethernet uses **CSMA/CD** to prevent collisions, as opposed to **token ring**s, which use token passing.

■ **EtherTalk** AppleTalk **protocol**s for Ethernet LANs, encapsulating DDP datagrams into Ethernet frames.

■ **EtherTalk Link Access Protocol (ELAP)** AppleTalk's Ethernet data link protocol.

A
B
C
D
E
F
G
H
I
J
K
L
M
N
O
P
Q
R
S
T
U
V
W
X
Y
Z

■ **ETLA** (*ee-tee-ell-ay*) *Extended three-letter acronym* (i.e., a four-letter acronym). The acronym is a facetious comment on the proliferation of bewildering **TLA**s in the technical world. Too many TLAs and ETLAs thrown around make **MEGO** (my eyes glaze over).

■ **.etx** File **extension** for a **setext** file.

■ **Eudora** An **e-mail** program for Windows or the Macintosh that can use the **Post Office Protocol** and function as an **offline mail reader**. Available via **anonymous FTP** from ftp.qualcomm.com.

■ **EUnet Communications Services** (*you-net*) [European **service provider**] info@EU.net, +31 20 623 3803.

■ **European Academic and Research Network (EARN)** A network of universities and research facilities in Europe that has e-mail and file-transfer connections to BITNET.

■ **even parity** A method of verifying the correctness of transmitted data by summing each **byte**, adding a **parity bit** of 1 if necessary to make the sum even before sending the data, and then repeating the summation on the receiving end.
See also **parity**.

■ **Evergreen Communications** [service provider] evergreen@libre.com, (602) 955-8315.

■ **eWorld** [online service] An Apple online service geared for Macintosh users; eac@ eworld.com, askeac@eworld.com, (800) 775-4556.
See also **service provider**.

■ **exclamation point (!)** 1. A bang—it precedes each site in a **bang path**; 2. In some **UNIX** programs, an exclamation mark enables the user to **shell out**; 3. Overuse of exclamation marks to punctuate Usenet **posts** is one of the hallmarks of a **newbie** or a **B1FF**.

■ **.exe** A DOS file **extension** used to indicate an executable file (such as a program or **self-extracting archive** file).

■ **execute** To perform a command or run a program, something **operating system**s do.

■ **exit** (v) To quit a program or leave a **shell**.

■ **expansion slot** Inside a PC, a connector that gives an adapter access to the system **bus**, allowing the installation of additional peripheral devices.

■ **expire** Applied to **Usenet** articles, to be removed after an expiration date to keep the **newsfeed** from growing too large.

■ **export** (v) 1. To save a file in a different format (that of another program); 2. To send a product to a foreign country (whether physically or over the Internet).

■ **Express Access Online Communications Service** [service provider] info@ digex.com, (800) 969-9090,(301) 220-2020.

■ **Extended Binary Coded Decimal Interchange Code (EBCDIC)** A proprietary **IBM** character set that is not entirely compatible with **ASCII**.

■ **extension** The portion of a file name after the last **dot**, often used to indicate the type of file. **DOS** extensions have a three-character maximum length.

■ **External Gateway Protocol (EGP)** A routing **protocol** by which connected networks signal their availability to each other.

■ **EZ-E-Mail** [service provider] info@lemuria.sai.com, (603) 672-0736.

■ **e-zine** Also *ezine*, an electronically distributed **fanzine** or magazine. Many are sent as **e-mail**. Others are made available via **gopher** or the **Web**.

A
B
C
D
E
F
G
H
I
J
K
L
M
N
O
P
Q
R
S
T
U
V
W
X
Y
Z

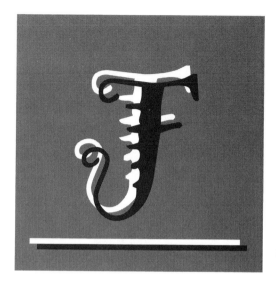

■ **f** 1. The **forward** command in many **UNIX** mail programs; 2. The **follow up** command in some **UNIX newsreaders**.

■ **face time** (n) Time spent meeting with a person, as contrasted with time spent communicating via e-mail, voice mail, etc.

■ **face-to-face** (adv or adj) Meeting in person.

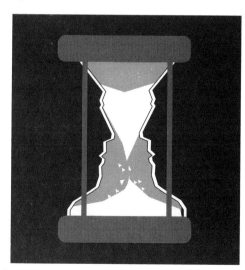

face time

■ **Fairfield Free-Net** [service provider] sterry@ins.infonet.net, (515) 472-7494.

■ **FairNet** [service provider] ffmob@ aurora.alaska.edu, (907) 474-5089.

■ **fair use** The legal doctrine that allows limited quotation of other people's work if the use of their work does not undercut its market value.

■ **fall off** (v) Said of a portion of data that exceeds the size of a memory register and is lost.

■ **fanzine** An underground, do-it-yourself magazine, often dedicated to a band, celebrity, or cult figure.

■ **FAQ** (*fack*, n) 1. A *frequently asked question*; 2. A file containing frequently asked questions and their answers, sometimes called a **FAQL** (*frequently asked question list*). To find FAQs, look in the *.answers **newsgroup**s or the **FTP** archive at rtfm.mit.edu. Many **mailing list**s and **Usenet** newsgroups maintain FAQs so that participants won't have to spend lots of time answering the same set of questions.

See also **RTFAQ**.

■ **FAQL** (*fackle*, n) *Frequently asked question list*, a file containing frequently asked questions and their answers, usually compiled and maintained by a **newsgroup**, **mailing list**, or Internet **site**.

■ **FAQ list**

See **FAQL**.

■ **FARNET (Federation of American Research Networks)** A nonprofit organization that works to promote the

A
B
C
D
E
F
G
H
I
J
K
L
M
N
O
P
Q
R
S
T
U
V
W
X
Y
Z

use of computer networks for research and education.

■ **fast packet** A standard for high-speed, high-traffic, **cell-switching** networks. Also called *Asynchronous Transfer Mode (ATM)*.

■ **fax** (n) 1. A *facsimile* of a document, digitized and transmitted over phone lines. While faxes are usually sent and received with a stand-alone fax machine, faxes may also be sent to and from computers using fax software and a **fax modem**; 2. A machine that can send and receive faxes.

(v) To send a fax.

■ **fax modem** A modem that can fulfill some of the functions of a **fax** machine.

■ **FDDI**

See Fiber Distributed Data Interface.

■ **Federal Information Exchange (FIX)** A **gateway** linking U.S. government networks with the Internet.

■ **Federal Information Processing Standards (FIPS)** A United States Department of Defense document specifying U.S. government networking plans.

■ **Federal Networking Council (FNC)** An organization that coordinates the networking standards of U.S. government agencies.

■ **Federation of American Research Networks**

See FARNET.

■ **FEDIX** An online information service linking educational institutions and the U.S. government. It offers the **Minority On-Line Information Service** (MOLIS).

■ **feed**

See newsfeed.

■ **fetch** (v) To transfer a file from a remote **site** on the Internet to your **host** computer.

(n) A Macintosh **FTP** program.

fetch

■ **Fiber Distributed Data Interface (FDDI)** A **backbone** system for large networks, employing two rings of fiber-optic cabling, with a signaling rate of 80 Mbps.

■ **fiber-optic cable** Glass cabling designed to carry light pulses, often used for **backbones**; more dependable, lighter, and smaller than copper cable carrying electronic signals, but much more expensive and more difficult to repair. (See illustration, opposite page.)

■ **FidoNet** A network of **BBSs** with Internet e-mail access.

■ **field** (n) A defined area containing a fixed number of characters, found in online forms and some databases.

■ **56K** (adj) Said of a telephone circuit with a 64 Kbps **bandwidth** that uses 8K for signaling and the remaining 56K for traffic.

fiber-optic cable

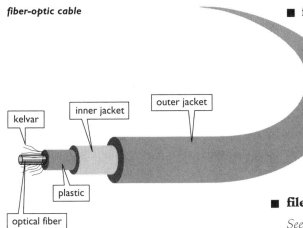

kelvar

inner jacket

outer jacket

plastic

optical fiber

- **Fight-o-net** A pejorative name for FidoNet, alluding to the frequent arguments on FidoNet **echo**es and **mailing list**s.

  See also **flame war**.

- **File Attach** A FidoNet procedure for attaching a file to an e-mail message to send it to another **BBS**.

- **file compression**

  See **compression**.

- **file locking** Preventing all but the first user from making changes to a file that is opened by more than one user on a network (see illustration below).

- **file name extension**

  See **extension**.

  - **File Request** A FidoNet procedure for transferring a file from one **BBS** to another.

  - **file server** A computer that makes files available to other users on a network.

    See also **FTP server**.

- **file site**

  See **FTP site**.

- **file transfer** The copying of a file over a network connection from a **remote site** to the **localhost**.

- **file transfer protocol**

  See **FTP**.

- **film at 11** A common tag line in **Usenet** **follow-up post**s mocking the timeliness (or lack thereof) of the original article. (This is an allusion to a once-popular evening news teaser.) Often follows "**Imminent death of the Net predicted!**"

- **filter** (n) 1. A program that converts one file format into another; 2. In e-mail, a program that allows certain messages to reach

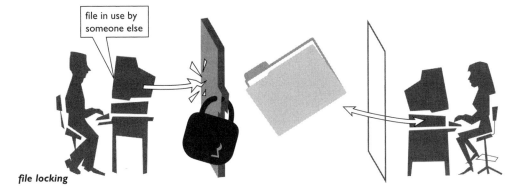

file in use by someone else

file locking

the user while eliminating other messages. On **UNIX** machines, it is easy to set up an e-mail filter to prevent unwanted mail from making it to your **inbox**.

(v) To ignore unwanted information by using a filter (definition 2).

■ **finger** (v) To seek the identity of a user or the status of a network.

(n) The **UNIX** command that performs the finger function.

finger

■ **finn** (v) To pull rank on someone else in IRC by showing that you've been around a lot longer than the other person—a relative **newbie** compared to you. (The IRC protocol was first used on servers in Finland, hence the term *finn*.)

■ **FIPS**

See **Federal Information Processing Standards**.

■ **firewall** (n) A security measure on the Internet, protecting information, preventing access, or ensuring that users cannot do any harm to underlying systems (see illustration below). Some networks are connected to the Internet via a firewall machine.

■ **FirstSearch Catalog** A catalog maintained by the **Online Computer Library Center** that gives member libraries access to many databases of books and magazines in print.

■ **FishNet** [service provider] info@pond.com, (610) 337-9994.

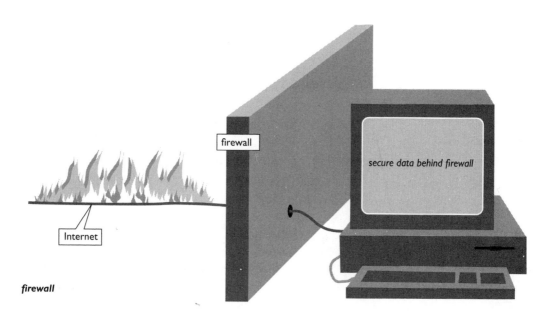

firewall

■ **FIX**

See Federal Information Exchange.

■ **flame** (n) An insulting **e-mail** or **Usenet post**. Flames are often ill-considered knee-jerk expressions of anger, but they can also be cruelly detailed and intended for the amusement of the general audience at the expense of the flamee.

(v) To post a flame.

flame

■ **flamebait** (n) A **post** to a **mailing list** or **newsgroup** designed to elicit **flames**. Flamebait can be recognized by the fact that it goes beyond the premises of the list or newsgroup. Nobody objects to provocative or even argumentative posts, but posts to the alt.fan.frank-zappa newsgroup saying "Zappa was a no-talent potty-mouthed dweeb" betray a lack of legitimate interest in the subject at hand.

See also **troll**.

■ **flamefest** A flame war, particularly one involving many participants.

■ **flame on** A comment in a **post** meaning either "Here is where I start flaming" or "I'm prepared to be flamed for the following comment."

See also **asbestos**.

■ **flamer** 1. One who **flames**; 2. One who flames habitually or incessantly.

■ **flames to /dev/null** A tag line in **posts** to **mailing lists** and **newsgroups** meaning "I'll ignore (or delete) any **flames**," from the **UNIX** name for the **null device**, a sort of trash can.

■ **flame war** Often written *flamewar*, a prolonged series of **flames** and counterflames, drowning out the on-topic **posts** in a **newsgroup** or **mailing list**. Traditionally, flame wars end when **Nazis** are mentioned.

■ **flavor** (n) A variety, as in "BSD is a flavor of UNIX."

■ **flood** (v) To **spam** an IRC channel, that is, to type or paste in huge amounts of text, effectively drowning out the conversation.

■ **floppy disk** A removable storage medium (see illustration, next page).

■ **flow control** The method by which two **devices**, generally **modems**, signal to each

A B C D E F G H I J K L M N O P Q R S T U V W X Y Z

floppy disk

other when to start and stop sending data.

See also **hardware flow control, XON/XOFF.**

- **FNC**

  See **Federal Networking Council.**

- **fnord** A nonsense word embedded in **posts** or **sig block**s, alluding to Robert Anton Wilson's *Illuminati!* trilogy (in which children are taught not to see the fnords as part of their fnord conditioning by fnord the state fnord).

- **FOAF** (written only, n) A *friend of a friend*, the most common source or attribution for **urban legend**s, implying that the teller doesn't personally know the participants, but knows someone who does.

- **folder** 1. A **directory**, especially on a Macintosh; 2. An e-mail file containing related messages.

- **follow up** (v) To respond to a **post** with a replying post.

- **follow-up** (n) A **post** that replies to and possibly quotes an earlier post.

- **follow-up line** A line in the **header** of some **Usenet post**s directing **follow-up**s to a particular **newsgroup** or newsgroups. **Newbie**s who fail to heed the follow-up line can be tricked into posting replies to inappropriate newsgroups (or worse, to *.test groups, resulting in thousands of automated replies stuffing their **inbox**).

- **foo** A dummy **variable** used by **programmer**s as a stand-in for a real variable, often paired with **bar**.

- **foobar** A dummy **variable** used by **programmer**s as a stand-in for a real variable. *See also* **FUBAR.**

- **footprint** The portion of a surface that a computer or other device occupies.

- **foreground** In a **multitasking** computer environment, a process that takes place in full view or with higher priority than other running processes is said to take place in the foreground.

  See also **background.**

- **Forsyth County Free-Net** [service provider] annen@ledger.mis.co.forsyth. nc.us, (919) 727-2597 ext. 3023.

  See also **free-net.**

- **FORTRAN** An early computer programming language (the name comes from *FORmula TRANslator*).

- **Fortrash** A pejorative term for **FORTRAN**.

- **fortune cookie** A program that spits out a different fortune every time you run it. Some systems run cookie as part of their **startup** or **login** procedure.

  See also **qotd.**

■ **forum** A discussion group on CompuServe and other online services and BBSs where users with similar interests may find valuable information, exchange, ideas, and share files.

See also newsgroup, echo.

■ **forward** (v) To send received e-mail along to another address, either manually or automatically.

■ **forward slash** /, used to divide directories in a path (in UNIX and, hence, in many Internet applications).

■ **404 Free-Net** [service provider] mike_bernath@solinet.net, (404) 892-0943.

See also free-net.

■ **FQA** *Frequently questioned acronym.*

See also ETLA, FAQ, TLA.

■ **FQDN**

See fully qualified domain name.

■ **frame** (n) A block of data encapsulated with a header and trailer for transmission over a network.

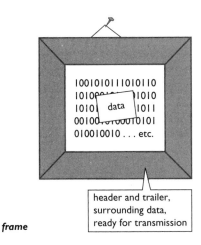

```
1001010111010110
1010        1010
1010  data  1011
00100       0101
010010010 . . . etc.
```

header and trailer, surrounding data, ready for transmission

frame

■ **frame relay** A standard for transmission of frames over a packet-switching network, a variant of the X.25 standard.

See also cell-switching.

■ **fred** 1. An easy-to-use X.500 interface; 2. A dummy variable used by programmers to stand for a real variable.

See also barney.

■ **FrEdMail** (*fred-mail*) A network of BBSs for students and teachers.

■ **Freelance Systems Programming** [service provider] fsp@dayton.fsp.com, (513) 254-7246.

See also free-net.

■ **free-net** A free public network providing Internet access to members of a community.

■ **Free Software Foundation (FSF)** An organization dedicated to the production and distribution of free software, the creators of GNU, reachable via FTP at prep.ai.mit.edu.

■ **Free State Free-Net** [service provider] aduggan@well.sf.ca.us, (410) 313-9259.

■ **free-WAIS** A free version of a WAIS server produced and distributed by CNIDR (Clearinghouse for Networked Information Discovery and Retrieval).

■ **freeware** Software distributed for free (or for bragging rights) via the Net. The culture of the Internet encourages freeware.

See also shareware.

■ **frequency** A measurement of the number of cycles per second of an electronic signal, roughly a measurement of the speed of a process or device.

A B C D E F G H I J K L M N O P Q R S T U V W X Y Z

■ **fringeware** Software of dubious stability, commercial value, or appeal, made available as **freeware**.

■ **frink** The sound that lemurs make, according to the alt.fan.lemurs **newsgroup**.

■ **front end** The part of a computer process that the **end-user** interacts with. In **client/server** applications, the **client** acts as a front end for the **server**.

■ **FSF**

See Free Software Foundation.

■ **FSLIST** The *Forgotten Site List*. A list of Internet **service provider**s available via **anonymous FTP** from freedom.nmsu.edu in the /pub/docs/fslist directory.

■ **ftp** The UNIX FTP program.

See also ncftp.

■ **FTP** Internet *file transfer protocol*, the standard **TCP/IP protocol** for transferring files over the Internet, across any **platform**s. (See illustration below.)

See also fetch, ftp, uucp.

■ **FTPmail** A way to use **FTP** by **e-mail** if you don't have an FTP application. One address for an FTPmail server is ftpmail@ pa.dec.com.

■ **FTP server** An **FTP file server**, a computer serving files from an FTP **archive**.

■ **FTP site** A **host** on the Internet containing archives and set up for **FTP**.

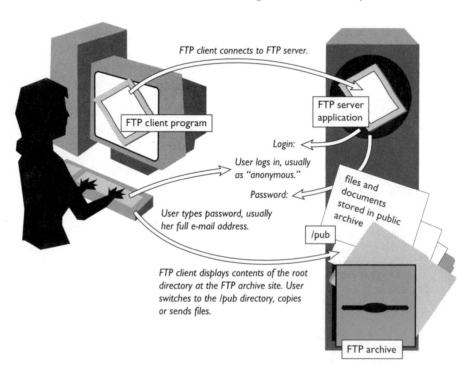

FTP client connects to FTP server.

FTP client program

FTP server application

Login:

User logs in, usually as "anonymous."

Password:

User types password, usually her full e-mail address.

files and documents stored in public archive

/pub

FTP client displays contents of the root directory at the FTP archive site. User switches to the /pub directory, copies or sends files.

FTP

FTP archive

■ **f2f** (written only, adv or adj) *Face-to-face,* meeting in person.

■ **FUBAR** (adj) *Fucked up beyond all recognition,* an old U.S. Army term used frequently on the Net.

See also **bar, foo, foobar.**

■ **full duplex** Two-way communication in which the computers at either end of the transmission both send and receive at the same time.

See also **half duplex, simplex.**

■ **full name** The **real name** associated with an e-mail address; can be an **alias.**

■ **full-screen editor** A text editor that allows the user to move around the screen, editing the entire file.

■ **fully qualified domain name (FQDN)** The complete **domain name** that identifies a specific computer (or **host** network, at the very least) on the Internet, including a **host name,** a **subdomain** name, and a domain name. (See illustration to right.) Also called *domain name address.*

■ **furrfu** (*fur-foo*) **rot13** for *sheesh!*

■ **fwiw** (written only) *For what it's worth.*

■ **FXNET** [service provider] info@fx.net, (704) 338-4670.

■ **fyi** (*eff-why-eye,* also *FYI*) *For your information.*

■ **FYI** (n) An Internet document that provides information about the Internet itself, but which does not define standards. Available via **anonymous FTP** from rtfm.mit.edu.

See also **RFC.**

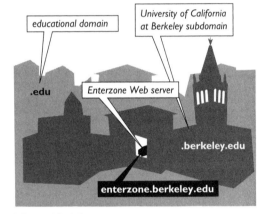

fully qualified domain name

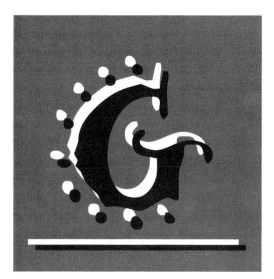

■ **g** The *go* command in the **UNIX** programs **gopher** and **lynx**, used to go to a specific address.

■ **G** Abbreviation for **gigabyte** (roughly one billion **byte**s).

■ **<g>** Also *<grin>*, indicates that the author is grinning, similar to

:-)

■ **Garrett Communiversity Central** [service provider] 71072.2304@ compuserve.com, (301) 387-3035.

■ **gate** (n) Also called a *gateway*, a computer providing a connection between two networks, two e-mail handling systems, or a **Usenet newsgroup** and a **mailing list** (see illustration below). A gate reformats the data so that it will be acceptable to the system it is passing into.

(v) To establish a gate.

■ **gated** (adj) Connected to another network or discussion group via a **gateway**.

■ **gated newsgroup** A newsgroup whose **post**s are sent to a **mailing list** and which receives (or includes) posts from the mailing list.

■ **gateway** Also called a *gate*, a computer providing a connection between two networks, two e-mail handling systems, or a **Usenet newsgroup** and a **mailing list**. A gateway reformats the data so that it will be acceptable to the system it is passing into.

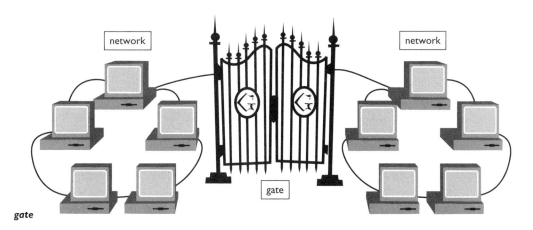

gate

■ **<gd&r>** *Grinning, ducking, and running*
(what you **post** after you've **tweak**ed someone). Also *<gr&d>*.

■ **geek** Someone who knows a lot about
computers, networks, or the Internet and
thinks they're interesting (not necessarily an
insult).

■ **geek code** A set of coded ratings in a **sig
block**, describing the **poster** in humorous,
geeky terms. For example, if I put the following geek code in my signature:

```
GLP d— H s-:+ g? p0 au— a w v+++
C++ US N++ K+++ W+ M+ !V
-po+ Y+ t+ j+ R— tv+ b++ !D B-
e++ u** h— f+ r++ !n y?
```

I'd be saying "I am a geek of literature and
philosophy, dress casually (jeans at work),
have normal hair, am shorter and rounder
than average, can't find my glasses, generally have no pens in my pockets, drive an
old car, am between 30 and 39, am slightly
weird, talk a mile a minute, use computers a
lot, work in the Sun OS/Solaris version of
UNIX, keep up with a number of **newsgroup**s, have gotten mail from **Kibo**, am
overly committed to Microsoft Windows,
like Macintoshes, have never used **VMS**,
hate both sides of the conventional political
debate, am concerned about privacy and
security in **cyberspace**, watch *Star Trek*,
enjoy Jeopardy, am down on role-playing
games, watch some TV just about every day,
read a lot, have never played Doom, find
Barney slightly annoying, have a bachelor's
degree, listen to lots of strange music, live in
a fairly nongeeky home, have a lot of geeky
friends, have dated my current **SO** for a long
time, will eat anything, and I'm male.

The code is maintained by Robert A.
Hayden. For a complete key to all of the
categories, **finger** hayden@vax1.mankato.
msus.edu.

■ **geek out** (v) 1. To get lost in the minutiae
of a computer process; 2. To talk computers
or networking in a social setting.

■ **General Public License (GPL)** Also
called *copyleft*, the license carried by **Free
Software Foundation** software (such as
GNU), granting reuse and reproduction
rights to anyone and everyone.

■ **General Public Virus (GPV)** A pejorative name for the **General Public License**
carried by **Free Software Foundation** software, so called because some developers
believe it opens them up to legal liability if
they include GPL code in their products.

■ **Genesee Free-Net** [service provider]
dcheslow@umich.edu, (810) 762-3309.

See also **free-net**.

■ **GEnie** [online service] info@genie.com,
(800) 638-9636.

■ **get** (v) To copy a file from a remote source
to your **host** computer, particularly via **FTP**
(see illustration, opposite page).

(n) The FTP command to get a file.

■ **Get a life!** A common **flame**, suggesting
that the flamee is too involved in the
Internet or her/his computer.

■ **Get a real...!** A common geeky type of
flame (such as "Get a real computer," "Get a
real operating system," "Get a real service
provider," and so on) directed at someone's
inferior hardware, software, or network
connection.

■ **Ghod** An alternative spelling for God preferred by some **hackers** and other **netizens** (also spelled *ghod*).

■ **Ghu** A deity some **hackers** and other **netizens** offer their praises and curses to, as in "Great Ghu! Where'd you get an idea like that?"

■ **.gif** The file extension for **GIFs**.

■ **GIF (Graphics Interchange Format)** 1. An extremely popular compressed graphics (image) file format originated by **CompuServe** but readable in most platforms; 2. A file in the GIF format.

■ **GIF! GIF! GIF!** A ritual **follow-up** to a **post** mentioning an image (such as a photograph), requesting that someone scan the image, save it as a **GIF**, **uuencode** it, and post it to the **newsgroup**.

■ **giga-** Prefix meaning one billion.

■ **gigabyte** Roughly one billion **bytes** (actually 1,073,741,824 bytes), a large amount of storage.

■ **GIGO** (written only) *Garbage in, garbage out*, a longstanding computer truism meaning that the computer won't produce meaningful results if you feed it useless data.

■ **gilley** (n) A unit of **bogosity**, specifically applied to bogus analogies.

■ **GLAIDS NET** [service provider] tomh@glaids.wa.com, (206) 323-7483.

■ **glitch** An unexplainable small computer lapse, causing a faulty result.

■ **global** Affecting an entire document or system (for example, a global search and replace is a search and replace operation

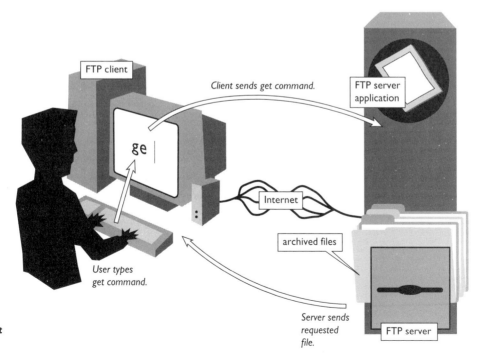

get

FTP client

Client sends get command.

FTP server application

ge

Internet

User types get command.

archived files

Server sends requested file.

FTP server

performed on an entire document, rather than a small selection or a single item).

■ **gnu.** A hierarchy in the Usenet mold devoted to the Free Software Foundation and to its free products, such as GNU and emacs.

■ **GNU** (*noo*) A freely distributed set of applications and utilities intended as a replacement for UNIX. GNU is distributed by the Free Software Foundation. (Its name is a recursive acronym that stands for *GNU's not UNIX*.)

■ **GNUMACS** A contracted form of GNU emacs.

■ **Godwin's Rule** Usenet Rule #4, which states that a thread in which Nazis or Hitler have been invoked has reached irrelevancy and will end soon. For some (but not all) of the other Rules see the net.legends FAQ at gopher://dixie.aiss.uiuc.edu:6969/00/urban. legends/net.legends/Net.Legends.FAQ.

■ **Good Thing** Something generally or widely accepted to be good. Tolerance is a Good Thing. So is reading the FAQ before asking questions.

See also Bad Thing.

■ **gopher** A client/server application that allows you to browse huge amounts of information by performing FTP transfers, remote logins, archie searches, and so on, presenting everything to the end-user in the form of menus. This saves the user from having to know (or type in) the addresses of the Internet resources being tapped. (See illustration to right.)

■ **Gopher Book for Windows** A gopher client for Windows, available via anonymous FTP from sunsite.unc.edu.

■ **gopher client** The gopher program that an end-user runs to get information from a gopher server. The gopher client retrieves

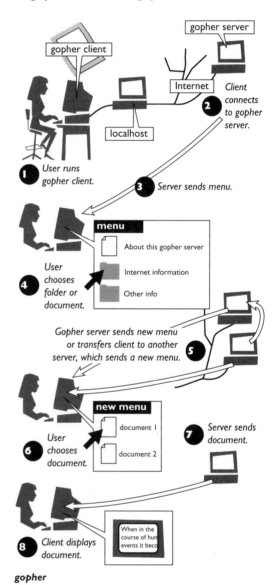

gopher

the menus and documents and displays them for the user.

■ **gopher.micro.umn.edu** The site of the University of Minnesota Gopher, the original **gopher server**.

■ **Gopher for Nextstep** A gopher client for the **Nextstep** operating system, available via **anonymous FTP** from sonata.cc. purdue.edu.

■ **gopher server** An application that provides documents and menus to **gopher clients**, a starting point for a gopher search.

■ **gopher site** A computer with a **gopher server** running on it.

■ **gopherspace** A conceptual space encompassing all of the menus and documents that can be reached via the interconnected system of **gopher server**s on the Internet.

■ **gorets** (n) A generic noun that can have any meaning, especially as elaborated in the alt.gorets **newsgroup**.

■ **go root** (v) To **log in** as **root**, a **UNIX** **superuser** or **system administrator** **account**, in order to exercise the extended **privileges** of that account.

■ **GOSIP** (*gossip*)
See Government OSI Profile.

■ **.gov** An Internet **domain** corresponding to U.S. government, including federal, state, and local governments.

■ **Government OSI Profile (GOSIP)** A set of **OSI** standards that the U.S. government follows in the procurement of computers in order to preserve compatibility among various government computer networks.

■ **GPL**
See General Public License.

■ **GPV**
See General Public Virus.

■ **Grand Rapids Free-Net** [service provider] andyb@bethany.org, (616) 459-6273.
See also **free-net**.

■ **The Granite State Oracle** [service provider] quentin.lewis@sun.com, (508) 442-0279.

■ **grape juice!** Something you yell at a computer when it isn't working, akin to banging it on the side.

■ **graphical user interface (GUI)** A full-screen graphical interface (meaning not limited to just letters and numbers) that allows users to run programs, execute commands, and generally interact with the computer by using a pointing device such as a mouse to manipulate graphical screen elements, as opposed to typing commands at a prompt.

Dial-up Internet users generally need **SLIP** or **PPP** access to be able to interact directly with Internet facilities within their GUI.

■ **Graphics Interchange Format**
See GIF.

■ **<gr&d>** (written only) *Grinning, running, and ducking* (what you **post** after you've **tweak**ed someone). Also *<gd&r>*.

■ **Greater Columbus Free-Net** [service provider] sgordon@freenet.columbus.oh.us, (614) 292-4132.
See also **free-net**.

A
B
C
D
E
F
G
H
I
J
K
L
M
N
O
P
Q
R
S
T
U
V
W
X
Y
Z

■ **Greater Detroit Free-Net** [service provider] raine@gdls.com, (313) 825-5293.

See also **free-net**.

■ **Greater Knoxville Community Network** [service provider] gcole@solar.rtd.utk.edu, (615) 974-2908.

See also **free-net**.

■ **Greater New Orleans Free-Net** [service provider] nrrmc@uno.edu, (504) 286-7187.

See also **free-net**.

■ **Greater Pulaski County Free-Net** [service provider] john.eichler@grapevine.lrk.ar.us, (501) 666-2222.

■ **Great Lakes Free-Net** [service provider] merritt_tumanis@fc1.glfn.org, (616) 961-4166.

See also **free-net**.

■ **Great Renaming** A day in 1985 on which nonlocal **Usenet newsgroup** names were changed from the form *net.** to the **hierarchy** still in use today.

■ **Great Worm** The 1988 **worm** that got out of control and **crash**ed systems all over the Internet, throwing a scare into many.

■ **green-card lawyer** A pejorative term for people who **spam** the Net with unwanted advertisements and then go on TV to defend their actions. (In 1993, a pair of lawyers posted an advertisement for their services in helping immigrants obtain green cards [to work in the United States] separately and individually to over six thousand **newsgroup**s, provoking a huge backlash of fury and indignation.)

■ **GreenCo-NET** [service provider] oukmddn@cluster1.clemson.edu, (803) 223-8431.

See also **free-net**.

■ **Greenet** [service provider] sgr002@sol1.solinet.net, (803) 242-5000 ext. 231.

See also **free-net**.

■ **grep** (rhymes with *prep*, v) To **globally** search a document, set of files, or **newsfeed** for a particular word or expression.

(n) The **UNIX** grep command.

See also **kiboze**.

■ **<grin>** Also <*g*>, just kidding, similar to

: -)

■ **grok** (v) To understand deeply or intimately, from Robert A. Heinlein's *Stranger in a Strange Land*.

■ **group** (n) Generally, a **newsgroup**, a **Usenet** or similar style discussion group.

Great Worm

■ **groupware** Software that gives multiple users access to the same information over a network, allowing collaboration on documents, scheduling of meetings, tracking of mission-critical projects, and so on.

■ **grovel** 1. To beg for something in a **Usenet newsgroup**; 2. For a programmer, to hunt through **code** looking for a problem.

■ **guest** A special **login** account reserved for visitors checking out a **BBS**, **online service**, or **service provider**.

■ **GUI** (*gooey*) A full-screen *graphical user interface* (meaning not limited to just letters and numbers) that allows users to run programs, execute commands, and generally interact with the computer by using a pointing device such as a mouse to manipulate graphical screen elements, as opposed to typing commands at a prompt.

Dial-up Internet users generally need **SLIP** or **PPP** access to be able to interact directly with Internet facilities within their GUI.

guiltware

■ **guiltware** **Shareware** that reminds you to register (and pay for) the product.

■ **gunzip** (n) The **UNIX uncompression** program for **gzip**ped files.

■ **guru** A helpful expert, someone to whom regular users turn to solve problems with their computer or network.

■ **Gutenberg**

See **Project Gutenberg**.

■ **.gz** A file extension for files that have been compressed with **gzip**.

■ **gzip** (n) A **UNIX** file **compression** program.

A
B
C
D
E
F
G
H
I
J
K
L
M
N
O
P
Q
R
S
T
U
V
W
X
Y
Z

■ **h**   The **help** command in some **UNIX** applications. Also try *?* (**question mark**).

■ **-h-**   The letter *h* is often stuck inside other words to make them appear odd, as in Ghod.

■ **^H**   The backspace character. Use of the **Backspace key** in **terminal emulation**s that don't support it sometimes leaves the original text on-screen, followed by one ^H character for every time Backspace is pressed, as in "Let me be the first to call you a fool^H^H^H^Hfriend."

■ **hack**   (v) To write **code**, to work on a computer, to cleverly diagnose and fix a problem, to dig beneath the surface of a computer process, reinventing things when necessary. (Outside of the Internet, the word *hack* suggests the action of breaking into computer networks. On the Internet, the word **crack** is used for that meaning.)

■ **hack around**   To figure a software program out for yourself, by trial and error, rather than by reading the manual.

■ **hacker**   A computer adept, someone who enjoys working with computers and testing the limits of systems, an enthusiastic or fast (or both) programmer. (Outside of the Internet, the word *hacker* has unsavory connotations, suggesting someone who breaks into computer networks and steals or vandalizes information. On the Internet, such malevolent hackers are called **cracker**s.)

■ **hacker ethic**   The philosophy, common among **hacker**s, that information, technology, and clever tricks should be shared and disseminated rather than hoarded.
See also **Free Software Foundation**, **information wants to be free**.

■ **Hacker's Dictionary**   *The New Hacker's Dictionary, Second Edition,* compiled by Eric S. Raymond and published by MIT Press: the paper book equivalent of the **jargon file**, an invaluable resource of **hacker** slang (much of which overlaps Internet slang and jargon).

■ **Halcyon**   [service provider] info@ halcyon.com, (206) 955-1050, (206) 426-9298.

■ **half bridge**   A device that connects a network to a communications link via a **modem** without passing routing information, which must be supplied by the network software (see illustration, next page, top).
See also **bridge**, **half router**.

■ **half duplex**   Two-way communication in which the computers at each end of the transmission take turns sending.
See also **full duplex**, **simplex**.

A B C D E F G **H** I J K L M N O P Q R S T U V W X Y Z

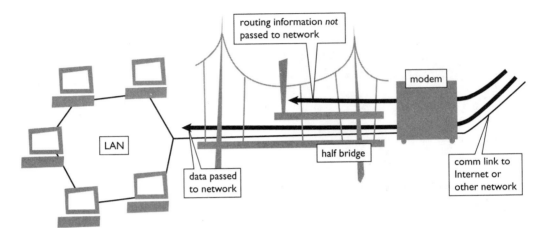

half bridge

■ **half router** A device that connects a network to a communications link via a **modem**, passing **routing** information along with data (see illustration below).

See also **half bridge, router**.

■ **HAND** (written only) *Have a nice day* (usually sarcastic).

See also **troll, YHBT. YHL. HAND**.

■ **handle** (n) A nickname or one-word name, such as a **nick** on IRC or a **username**. Network connections provided by employers often assign a strung-together version of a person's full name (using hyphens, underlines, dots, or capitalization to separate first and last name and sometimes even middle initials) as their username, instead of a handle.

■ **handshaking** For two connected devices, the sending of signals to alert each other when ready to receive data (see illustration, next page).

See also **flow control**.

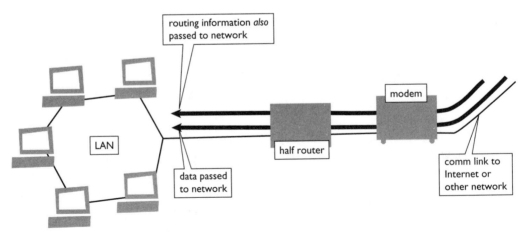

half router

handshaking

■ **hang** Said of a computer, to stop working, to freeze, to become unresponsive, to wait for something that will never happen.

See also **crash**.

■ **HappyNet** Kibo's proposed reorganization of **Usenet** into three major hierarchies —*nonbozo.*, *bozo.*, and *megabozo.* The entire text of the original HappyNet proclamation and manifesto can be found on the **Web** at ftp://ftp.std.com/pub/alt.religion.kibology/ happynet/HappyNet.1994.

■ **hard disk** A fixed computer storage medium.

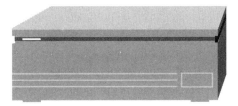

hard disk

■ **hardware** Computer equipment—the actual pieces of metal and plastic, as opposed to the programs that run on computers (**software**).

■ **hardware address** A specific **physical** address (as contrasted with a variable **logical** address) assigned to a device.

■ **hardware flow control** A form of **flow control** that is governed by devices themselves, instead of by communications software.

■ **Harris' Lament** "All the good ones are taken!" (that is, all the good **domain name**s).

■ **hash** 1. A symbol (usually #) **echo**ed at regular intervals to show that a process is still underway; 2. The **ftp** command that causes the hash symbols to be displayed.

■ **hat** A common name for the caret character, ^ (ASCII 94), used to indicate exponents and to underscore text on the previous line in e-mail and **Usenet post**s.

■ **Hayes-compatible** Said of a **modem** that understands the Hayes AT instruction set. (Hayes is a name-brand modem maker.) Most modems today are Hayes-compatible.

■ **HDLC**
See **High-Level Data Link Control**.

■ **header** 1. The rows of information at the top of an e-mail message that include who the message is from, who it's to, when it was sent, and what it's about; 2. Information preceding the data in a **packet**, specifying the addresses of the source and the destination as well as error-checking information.

■ **Hello world.** The output of most **C** programmers' first program, from Kernighan & Ritchie's **canonical** C text, *The C Programming Language*.

■ **help** A command that will bring up help information in some programs and in some operating systems. When you are stuck, it never hurts to type *help*, or *h*, or *?*, and press Enter to see what happens.

A B C D E F G H I J K L M N O P Q R S T U V W X Y Z

■ **HEPnet** A network for physicists, not part of the Internet, but accessible via the **Web** at http://info.cern.ch/hypertext/DataSources/bySubject/Physics/HEP.html.

■ **hetboy** A heterosexual male, used most often in alt.sex groups.

■ **heterogeneous network** A network that includes various types of computers, operating systems, network cards, and so on, which therefore must be capable of different network **protocols**.

See also **homogeneous network**.

■ **hetgirl** A heterosexual female, used most often in alt.sex groups.

■ **hex**

See hexadecimal.

■ **hexadecimal** (adj) Pertaining to a numerical system using base 16 (as opposed to our more common decimal system, which uses base 10, or the **binary** system, which uses base 2). Hexadecimal digits are represented by the numerals 0 through 9 and the letters A through F. Because 16 is a multiple of 2, it is easy to convert binary numbers into hexadecimal numbers, and some programs display data in hexadecimal form.

■ **HGopher** A gopher client for **Windows**, available via **anonymous FTP** from lister.cc.ic.ac.uk.

■ **hiccup** (v) Said of a network or application, to mistakenly skip some data or send it more than once.

■ **hierarchical file system** A system of arranging files in directories and subdirectories in order to maintain hierarchical

relationships between the files and make them easier to find and retrieve.

■ **hierarchical name**

See **domain name**.

■ **hierarchical routing** A system of **routing** in which different parts of a large network are arranged in a hierarchical tree and each level takes care of routing information to subordinate levels (see illustration).

The Internet maintains three different routing levels: **backbone** networks, **mid-level** networks, and **stub** networks.

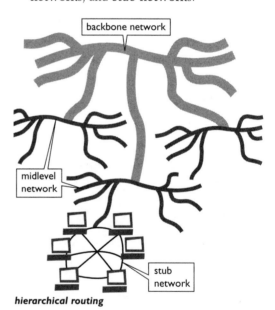

hierarchical routing

■ **hierarchy** 1. In file storage, the arrangement of directories into a tree of parents and children; 2. In networks, the arrangement of levels for routing purposes; 3. In **Usenet**, the organization of **newsgroups** into general areas, topics, and subtopics, or the major groupings themselves.

■ **High-Cap**
See T1.

■ **High-Level Data Link Control (HDLC)** An ISO protocol for the **data link layer** of **X.25** and **OSI** networks. It specifies that data is sent in **frames** that may vary in length.

■ **High Performance Parallel Interface (HPPI)** An ANSI standard for connecting **supercomputer**s to other devices, such as **router**s and other computers.

■ **hing** (n) A hint (originally from a typo) on IRC, used in **initgame**.

■ **history** 1. A list of a user's recent actions or commands; 2. A list of the **gopher** menus a user has passed through; 3. A list of the **hypertext link**s a **Web** browser has followed.

■ **hit** 1. A successful match in a database search (in some searches, you can specify a maximum number of hits); 2. A connection made to a **Web server**.

■ **hog** (v) To reserve an undue amount of some resource for yourself, as in "hogging **bandwidth**." (n) One who hogs some resource.

■ **HoloNet** [service provider] info@holonet.net, (510) 704-0160.

■ **holy war** An neverending argument between intractable sides, such as over gun control, abortion, or IBM vs. Mac. There are usually special **talk. newsgroup**s set up for the people who can't resist arguing with their opposites, and it's considered bad form to bring up a holy war topic in an inappropriate forum. (Newsgroups and **mailing list**s often have their own local holy wars.)

■ **$HOME** In UNIX, a variable that serves as an abbreviation for the **path** of your home directory.

■ **home directory** The directory allotted to your specific **account**, where you start off when you log into your **UNIX** account, and where you store your files.

■ **home page** On the **Web**, a starting **page** with links to other related pages. Many people have personal home pages with

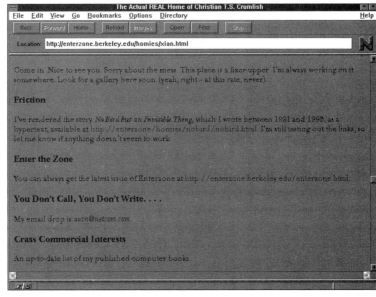

home page

A B C D E F G H I J K L M N O P Q R S T U V W X Y Z

biographical information and a **hotlist** of favorite Web destinations. The figure on the previous page shows my home page.

- **homogeneous network** A network that includes only one type of computer, operating system, network card, and so on, and therefore a single network **protocol**.

  See also **heterogeneous network**.

- **HookUp Communication Corporation** [service provider] info@hookup.net, (519) 747-4110.

- **hop** (n) Each short, individual trip that **packet**s (or e-mail messages) make many times over, from **router** to router, on their way to their destinations (see illustration below).

- **hop count** The number of **hop**s it will take for a **packet** to make it from a source to a destination.

- **host** (n) A computer on a network that allows many users access at once. If you connect to the Internet by dialing up a provider via a **modem**, then the computer you log into is your **local host**. If you

connect via **FTP** to an **archive site**, then the computer you're getting the files from is a **remote host**.

- **host address** A numerical **IP address** of the form *number-dot-number-dot-number-dot-number* (such as 192.100.81.101).

- **host name** Also *hostname*, the leftmost portion of a **fully qualified domain name**, uniquely identifying a specific computer (**host**) on a network in a **subdomain** in a **domain**.

- **host number**

  See **host address**.

- **hotlist** A list of frequent destinations, or **site**s, arranged on a menu, such as a list of Web pages.

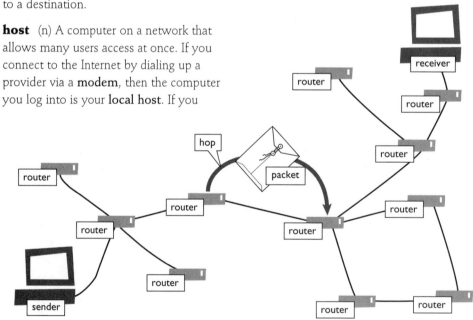

hop

■ **HotWired** The online sibling of *Wired* magazine, a **Web** **site**, a publication, and an **online** **service**, at http://www.hotwired.com/.

■ **Houston Civnet** [service provider] paul@sugar.neosoft.com, (713) 869-0521.

■ **HPPI**

See **High Performance Parallel Interface**.

■ **HP-SUX** A derogatory term for **HP-UX**.

■ **HP-UX** Hewlett-Packard's version of UNIX.

■ **.hqx** A file **extension** that indicates the file has been **compress**ed with the Macintosh BinHex compression.

■ **HTML** *Hypertext markup language*, the **hypertext** language used in **Web** **page**s. It consists of regular text and **tag**s that tell the **browser** what to do when a **link** is activated. It is a subset of **SGML**, a pre-existing markup language.

■ **HTTP** *Hypertext transport protocol*, the Internet **protocol** that defines how a **Web** **server** responds to requests for files, made via **anchor**s and **URL**s.

■ **hub** In networks arranged with **star topology**, the central connecting device, a device that allows a network to add workstations by extending the transmission signal (see illustration below).

■ **humma** A nonsense word used to fill dead air on **IRC**.

■ **hung** (adj) Said of a computer, unresponsive, frozen, and possibly stuck in an **infinite loop**.

■ **Huron Valley Free-Net** [service provider] michael.todd.glazier@umich.edu, (313) 662-8374.

See also **free-net**.

■ **HyperCard** The Macintosh hypermedia program that features **card**s that may contain text, pictures, sounds, movies, and so on, with clickable **link**s to other cards.

■ **hyperlink** A hypertext link or a hypermedia link.

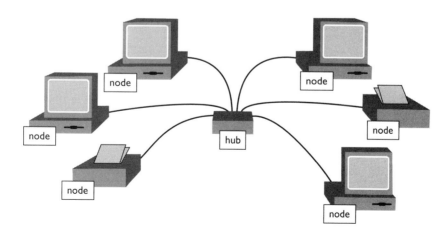

hub

- **hypermedia** An extension of the concept of **hypertext** to include pictures, sounds, movies, and so on, along with text and **link**s to other documents.

- **hypermedia link** A link from one document to another, from an **anchor** to a named location, or from an anchor to another form of media entirely, such as a picture, sound, or movie.

- **Hypernews** An experimental **Web** news format, in some ways analogous to **Usenet**, found at http://ginko.cecer.army.mil:8000/hypernews/hypernews.html.

- **HyperTelnet**

   See **Hytelnet**.

- **hypertext** Text that contains **link**s to other text documents, allowing the reader to skip around and read the documents in various orders.

- **hypertext link** A link from one text document to another or from a text **anchor** to a named location.

- **hypertext markup language**

   See **HTML**.

- **hypertext transport protocol**

   See **HTTP**.

- **HyperWais** A **WAIS** client for Hyper-Card (for the

Macintosh), available via **anonymous FTP** from sunsite.oit.unc.edu.

- **hyperzine** An electronic **hypermedia** magazine or 'zine.

- **hyphen** On computer keyboards, the – character, used also to indicate a dash. Compound portions of **newsgroup** names are hyphenated, as in alt.fan.dave-barry (alt.fan.dave.barry would be incorrect), as are some **username**s.

- **Hytelnet** A **telnet shell** that runs in UNIX; it helps you find the telnet site you want and then runs the telnet session for you (see figure). It contains a huge list of university and public library catalogs, as well as **gopher** servers, **WAIS** servers, BBSs, and so on.

- **Hytelnet for DOS** A version of Hytelnet that runs in **MS-DOS** on a PC, available via **anonymous FTP** from access.usask.ca.

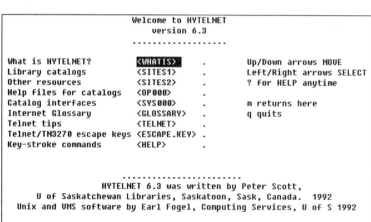

```
                        Welcome to HYTELNET
                           version 6.3
                        ...................
What is HYTELNET?        <WHATIS>    .    Up/Down arrows MOVE
Library catalogs        <SITES1>    .    Left/Right arrows SELECT
Other resources         <SITES2>    .    ? for HELP anytime
Help files for catalogs <OP000>     .
Catalog interfaces      <SYS000>    .    m returns here
Internet Glossary       <GLOSSARY>  .    q quits
Telnet tips             <TELNET>    .
Telnet/TN3270 escape keys <ESCAPE.KEY> .
Key-stroke commands     <HELP>      .


                  .....................
            HYTELNET 6.3 was written by Peter Scott,
     U of Saskatchewan Libraries, Saskatoon, Sask, Canada.  1992
   Unix and VMS software by Earl Fogel, Computing Services, U of S 1992
```

Hytelnet

■ **IAB**

See Internet Architecture Board.

■ **IANA**

See Internet Assigned Numbers Authority.

■ **IANAL** (written only) *I am not a lawyer* (used as a disclaimer before offering quasi-legal advice on the Net).

■ **IBM** *International Business Machines*, at one time the world's dominant computer company, maker of **mainframe**s and **PC**s.

■ **ice** Slang for security software, popularized in William Gibson's *Neuromancer* trilogy.

See also **firewall**.

■ **ICMP**

See Internet Control Message Protocol.

■ **I-D**

See Internet-Draft.

■ **The IDS World Network** [service provider] sysadmin@ids.net, (401) 884-7856.

■ **IEEE** (*eye triple ee*) *See* Institute of Electrical and Electronic Engineering.

■ **IEN**

See Internet Experiment Note.

■ **IESG**

See Internet Engineering Steering Group.

■ **IETF**

See Internet Engineering Task Force.

■ **IGC (Institute for Global Communications)** [service provider] support@igc.apc.org, (415) 442-0220.

■ **IgLou Internet Services** [service provider] info@iglou.com, (800) 436-IGLOU.

■ **ignore** On IRC or in any other type of **chat**, to screen out the contributions of a participant who is annoying you.

ignore

■ **IGP**

See Interior Gateway Protocol.

■ **IINREN**

See Interagency Interim National Research and Education Network.

■ *Illuminati!*   Robert Anton Wilson's crazed, paranoid novel of conspiracy theories, sex, and eschatology.

See also **fnord**.

■ **Illuminati Online**   [service provider] info@io.com, (512) 447-7866.

■ **image file**   Another name for a **binary file**.

■ **IMAP**   *Internet Message Access Protocol*, a **protocol** for the storage and retrieval of e-mail, not yet a widespread standard.

See also **Post Office Protocol**.

■ **imho**   (written only, also *IMHO*) *In my humble opinion*.

■ **Imminent Death of the Net Predicted!**   A parody of the perennial warnings that traffic on the Net has gotten to be too much. Often followed by "**film at 11**."

■ **imnsho**   (written only, also *IMNSHO*) *In my not so humble opinion*.

■ **imo**   (written only, also *IMO*) *In my opinion*.

■ **IMR**

See Internet Monthly Report.

■ **inbox**   Also *in box* and *in-box* a file in which a **mail program** stores incoming **e-mail** messages.

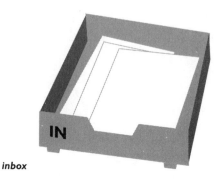

inbox

■ **include**   To copy some or all of the message to which you are responding. Most e-mail programs and **newsreaders** will add a character such as > before each line of included text.

■ **#include <disclaimer.h>**   A C joke that appears in **sig block**s, meaning that a standard **disclaimer** should be understood to have been included there.

■ **include war**   (n) A flame **war** in which so many previous **posts** have been **include**d that it's impossible to follow the argument amidst all the >s (see figure).

```
junior@site.net wrote:
>ljarden@megaco.com wrote:
>|rtm@dweezil.bigu.edu wrote:
>|>junior@site.net wrote:
>|>>You Macintosh weenies couldn't handle a computer with a
>|>>command line.
>|Oh, so I suppose your Windoze computer is so cool that it
>|has to try to fake a Macintosh front end on top of a
>|clunky old crippled operating system.
>Yeah, right. In your dreams I'd have an IBM PC.
>|>Most of the so-called weenies in this newsgroup were
>|>programming in machine language before you were out of
>|>diapers, junior. Don't let the door slam your ass on the
>|>way out of here.
>|Well, I'm probably younger than junior and a Mac was my
>|first computer and I don't need some old technogeek
>|speaking up on my behalf, thank you very much. As for you,
>|junior, what are you gonna do when you're daddy finds out
>|you're using his account?
>Yah, you're both lusers. If you had any sense you'd be
>cruising around with an Amiga, just like me.
Looks like it's time to mention Nazis and end this thread.
    --net.cop
```

include war

■ **index** (n) 1. A file in a **directory** at a **site** that describes the contents of the directory; 2. An **archie** database; 3. A default **Web page** that a **Web server** provides when no file is specified.

■ **INET** 1. An annual conference put on by the **Internet Society**; 2. An abbreviation for Internet.

■ **Inet services**

See Internet Services List.

■ **InfiNet, L.C.** [service provider] comment@infi.net, (800) 849-7214.

■ **infinite loop** A computer process that repeats forever due to a programming error, causing the computer to **hang**. The instructions on the back of many a shampoo bottle—lather, rinse, repeat—would cause an infinite loop in a computer.

■ **info** A common username for a **mailbot** (info@*host.subdomain.domain*) providing information about a network, **service provider**, or information service.

■ **info-deli** Peter Kaminski's information server (e-mail info-deli@netcom.com).

■ **Info-Mac archives** A huge collection of **Macintosh** software at the sumex-aim. stanford.edu FTP site, in the /info-mac directory. It's also **mirror**ed at wuarchive. wustl.edu in the /mirrors/info-mac directory.

■ **information agent** A program that searches databases for information without requiring that the user know where the information is stored.

■ **information pooper-highway** Some people think that the Internet won't reach its ultimate potential until computers are taken into the bathroom as easily as newspapers.

■ **information wants to be free** A slogan popular on the Internet, suggesting that it is impossible, ultimately, to hoard information, as it finds its way into general availability much as water proverbially seeks its own level.

■ **InforMNs** [service provider] howe@ informns.k12.mn.us, (612) 638-8786.

■ **info-server** An e-mail **address** that triggers a **mail server**, responding to messages that contain key words by sending stored information.

■ **initgame** An IRC variation on the guessing game called Botticelli, in which one participant changes their **nick** to the initials of a famous or fictional person and the other participants ask yes-or-no questions trying to guess the secret identity. Winner gets to start the next game.

initgame

■ **initialization string** A string of seemingly nonsense characters (really **AT commands**) sent to a **modem** to get it ready to make a connection.

■ **Inland Northwest Community Network** [service provider] kmichaelson@ewu.edu, (509) 359-6567.

■ **inline graphic** An illustration on a **Web page** (as opposed to a **linked** graphic).

■ **insert mode** In text editors such as **vi**, a special mode the user has to switch into (from **command mode**) to insert text.

■ **Institute of Electrical and Electronic Engineering (IEEE)** A professional organization that, among other things, has defined a number of networking standards, such as the **802.x protocols**.

■ **Institute for Global Communications** *See* IGC.

■ **INTAC Access Corporation** [service provider] info@intac.com, (201) 944-1417.

■ **integrated circuit** A computer chip— a tiny circuit housing many electronic components.

■ **Integrated Services Digital Network** *See* ISDN.

■ **InteleCom Data Systems** [service provider] info@ids.net, (800) IDS-1680.

■ **intelligent agent** A (mostly theoretical so far) type of computer program that can handle a user's mail, database searches, file transfers, and so on over the Internet without the user having to oversee the process directly or even remain connected to the Net.

■ **InterAccess** [service provider] info@interaccess.com, (800) 967-1580.

■ **interactive** (adj) Said of programs or environments, able to respond and give feedback to a user and to take instruction from user commands.

■ **interactive talk**

See IRC, talk.

■ **Interagency Interim National Research and Education Network (IINREN)** A set of network and operating system **protocols** under development for the National Research and Education Network.

■ **INTERCAL** A mock programming language designed to be written only (INTERCAL is said to stand for *Compiler Language with No Pronounceable Acronym*) that is the subject of the alt.lang.intercal **newsgroup**.

■ **interface** The "face" presented to a user by a computer **operating system** or application, and the set of rules governing how

intelligent agent

information is displayed and how users may enter commands.

See also front end.

- **Interior Gateway Protocol (IGP)** A protocol that defines how routing information is distributed among routers in a network.

- **Intermediate System (IS)** An OSI system that moves packets across a network.

See also router.

- **Intermediate System to Intermediate System Protocol (IS-IS)** An OSI Interior Gateway Protocol that can route both OSI and IP packets.

- **intermittent** (adj) Said of a connection, not constant, occurring irregularly.

- **internal modem** A modem chip mounted on a board installed inside a computer.

See also external modem.

- **International Organization for Standardization (ISO)** An international standards organization attempting to foster international cooperation in science, engineering, and technology. Creator of the OSI Model.

See also American National Standards Institute.

- **International Telegraph and Telephone Consultative Committee (Comite Consultatif International de Telegraphique et Telephonique— CCITT)** An international standards organization comprising telecommunications companies, part of the United Nations' International Telecommunications Union, creator of the X.25, X.400, and X.500 standards.

- **internet** Any network that uses the TCP/IP protocol suite.

See also Internet.

- **Internet** An international network of well over ten thousand networks linked using the TCP/IP protocols (see illustration, next page). Also used more loosely to mean either the world-wide information net or the conglomeration of all computers and networks that can be reached via an Internet e-mail address.

- **Internet Access Cincinnati** [service provider] info@iac.net, (513) 887-8877.

- **Internet Adapter, The (TIA)** A UNIX program that enables a dial-up shell account to emulate a SLIP connection, allowing the user to run Internet software native to his or her desktop environment without the full costs (or full functionality, either) of real SLIP. TIA is available from Cyberspace Development at http://marketplace.com/.

- **Internet address**

See IP address.

- **Internet Architecture Board (IAB)** A group that oversees the maintenance of TCP/IP protocols and promulgates other Internet standards.

- **Internet Assigned Numbers Authority (IANA)** A group that assigns the standard numbers used for ports, sockets, and so on. Assigned numbers can be found in the Internet document called STD2 (one of the RFCs).

- **Internet Control Message Protocol (ICMP)** An Internet protocol that defines error messages and governs how test packets and the ping command function.

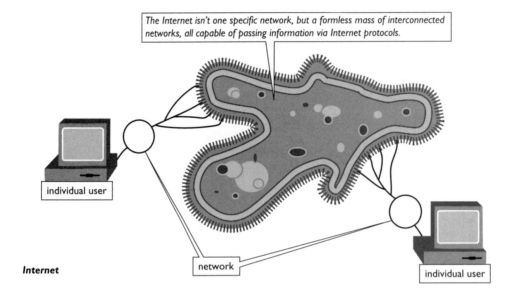

The Internet isn't one specific network, but a formless mass of interconnected networks, all capable of passing information via Internet protocols.

individual user

Internet

network

individual user

■ **Internet Direct, Inc.** [service provider] info@indirect.com (automated), support@ indirect.com (human), (602) 274-0100 (Phoenix), (602) 324-0100 (Tucson).

■ **Internet-Draft (I-D)** Draft documents written by the **Internet Engineering Task Force** dealing with potential problems and networking developments. They are archived at the ftp.internic.net **anonymous FTP** site.

See also **RFC**.

■ **Internet Engineering Steering Group (IESG)** A group that manages the **Internet Engineering Task Force** and reviews Internet standards.

■ **Internet Engineering Task Force (IETF)** A voluntary group made up of researchers that studies technical problems and proposes solutions to the **Internet Architecture Board**.

■ **Internet Experiment Note (IEN)** A now-obsolete series of reports on the development of the Internet, parallel to the **RFC**s.

■ **Internet Hunt** A monthly contest consisting of ten questions whose answers must be dug up on the Internet. The contest is reachable by **gopher** via gopher. cic.net in the hunt directory. Here's a sample question from the October, 1994 hunt (question designed by Dan Marmion):

"Surrey With the Fringe on Top." How many stars did Down Beat magazine give that album?

■ **Internet Monthly Report (IMR)** A monthly publication about the Internet, produced for the **Internet Research Task Force**.

■ **Internet Network Information Center**
See InterNIC.

■ **Internet number**
See IP address.

■ **Internet On-Ramp, Inc.**
[service provider] info@on-ramp.ior.com,
(509) 927-7267.

■ **Internet Protocol (IP)** The protocol
that handles routing of **datagrams** from one
Internet **host** to another. It works along
with the **Transmission Control Protocol**
(TCP) to ensure that data is trasmitted accurately across the Internet.
See also TCP/IP.

■ **Internet Relay Chat**
See IRC.

■ **Internet Research Steering Group
(IRSG)** A group that manages the Internet
Research Task Force.

■ **Internet Research
Task Force (IRTF)**
A voluntary group
that projects long-
term issues and prob-
lems for the Internet
and proposes solut-
ions and new direc-
tions, reporting to
the Internet
Architecture Board.

■ **Internet Services
List** An exhaustive
list of Internet ser-
vices, maintained by
Scott Yanoff and avail-
able via **anonymous**

FTP from csd4.csd.uwm.edu, in the /pub
directory, with the file name inet.services.txt.

■ **Internet Society (ISOC)** A nonprofit
organization that promotes the use of the
Internet in academic and research communities and supports networking research, publishing the *Internet Society News* and putting
on the **INET** conference every year.

■ **Internet Talk Radio (ITR)** A set of
audio programs, similar to radio broad-
casts, distributed over the Internet via
the **MBONE**. For more information, send
e-mail to info@radio.com.

■ **Internet tools** A set of utility programs
that can use various Internet facilities and
that have **interoperability**.

■ **Internet Underground Music Archive
(IUMA)** A database of (mostly unsigned)
bands, including sound clips, video clips,
information, and many other music-related

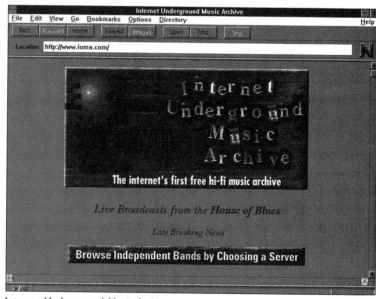

Internet Underground Music Archive

links, available via the Web at http://www. iuma.com/.

■ **Internetwork Packet Exchange (IPX)**
Novell's NetWare network layer protocol that specifies addressing, routing, and switching packets between a server and workstations and across interconnected LANs. **Encapsulated** IPX packets can be carried by **Ethernet** packets and **token ring** frames.

■ **InternetWorks**
A **Web browser** for **Windows** available via **anonymous FTP** fromftp.booklink. com. (See figure, opposite.)

■ **Internet Worm**
See **Great Worm**.

■ **InterNIC**   Short for the Internet Network Information Center, a service of the **National Science Foundation**. It provides information about the Internet and registers **domain name**s, available via e-mail at info@internic.net or on the **Web** at http://www.internic.net/.

■ **interoperability**   The ability of devices made by different manufacturers or as part of different computer systems to communicate and share information over a network.

■ **Interport Communications**
[**service provider**] info@interport.net, (212) 989-1128.

■ **InterSLIP**   Macintosh SLIP software, developed by InterCon Systems Corporation and available as **freeware** via **anonymous FTP** from ftp.intercon.com.

■ **InterText**   A online fiction magazine distributed via the **Web** from http://www. etext.org/Zines/InterText/.

InternetWorks

■ **Iowa Knowledge Exchange**
[**service provider**] garyb@ins.infonet.net, (515) 242-3556.

■ **IP**   *Internet Protocol*, the **protocol** that handles routing of **datagram**s from one Internet **host** to another. It works along with the Transmission Control Protocol (**TCP**) to ensure that data is trasmitted accurately across the Internet.
See also **TCP/IP**.

■ **IP address**   Also called a *dotted quad,* the numerical **Internet Protocol** address that uniquely identifies each computer on the Internet, made up of four numbers separated by three dots.

■ **IPX**

See **Internetwork Packet Exchange.**

■ **irc** UNIX **client** software for IRC.

■ **IRC** *Internet Relay Chat*, a **protocol** for **client/server** programs that allows you ito **chat** with people in **real time** (synchronously) all over the Internet in **channels** devoted to different topics.

■ **Ircle** Macintosh **client** software for Internet Relay Chat, available via **anonymous FTP** from mac.archive.umich.edu.

■ **IRSG**

See **Internet Research Steering Group.**

■ **IRTF**

See **Internet Research Task Force.**

■ **IS**

See **Intermediate System.**

■ **ISDN** *Integrated Services Digital Network*, a digital **circuit-switched network** that can carry both voice and data communication over a single cable. ISDN standards have been specified by the **CCITT**. (Some people joke that ISDN stands for *It Still Does Nothing*.)

■ **IS-IS**

See **Intermediate System to Intermediate System Protocol.**

■ **ISO** The *International Organization for Standardization*, which attempts to foster international cooperation in science, engineering, and technology. Creator of the **OSI** Model.

See also **American National Standards Institute.**

■ **ISOC**

See **Internet Society.**

■ **ISODE**

See **ISO Development Environment.**

■ **ISO Development Environment (ISODE)** Software that enables networks using **OSI** standards to communicate with **TCP/IP** networks.

■ **ITR**

See **Internet Talk Radio.**

■ **IUMA**

See **Internet Underground Music Archive.**

■ **IWBNI** (written only, also *iwbni*) *It would be nice if*.

■ **IYFEG** (written only) *Insert your favorite ethnic group*.

A B C D E F G H I J K L M N O P Q R S T U V W X Y Z

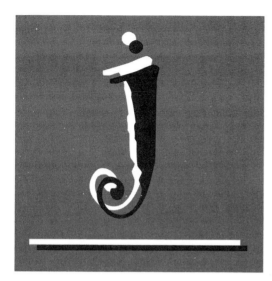

■ **jack in** To log onto the Internet (from a cyberpunk term popularized by William Gibson).

jack in

■ **Jackson Area Free-Net** [service provider] dlewis@jscc.cc.tn.us, (901) 425-2640.

■ **Janet** The major United Kingdom **backbone** network.

■ **jargon file** A list of **hacker** jargon and slang—compiled and maintained collec-

tively since the 1960s—with excellent definitions, great humor, and lots of interesting anecdotes, available via the **Web** at http://www.ccil.org/jargon/jargon.html and as a paper book from MIT Press under the name *The New Hacker's Dictionary, Second Edition* (buy the book!).

■ **joe** A UNIX text editor.

■ **Joint Photographics Experts Group** An **ISO** committee that proposed the JPEG image compression standard.

■ **JPEG** A compressed file format for images that is more efficient than **GIF** (but newer and therefore not so widespread).

■ **.jpg** A file **extension** that indicates JPEG compression.

■ **Jughead** An **index** of high-level **gopher** menus. (After the creation of **archie**, other Internet tool developers have not been able to resist naming their applications after other Archie Comics characters. Besides Jughead, there is also **Veronica**. What's next, Big Moose?)

■ **jupiter** (v) To **kill** an IRC 'bot or **kick** a user and then keep the 'bot or user from reconnecting by adopting its **nick**. (Jupiter is the **handle** of the first user to use this tactic.)

■ **JvNCnet (The John von Neumann Computer Network—Dialin' Tiger)** [service provider] info@jvnc.net, market@jvnc.net, (800) 358-4437, (609) 897-7300, (609) 258-2400.

A B C D E F G H I J K L M N O P Q R S T U V W X Y Z

■ **k** 1. An abbreviation for **kilobit**; 2. The **kill** command in many **UNIX** newsreaders.

■ **K** An abbreviation for **kilobyte**.

■ **k12.** An alternative newsgroup hierarchy in the **Usenet** mold, dedicated to elementary and secondary school (kindergarten through 12th grade) education.

■ **KAIWAN Public Access Internet Online Services** [service provider] info@kaiwan.com, (714) 638-2139.

■ **KA9Q** An adaptation of TCP/IP protocols for radio systems.

■ **Kb** An abbreviation for **kilobit**.

■ **KB** An abbreviation for **kilobyte**.

■ **Kbps** An abbreviation for **kilobits per second**, a measurement of transmission speed (such as **modem** speed or network speed).

■ **Kbyte** An abbreviation for **kilobyte**.

■ **KC Free-Net** [service provider] josbourn@tyrell.net, (816) 340-4228. *See also* **free-net**.

■ **Kermit** A very common, but now relatively slow, **protocol** for **download**ing and **upload**ing via a **modem**. *See also* **Xmodem, Ymodem, Zmodem**.

■ **kevork** (v) To abort a process or **reboot** a computer (from Dr. Jack Kevorkian, a.k.a. Dr. Death, a Michigan physician who routinely assists terminally ill patients in committing suicide).

■ **key** 1. In **encryption**, a phrase or string that allows you to **decrypt** encrypted text. In **public-key encryption**, there are two kinds of keys, **public keys** and **private keys**; 2. A key word.

■ **keyboard buffer** *See* **buffer**.

■ **key encryption** A form of **encryption** that relies upon **keys** for the **encrypt**ing and **decrypt**ing of messages or files (see illustration, next page). *See also* **private key, public key, public-key encryption**.

■ **key word** (Also *keyword*.) 1. In a database search, a word to search for in target documents—**hits** (successful matches) must include the key word; 2. In **online services**, a word used to jump directly to a topic area.

■ **kgbvax** One of the machines on the **bang path** of the famous April Fool's **kremvax** post.

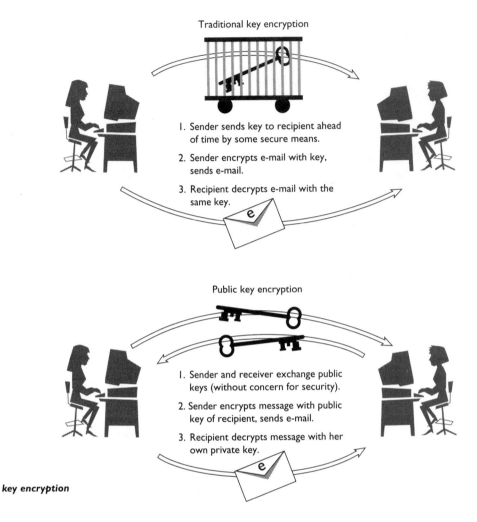

Traditional key encryption

1. Sender sends key to recipient ahead of time by some secure means.

2. Sender encrypts e-mail with key, sends e-mail.

3. Recipient decrypts e-mail with the same key.

Public key encryption

1. Sender and receiver exchange public keys (without concern for security).

2. Sender encrypts message with public key of recipient, sends e-mail.

3. Recipient decrypts message with her own private key.

key encryption

■ **Kibo** The **username** of James F. Parry, acclaimed by some as the first deity of the Internet. Also known as "he who **greps**," Kibo reportedly notes every mention of his name on **Usenet** and follows up worthy **post**s. He is also the founder of **HappyNet**. Students of **kibology** can read more on the subject in the alt.religion.kibology newsgroup.

See also **troll**, **Xibo**.

■ **KIBO** *Knowledge in, bullshit out.*

■ **kibology** The religion (or is it a science?) of **Kibo**. Its main doctrine is You're Allowed. Only Spot, Kibo's dog, is Not Allowed. For more adept instruction in the ways of kibology, try to follow the alt.religion.kibology **newsgroup** or wait for the kibologists to start **cross-post**ing their **metapost**s into your favorite newsgroup. Beware of **trolls**.

See also YHBT. YHL. HAND, You misspelled…

■ **Kibo number** Also *Kibo #*, a number that represents how close you are to **Kibo** in terms of e-mail. Kibo's Kibo number is 0. Anyone who has gotten mail from Kibo has the Kibo number 1. Mail from someone with a lower Kibo number than yours lowers your Kibo number to that person's Kibo number plus 1.

■ **kiboze** (v) To **grep** the **newsfeed** to find every single **post** that mentions the **key word** you're grepping for.
See also **Kibo**.

■ **kick** (v) To eject a participant from an **IRC** conversation and prevent the user from rejoining (done by the **channel op**).

■ **kill** (v) 1. To delete a **post** (mark it as having been read); 2. To delete posts automatically, using a **kill file**; 3. To stop a process; 4. To erase a file.

■ **kill file** Also *killfile*, a file containing search instructions for automatically **kill**ing or **autoselect**ing **Usenet post**s. Sometimes called a **bozo filter**, a kill file can be used to screen out annoying posters and avoid uninteresting **thread**s.
See also **plonk**.

■ **kilobit** (Abbreviated *k* or *Kb*.) Roughly one thousand (actually 1,024) **bit**s. Kilobits per second (kps or Kbps) is a common measurement of transmission speed (such as **modem** speed or network speed).

■ **kilobits per second** (Abbreviated *kps* or *Kbps*.) A measurement of the speed of a **medium**, meaning the number of **kilobit**s that can pass through the medium in one second.
See also **bits per second**.

■ **kilobyte** (Abbreviated *K*, *KB*, or *Kbyte*.) Roughly one thousand (actually 1,024) **byte**s, usually a measurement of **memory** or storage capacity.

■ **KIS**
See **Knowbot Information Services**.

■ **Kitsap Free-Net** [service provider] michael@kitsap.lib.wa.us, (206) 377-7601.
See also **free-net**.

■ **kludge** (*klooj*, n) The more common spelling of *kluge*, a clumsily assembled program or feature of a program that functions well enough but is not elegant, similar to the noncomputer expression *jury-rigged*.

■ **kluge** (*klooj*, n) The original and more phonetically correct spelling of *kludge*, a clumsily assembled program or feature of a

kill file

program that functions well enough but is not elegant, similar to the noncomputer expression *jury-rigged*.

■ **Knowbot**

See Knowbot Information Services.

■ **Knowbot Information Services (KIS)**
An experimental information service on the Net, intended to function as a robotic librarian that can search databases and, among other things, help find e-mail addresses. To access the Knowbot, **telnet** to nri.reston.va.us. For more information, send e-mail to kis@nri.reston.va.us.

■ **Korn shell**   A common flavor of UNIX shells.

■ **kps**   An abbreviation for **kilobits per second**, a measurement of transmission speed (such as **modem** speed or network speed).

■ **kremvax**   An imaginary **Usenet** site, the source of a famous April Fool's hoax **posting** in 1984, supposedly the first Soviet communication over the Internet, a direct message from Premier Konstantin Chernenko (actually written by Piet Beertema). The post was met with both welcoming and scornful responses.

■ **l** The UNIX *directory list* command, producing full information about the files (except dot files) in the working directory.

■ **Lamoille Net** [service provider] braman@world.std.com, (802) 888-2606.

■ **LAN** (n) *Local area network*, a computer **network**, usually confined to a single office or building, that allows for the sharing of files and other resources (such as printers) among several users and makes **interoperability** among various systems possible.

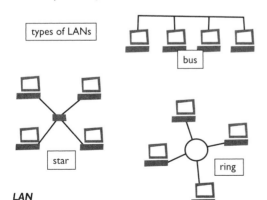

LAN

■ **LAN adapter** Also called a *network interface card* or *network interface controller*, a **card** installed into a PC to attach it to a **LAN**.

■ **LAN Workplace** Novell's TCP/IP **client** software for **Macintosh** and DOS computers.

■ **LAP**
See Link Access Protocol.

■ **LAT**
See Local Area Transport.

■ **layer**
See OSI Model.

■ **lcd** The UNIX ftp command to change the local directory (as opposed to the working directory at the ftp **host site**).

■ **leaf** 1. In network architecture, a computer that receives a signal from a more central computer but does not pass a signal along to a more remote computer; 2. In (audio cassette) **tape tree**s, a participant who receives a copy of the tape being distributed but does not make copies of the tape for anyone else.

■ **leaf site** A **Usenet** computer that receives a **newsfeed** from another site but does not distribute news to any other computers (see illustration, next page).

■ **League for Programming Freedom** A group that opposes software patents and **copyright**s; information available via **anonymous** FTP at prep.ai.mit.edu in the pub/lpf directory or by e-mail at league@prep.ai.mit.edu.

A
B
C
D
E
F
G
H
I
J
K
L
M
N
O
P
Q
R
S
T
U
V
W
X
Y
Z

The mixed metaphors of net news:

leaf site

■ **Learning Village Cleveland** [service provider] jmk@nptn.org, (216) 247-5800.

■ **leased line** A telephone line leased from the telephone company to provide a permanent connection from a **LAN** to an Internet service provider or to a **WAN**.

■ **Lehigh Valley Free-Net** [service provider] tpl2@lehigh.edu, (610) 758-4998. *See also* **free-net**.

■ **letterbomb** An e-mail message containing either **escape characters** that can **lock up** certain types of terminals, or harmful commands to be interpreted by the user's **shell**. *See also* **mailbomb**.

■ **Lexis/Nexis** A proprietary system of **searchable** databases of legal briefs (Lexis) and newspaper and magazine articles (Nexis).

■ **lharc** A file **compression** program for **DOS**.

letterbomb

■ **.lhz** A file **extension** that indicates **lharc** compression.

■ **library catalogs** Most university and public library catalogs are available via **telnet** (and some via **gopher**). **Hytelnet** has an excellent index of library catalogs.

■ **Library of Congress** The main repository of information of the U.S. government, available by **telnet** at locis.loc.gov or on the Web at http://www.loc.gov/ (see figure).

See also **Thomas.**

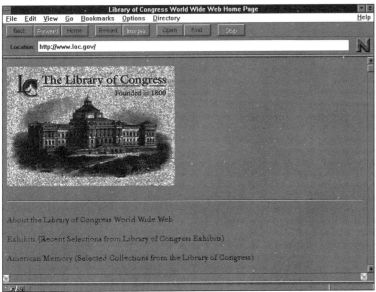

Library of Congress

■ **Lightside, Inc.** [service provider] (818) 858-9261.

■ **Lima Free-Net** [service provider] monus@clipo1.usachem.msnet.bp.com, (419) 226-1218.

See also **free-net.**

■ **line eater** A **bug** in older versions of **Usenet newsreader** software for **UNIX** that caused certain lines at the beginning of **post**s to vanish. To appease the line eater, posters would include lines of spurious text to be sacrificed instead of the actual contents of the message.

■ **line feed** Also *linefeed*, a character that moves the cursor down one line (ASCII 10), usually starting a new line in combination with a **carriage return** character.

See also **newline.**

■ **line length** The number of characters that fit on a line—fixed on some systems, settable on others. The standard line length on the Internet is 80 characters; e-mail or **Usenet post**s produced with software using longer line lengths will wrap irregularly and appear awkward to users with 80-character lines.

■ **line noise** Static or interference on a wire that corrupts the signal. On a **character-based modem** connection, for example, line noise might result in random gibberish and **escape characters** interpolated with the intended text.

■ **line-oriented** (adj) Said of applications and interfaces that display text one line at a time, rather than making an entire screenful of text available at once.

See also **screen-oriented.**

■ **link** (n) 1. In **UNIX**, a reference to a directory or file contained elsewhere that appears in directory listings just as if the remote directory or file were in the current directory (also called a *symbolic link*); 2. On **Web** pages, a **hypertext** connection, a button or highlighted bit of text that, when selected, jumps the reader to another page.

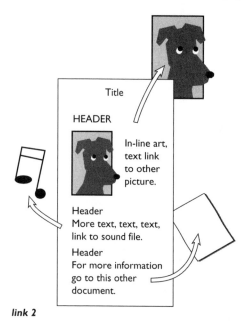

link 2

■ **Link Access Protocol (LAP)** A data link layer protocol for **AppleTalk** that specifies the interface to network hardware.

■ **Linux** (*line-ux*) An implementation of **UNIX** for IBM PC-compatibles. It has been developed as a collaborative effort by widespread Internet users and is distributed for free.

■ **LISP** The acronym for *List Processor*, a popular **Artificial Intelligence** programming language.

■ **list** (v) 1. To view the names of files in a **directory**; 2. To display the contents of a file. (n) An Internet or **BITNET** mailing list.

■ **listserv** A type of automated **mailing list** software that runs on IBM **mainframes** and originated on the **BITNET** network.

■ **little-endian** (adj) A storage format in which the most significant **byte** has the highest **address**, as opposed to **big-endian**.

■ **liveware** People (as opposed to **hardware** or **software**), also known as *wetware*.

■ **LLC**
  See Logical Link Control.

■ **local** (adj) Said of a computer to which a user is connected directly or of a device (such as a printer) or process under the user's direct control, as contrasted with remote **hosts**, devices, and processes.
  See also localhost.

■ **local area network**
  See LAN.

■ **Local Area Transport (LAT)** Digital (DEC) architecture for connecting **terminal servers** on Ethernet networks to **host** computers.

■ **local echo** 1. A copy of the data being sent (usually typed) over a communications device (such as a **modem**) displayed in a **terminal window** so that the sender can monitor the process; 2. A terminal mode in some communications programs, specifying **half duplex** transmission, in which the communications program displays the user's input on the screen, instead of relaying an **echo** from the **host**.

■ **localhost** (n) Also *local host*, the **host** computer a user is currently logged in to. The *loopback address* of any user's current localhost is always 127.0.0.1.

■ **local node** The computer on a network to which a user is connected directly.

■ **LocalTalk** Shielded, **twisted-pair** wiring and connectors for using the **Macintosh**'s built-in **AppleTalk** network hardware.

■ **locative domain name** A two-letter geographical **domain name**, such as *.us* for the United States, *.uk* for the United Kingdom, *.de* for Germany (Deutschland), and so on.

■ **LOCIS** The *Library of Congress Information Service*, available by **telnet** at locis.loc.gov or on the **Web** at http://www.loc.gov/.
See also **Thomas**.

■ **lock up** (v) To freeze, as when certain sequences of characters freeze a keyboard, preventing the user from typing.

■ **logical** Said of a computer address or device, identified by a numerical reference, which may or may not correspond to a **physical** address or device.

■ **logical conjunction** A word that joins two or more key words by specifying a logical relationship between them.

■ **Logical Link Control (LLC)** 1. The Institute of Electrical and Electronic Engineering 802 standard that specifies a uniform user interface; 2. A **data link layer** defined in IEEE 802.2.

■ **logical tree** Any **logical** arrangement of devices, files, data, and so on in which all relationships stem from a **root**; **child**

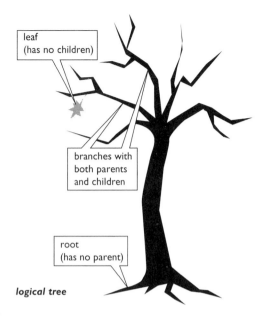

logical tree

branches are subordinate to **parent** branches, and an element without any children is called a **leaf**. (See illustration above.)

■ **Logical Unit** Software that communicates with an IBM **SNA** network.

■ **log in** (v) To connect to a network or computer, identify oneself as a user, supply a password, and start a session.

■ **login** (n) 1. A **username**, the *handle* a user logs in with, corresponding to an **account**; 2. An instance of logging in.

■ **login script** A prerecorded sequence of **login** (definition 2) steps that can play back automatically to connect a user to a computer or network. Login scripts can breach security if they automate the process of supplying a **password**, thereby allowing anyone who runs the script to log in.

■ **log off**
See **log out**.

■ **log on**

See log in.

■ **log out**　(v) To end a session and disconnect from a computer or network.

■ **LOL**　(written only, also *lol*) *Laughing out loud*.

■ **Long Island Information, Inc.**　[service provider] info@liii.com, (516) 248-5381.

■ **loopback**　(n) A test in which a signal is sent from a source to an intermediate point and then back to the original source to evaluate the accuracy of the transmission.

■ **loopback address**　The Internet address (127.0.0.1) that always points back to the localhost.

■ **Lorain County Free-Net**　[service provider] aa003@freenet.lorain.oberlin.edu, (800) 227-7113 ext. 2451, (216) 277-2451.

See also free-net.

■ **Los Angeles Free-Net**　[service provider] aa101@lafn.org, (818) 954-0080.

See also free-net.

■ **Los Nettos**　[service provider] los-nettos-request@isi.edu.

■ **low-bandwidth**
1. Said of a connection that can only manage a slow connect speed or of a resource on the Internet that a user with a slow connection will still find useful; 2. Colloquially, containing little useful information.

■ **ls**　The UNIX *short directory list* command.

■ **LU**

See Logical Unit.

■ **lurk**　To read a **mailing list** or **newsgroup** without **posting** to it. Every new user should lurk for a while before posting to get a feel for what the group is all about and how others in the group behave.

See also delurk.

■ **lurker**　One who lurks. On any **mailing list** or in any **newsgroup**, there are usually many times more lurkers than regular contributors.

■ **luser**　(*loser*) A hacker's term for a **clueless newbie**.

■ **lynx**　An excellent, text-based, UNIX **browser** for the **Web** that was created at the University of Kansas (see figure). To try out lynx (if it's not installed on your system), **telnet** to ukanaix.cc.ukans.edu and log in as *www*.

lynx

■ **m** The **mark as unread** command in some UNIX **newsreader**s.

■ **M** Abbreviation for **megabyte**.

■ **^M** One way that the **carriage return** character (**ASCII** 13) can appear. Some computers use a carriage return to indicate a **newline**, some use a **linefeed**, and some use both. If an ASCII file is transferred from a computer that uses carriage returns to one that doesn't, and a **binary file transfer** rather than an **ASCII file transfer** is used, ^M may appear at the end of each line.

■ **MaasInfo Package** A set of documents written by Robert E. Maas explaining how to use various Internet resources, available via **anonymous FTP** from aarnet.edu.au in the pub/doc subdirectory.

■ **Mac**

See Macintosh.

■ **MAC**

See Media Access Control.

■ **MAC address** The **address** that identifies a particular piece of hardware out of several connected to shared media.

■ **MacBinary** A Macintosh file transfer **protocol** that specifies how files should be transmitted over **modem**s.

■ **Macintosh** A personal computer made by **Apple** with a built-in **graphical user interface**. Macintosh users constitute a computer subculture of sorts and are usually fiercely loyal to their brand, some taking every opportunity to proselytize.

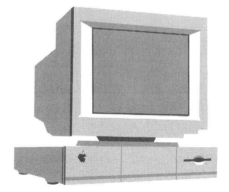

Macintosh

■ **Macintosh archive** The largest source of **Macintosh shareware** and files is the Macintosh archive at Stanford University. Connect via **anonymous FTP** to sumex-aim.stanford.edu and look in the info-mac directory. This site is also **mirror**ed at the wuarchive.wustl.edu FTP site in the /mirrors/info-mac directory.

■ **Macintoy** A derogatory term for a Macintosh, implying that it is a toy computer, not suitable for hardcore computing.

A
B
C
D
E
F
G
H
I
J
K
L
M
N
O
P
Q
R
S
T
U
V
W
X
Y
Z

■ **Macintrash** A derogatory term for a Macintosh.

■ **MacPPP** PPP (Point-to-Point Protocol) software for the **Macintosh**, developed by Merit Computer Network and available as **freeware** via **anonymous FTP** from ftp.merit.edu in the internet.tools/ppp/mac directory.

■ **macro** A shortcut consisting of a sequence of memorized keystrokes or a more elaborate set of **script**ing commands used to automate repetitive tasks, similar to a rudimentary program.

■ **MacSLIP** SLIP (Serial Line Internet Protocol) software for the **Macintosh**, developed by Hyde Park Software.

■ **MacTCP** TCP/IP protocol software for the **Macintosh**, built into version 7.5 of the Macintosh **operating system**. For more information, send e-mail to apda@ applelink.apple.com.

■ **MacWeb** A Web browser for the **Macintosh**, created by EINET and available via **anonymous FTP** from ftp.einet.net in the /einet/mac/macweb directory (see figure).

See also **WinWeb**.

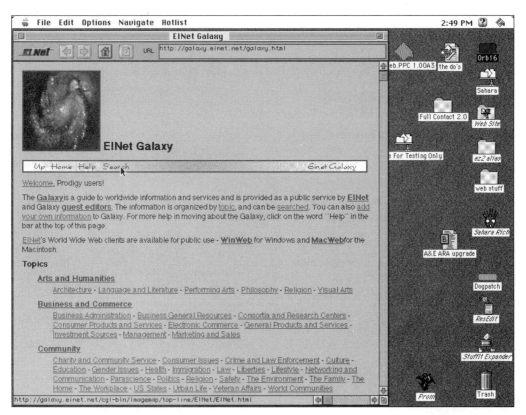

MacWeb

■ **Mac weenie** A pejorative or affectionate term for a **Macintosh** aficionado.

■ **Maestro** [service provider] info@ maestro.com (autoreply), staff@maestro. com, rkelly@maestro.com, ksingh@mae-stro.com, (212) 240-9600.

■ **magick** Magic in the sense of the occult, natural or supernatural mysteries, study of the kaballah, and so on, spelled with a *k* to distinguish from stage magic. For more information, See **newsgroup**s such as alt.magick, alt.sex.magick, alt.magick. ethics, etc.

■ **mail** (n) 1. On the Internet, synonymous with **e-mail**, that is, *electronic mail*, messages carried electronically from computer to computer; 2. The name of a simple **UNIX** **mail program**.

(v) To send an e-mail message.

■ **mail address** 1. An Internet **e-mail** **address** of the form *username@host.domain*; 2. The *username* portion of a mail **account** on a network.

■ **mailbomb** (n) A huge number of messages or an enormous chunk of data, such as a **core dump**, sent to an e-mail address as a prank or attack on the recipient, in hopes that the bomb will overload or even **crash** the user's mailer program.

(v) To send or encourage others to send a huge number of messages or an enormous chunk of data.

■ **mailbot** A *mail server*, a program that automatically responds to mail by sending information or performing functions specified in the incoming mail.

See also '**bot**.

■ **mailbox** A file, directory, or area of hard disk space used to store **e-mail** messages.

mailbox

■ **mail bridge** A device that connects networks and filters mail between them, passing only messages that meet certain criteria. (See illustration below.)

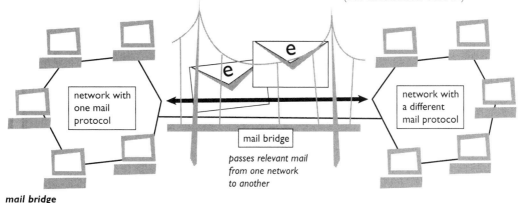

mail bridge

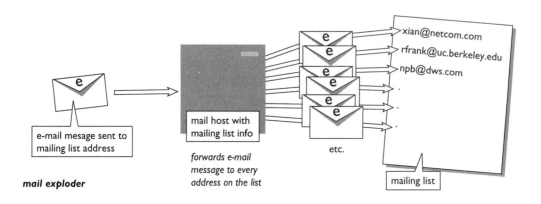

e-mail message sent to mailing list address

mail exploder

mail host with mailing list info

forwards e-mail message to every address on the list

etc.

xian@netcom.com
rfrank@uc.berkeley.edu
npb@dws.com

mailing list

■ **mail-enabled application** A program that, in addition to its normal capabilities, can also handle the sending and receiving of mail.

■ **mailer**

See mail program.

■ **Mail Exchange Record** A record type in the Domain Name System that identifies the mail-serving host for a given domain.

■ **mail exploder** A program that forwards an e-mail message to all the addresses on a mailing list (see illustration above).

See also listserv, mail reflector.

■ **mail gateway** A computer that passes e-mail from one network to another, from a network to the Internet, or vice versa, reformatting the headers as necessary (see illustration below).

■ **mailing list** A discussion group, commonly referred to on the Internet simply as a *list*, consisting of people with a common interest, all of whom receive all the mail sent, or posted, to the list. Mailing lists are often more specialized than Usenet newsgroups. Lists can be moderated or unmoderated.

See also mail exploder, mail reflector.

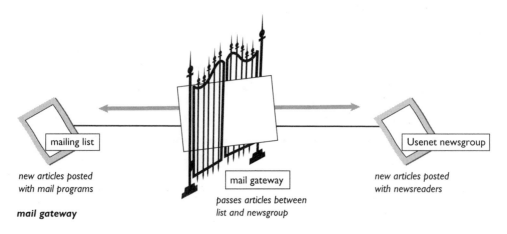

mailing list

new articles posted with mail programs

mail gateway

mail gateway

passes articles between list and newsgroup

Usenet newsgroup

new articles posted with newsreaders

■ **mail-news gateway** A computer that collects posts from a **mailing list** and forwards them to a corresponding **newsgroup**, and vice versa.

■ **mail path** Also *bang path*, a list of **sites** an e-mail message must pass through on the way from the sender to the receiver. Although it is rarely necessary any longer to specify the route your mail will take, mail **headers** still often include the entire mail path back to the sender.

■ **mail program** Also *mail reader*, the program a user reads, replies to, forwards, and saves mail with. Common **UNIX** mail programs include **mail**, **elm**, and **pine**. Eudora is a popular mail program for PCs and Macs.

■ **.mailrc** A setup file for **UNIX** mail programs (other than **elm**).

■ **mail reader**

See **mail program**.

■ **mail reflector** A mail **address** that automatically forwards any mail it receives to a list of other addresses.

See also **listserv**, **mail exploder**, **mailing list**.

■ **mail server** A *mailbot*, a program that automatically distributes files or information in response to e-mail requests.

■ **Maine Free-Net** [service provider] efrey@mmp.org, (207) 287-6615.

See also **free-net**.

■ **MAINE.NET Internet Connectivity Services** [service provider] sales@maine.net, (207) 780-6381.

■ **mainframe** (n) A large, fast, multiuser computer (larger than a **minicomputer** or microcomputer) capable of handling large quantities of data and complicated tasks, generally designed for **batch** (as opposed to **interactive**) use, most often used by large corporations, universities, and military organizations.

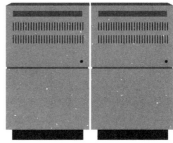

mainframe

■ **majordomo** A type of automated **mailing list** software, similar to **listserv**.

■ **MAKE.MONEY.FAST** A chain letter still making its rounds on the Net after many years. It's a classic Ponzi/pyramid scheme.

As someone replied last time I saw this garbage reposted, "Don't make your first Federal crime one that includes your name and address at the top!"

■ **man** The **UNIX** command that displays the **man pages**, online documentation for UNIX programs and commands.

■ **MAN** A Metropolitan Area Network, a high-speed (100 Mbps) public network, capable of voice and data transmission over long distances (but smaller than a **WAN**), connecting **LANs** across a city or campus (see illustration, next page).

■ **Management Information Base (MIB)** A database on a **host**, **router**, or **bridge** that

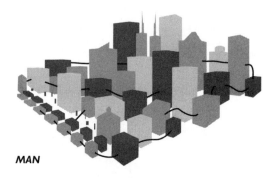

MAN

stores information about a network's configuration and performance.

■ **Management Information System (MIS)** A computer-organized system of synthesizing information from various departments in a corporation in order to provide information, assessments, and recommendations to management; a corporate computer center.

■ **Manchester encoding** A method of data-transmission that enables network interface cards to transmit digital signals using direct current, encoding data, and timing signals in the same data stream, as opposed to **non-return to zero (NRZ) encoding**, which employs two voltage levels—negative and positive—to represent 0 and 1.

■ **mang** 1. An undefined expletive, uttered or written in response to statements or actions so outrageous or bewildering as to overload a civilized person's ability to respond; 2. The sound the boo tree makes, straining to express the ineffable. (See **newsgroup** rec.music.gdead.)

■ **man pages** The *manual pages*—online documentation for **UNIX** commands and programs.

■ **manual pages**
See man pages.

■ **Marble Teleconnect** SLIP (Serial Line Internet Protocol) software for the Nextstep operating system, developed by Marble Associates.

■ **mark as unread** To save a **newsgroup** article as if it were still unread.

■ **Martian** (adj) Said of a **packet** that arrives with an incorrect or impossible source address.

■ **Mass ACK** A message sent to a **mailing list** requesting a response, in order to test the currency of the addresses on the list.

■ **massage** (v) To edit, extract information from, or format a file, as in "I'll have to massage this data some to figure out what it means."

■ **match** (n) In a **search**, a record or document that meets the specified criteria, also called a *hit*.

■ **Matrix News** A newsletter of the Matrix Information and Directory Services, on the subject of networks, avaible via **WAIS** at matrix_news.src.

■ **Maui Free-Net** [service provider] don.regal@tdp.org, (808) 572-0510.

■ **Maximum Transmission Unit (MTU)** The greatest **datagram** length allowed on a particular network.

■ **Maxwell's Demon** Nineteenth-century Scottish philosopher James Clerk Maxwell postulated that temperature could be regulated in a room by posting a demon at the entrance who would only allow air

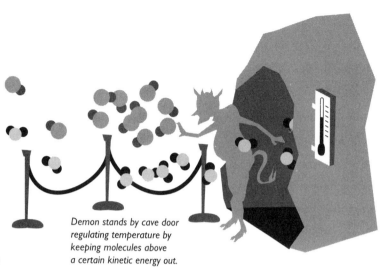

Maxwell's Demon

Demon stands by cave door regulating temperature by keeping molecules above a certain kinetic energy out.

molecules moving at a certain speed or higher to enter. This theory is the probable source for the computer terms **daemon** and **demon**.

■ **Mb** Abbreviation for **megabit**.

■ **MB** Abbreviation for **megabyte**.

■ **MBONE** The *multicast backbone*, an experimental, high-speed **virtual network** that can send **packet**s simultaneously to a large number of Internet sites, suitable for audio and visual transmission. In 1994, a Rolling Stones concert was multicast to **workstation**s around the world via the MBONE (see illustration to right).

■ **Mbps** Abbreviation for **megabits per second**.

■ **MCI Mail** [online service] An online service with e-mail connections to the Net; 2671163@mcimail.com, 3248333@mcimail.com, (800) 444-6245, (202) 833-8484.

■ **MCNet** [service provider] hammerg@firnvx.firn.edu, (407) 221-1410.

■ **MCSNet** [service provider] info@mcs.net, info@genesis.mcs.com, (312) 248-8649.

multicast feed

multicast backbone

Simultaneously sent to participating workstations connected to the MBONE

MBONE

■ **Media Access Control (MAC)** The lower component of the **data link layer**, which defines how computers on a **LAN** share access to a transmission medium, used in CSMA/CD (**Carrier Sense Multiple Access with Collision Detection**) and **token ring** LANs.

■ **media filter** A device that converts the signal from a **token ring** adapter board for a particular type of wiring.

■ **Medina County Free-Net** [service provider] gfl@freenet.medina.edu, (216) 725-1000 ext. 2550.

See also **free-net**.

■ **medium** Any substance that conveys a signal from a sender to a receiver, such as copper or other wire, coaxial cable, optical fiber, and so on.

■ **meg**

See **megabyte**.

■ **megabit** Roughly one million (actually 1,048,576) **bit**s.

■ **megabits per second** A measurement of transmission speed (such as **modem** speed or **network** speed).

■ **megabyte** Roughly one million (actually 1,048,576) **byte**s, usually a measurement of memory (RAM) or storage (HD).

■ **MEGO** (written only) *My eyes glaze over.*
See also **ETLA**, **TLA**.

■ **meltdown** What happens when a network is so overloaded that it **crash**es.

■ **meme** (rhymes with *seem*, n) A self-replicating and self-perpetuating idea, concept, saying, pun, or way of thinking. For example, how many times have you heard "The Eskimo language has a thousand words for *snow*" or words to that effect? It doesn't matter that it's not actually true; it is such an infectious or useful metaphor that it sticks in the mind and circulates from person to person perpetually.

The word *meme* was coined as an analogy to *gene* (in the sense of the "selfish" gene that propagates itself, using people as a medium) as well as *phoneme* and *morpheme* (in the sense of a "unit" of thought). The study of memes is called *memetics*. When a powerful set of memes (such as a religious philosophy) is unleashed on the Internet, it is called a *meme plague*.

See also **sig virus**.

■ **memory** Generally synonymous with RAM (random access memory), a location where files and processes a computer is currently working on are stored. The **operating system read**s applications and documents into memory and also **write**s (saves) the results back to the disk (or other storage medium).

■ **menu** A list of options available to a user. Options can usually be selected with a mouse or other pointing device, or by typing the number of the desired menu item and pressing Enter (see illustration, opposite page).

■ **menu-driven program** A program whose commands are accessible via **menu**s, relieving the user of the need to memorize commands.

- **Meridian Area Free-Net** [service provider] ric4aardvark@delphi.com, (601) 482-2000.

  See also **free-net**.

- **Merit Network** [service provider] jogden@merit.edu, (313) 764-9430.

- **message** 1. An e-mail letter; 2. A comment sent to a specific person on IRC and not to the entire channel; 3. A packet.

- **message cancel** A feature of some mail programs that allows the user to catch a message and "unsend" it (for only a short while after sending).

- **message of the day** A message from a network's system administrator that is displayed whenever a user logs in.

  See also **cookie**.

- **message handling service (MHS)** A popular e-mail protocol for storage,

menu

management, and exchange, especially in corporate offices, licensed by Novell.

- **message handling system** The CCITT X.400 protocol for store-and-forward messaging.

- **message switching** Also called *packet switching*, a store-and-forward method for routing messages in which each message is passed from a source through intermediate nodes to a destination address.

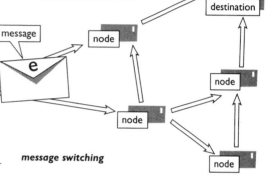

message switching

- **mess-dos** A pejorative term for MS-DOS, impugning its elegance.

- **metanetwork** A network made up of other networks. The Internet is one.

- **The Meta Network (TMN)** [service provider] info@tmn.com, (703) 243-6622.

- **metapost** A Usenet post, such as a troll, whose actual purpose is different from its literal content.

- **metasyntactic variable** A dummy variable, a stand-in variable used in an example to clarify a point of syntax.

- **Metropolitan Area Network**
  See **MAN**.

■ **mget** The command in the UNIX ftp program for *multiple get*, to get a number of files at once.

■ **MHS**

See message handling service.

■ **Miami Free-Net** [service provider] currye@mail.seflin.lib.fl.us, (305) 357-7318.

See also free-net.

■ **MIB**

See Management Information Base.

■ **Michiana Free-Net Society** [service provider] dmclaugh@darwin.cc.nd.edu, (219) 282-1574.

See also free-net.

■ **MichNet (Merit Network, Inc.— MichNet project)** [service provider] info@merit.edu, jogden@merit.edu, (313) 764-9430.

■ **Microcom Networking Protocol (MNP)** An error-checking feature built into many **modems**. MNP organizes data into frames, then transmits the frames, sometimes compressing the data as well.

■ **microcomputer** A small computer with a single-chip processor, smaller than a **minicomputer** or a **mainframe**, though currently as powerful as either of these earlier computer types once were. Scorned at first by the mainframe establishment, **PCs** (personal computers) ushered in the microcomputer revolution, bringing computing power into the hands of laypeople for the first time.

Microcomputers can range in size from desktops to portables to laptops to notebooks (see illustration, to right).

See also **Apple, IBM, Macintosh, Windows.**

■ **MicroDroid** An employee of Microsoft, especially one who defends the company in Usenet newsgroups.

■ **Microphone** A communications program for the Macintosh.

■ **microprocessor** A CPU (central processing unit) housed on a single integrated circuit, as in a **microcomputer**. The **processor** is the part of the computer that communicates with RAM, the storage medium (hard disk), the keyboard, the printer, and any other devices; performs arithmetic and logical comparisons; and controls the operations of the computer.

The Pentium, PowerPC, 680x0 series, 80x86 series, and 80x8 series are all microprocessors.

■ **MicroSerf** An employee of Microsoft.

■ **Microsloth Windows** A derogatory term for **Microsoft Windows**.

■ **Microsoft** A computer company founded in 1975 that sells **MS-DOS** (the **operating**

microcomputer

system for IBM PCs and compatibles), the Microsoft Windows operating environment, and a host of applications for PCs and Macintoshes. Some believe it to exert hegemony over the PC market.

■ **Microsoft Network** An upcoming online service from Microsoft (due to appear in late 1995), access to which will come built-in with Windows 95.

■ **Microsoft Windows** A multitasking operating environment that runs on top of MS-DOS and provides IBM PCs and compatibles with a GUI (graphical user interface) not unlike that of the Macintosh, including icons, dialog boxes, menus, and a mouse pointer.

The upcoming version of Windows, called *Windows 95*, is rumored to include TCP/IP support as well as direct access to Microsoft Network, which itself will include full access to the Internet (including the Web).

See also Windoze.

■ **mid-level network** A regional network, a vague Internet level category between backbone and rib levels (see illustration, to right).

■ **MIDnet** [service provider] info@mid.net, (800) 682-5550 (no dial-up services).

■ **MidNet—Columbia** [service provider] bajjaly@univscvm.csd.scarolina.edu, (803) 777-4825.

■ **.mil** An Internet domain corresponding to U.S. military organizations.

■ **Military Network (MILNET)** A network of U.S. military sites (it was part of the original ARPAnet) that carries non-classified military communication.

■ **Millennium Online** [service provider] jjablow@mill.com, (800) 736-0122.

■ **MILNET**
See Military Network.

■ **Milwaukee Internet X** [service provider] sysop@mixcom.com, (414) 962-8172.

■ **MIME** *Multipurpose Internet Mail Extensions*, a protocol that allows e-mail to contain simple text plus color pictures, video, sound, and binary data. Both the sender and the receiver need MIME-aware mail programs to use it.

■ **MindSpring Enterprises, Inc.** [service provider] info@mindspring.com, (404) 888-0725.

■ **MindVOX** [service provider] info@ phantom.com, (212) 989-2418, (212) 989-4141.

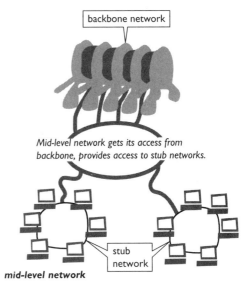

backbone network

Mid-level network gets its access from backbone, provides access to stub networks.

stub network

mid-level network

■ **minicomputer** A medium-sized computer (larger than a **microcomputer** but smaller than a **mainframe**), such as DEC's **VAX**, which can handle multitasking and over one hundred users (compared with over one thousand for mainframes).

■ **Minnesota Regional Network**

See **MRNet**.

■ **Minority On-Line Information Service (MOLIS)** A service maintained by the U.S. government offering educational and other information, as part of **Fedix**, available via **telnet** at fedix.fie.com (log in as *fedix*).

■ **MIPS** *Millions of instructions per second*, a measurement of chip (**CPU**) processing speed. Also, humorously, *meaningless indication of processor speed*.

■ **mirror** (v) To store an exact copy of files at another **archive site** (in order to minimize the load at the original site or provide an archive site geographically closer to some users).

■ **mirror archive**

See mirror site.

■ **mirror site** An **archive site** (generally FTP) containing an exact copy of the files at another site (see illustration, to right).

■ **MIS**

See Management Information System.

■ **misc.** A Usenet hierarchy devoted to whatever doesn't fit in the other hierarchies.

■ **mkdir** The UNIX command to make a directory.

■ **mnemonic** (*ne-mon-ic*, n) A word that helps one remember a command or shortcut. For example, in WordStar (an archaic word processing language), the *cut text* command is Ctrl-Y; the mnemonic to help remember this is *yank* (because you're yanking the text out of the document).

By association, the term has also taken on the meaning of the shortcut or command itself; thus, in the WordStar example, *Ctrl-Y* can also be called the mnemonic for *cut*.

■ **MNP**

See Microcom Networking Protocol.

■ **Mobile Free-Net** [service provider] geoffp@netcom.com, (205) 344-7243.

■ **mode** One of several possible states a program can be in. The most common

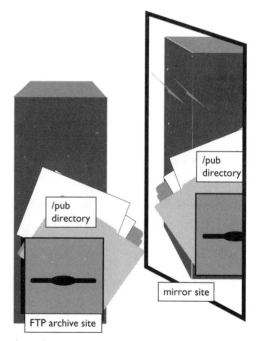

mirror site

example of this is the requirement some older **text editor**s such as **vi** have that the user must first enter **insert mode** before typing anything.

■ **modeless editor** A **text editor** that does not require the user to execute a special command to enter **insert mode** in order to begin typing. Most new text editors are modeless. On **UNIX** systems, **pico** is a modeless editor and **vi** is not.

■ **modem** (n) Short for *modulator/dem*odulator, a device that connects your computer to a phone jack and, through the phone lines, to another modem and computer, transmitting data by converting the computer's **digital** signal into the telephone's **analog carrier** signal, and vice versa. (See illustration below.)

The standard 14400 bps modem is 46 times faster than the 300 bps modems of 15 years ago.

■ **modem bank** A set of shelved **modem**s connected to a **host** or **BBS** to allow many callers to log in.

■ **moderate** (v) To review **article**s submitted to a **list** or **newsgroup** and **post** only those which meet certain criteria (minimally, they must be on topic).

■ **moderated** (adj) Said of **list**s and **newsgroup**s whose **post**s must pass muster with a **moderator** before appearing.

■ **moderator** The volunteer who decides which submissions to a **moderated list** or **newsgroup** will be **post**ed.

■ **monospace font** A font in which all the characters are the same width (as opposed to a proportional-width font, in which the letters *w* and *i*, for instance, vary greatly in width).

```
This text is written in a monospace
font.
```

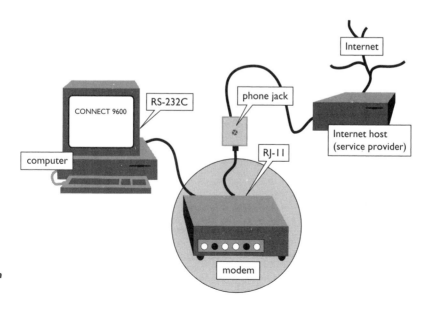

modem

For **e-mail** and **newsgroup post**s, the 80-character **line length** standard presupposes a monospace font (as do **ASCII** graphics and many people's **sig block**s).

■ **MOO**

See MUD.

■ **Mordor—Public Access Unix** [service provider] info@ritz.mordor.com.

■ **more**   A common **UNIX** paging program. Type

more *filename*

to see *filename* displayed one screenful at a time.

■ **MorF**   (written only) Short for *Male or Female*, asking about another user's sex.

■ **Morning Star PPP**   PPP (Point-to-Point Protocol) software for **Nextstep**, developed by Morning Star Technologies.

■ **Mosaic**   The first graphical **Web browser**, developed by **National Center for Super-computing Applica-tions**, which greatly popularized the Web in the last few years, and by extension the Internet, as it made the multimedia capabilities of the Net accessible via mouse clicks.

Mosaic exists in **freeware** and **shareware** versions for the **Macintosh**, **Windows**, and X **Window** systems and is available via **anonymous** FTP at ftp.ncsa.uiuc.edu.

Mosaic is often used (incorrectly) as a synonym for the **World Wide Web**.

See also **lynx**, Netscape, **www**.

■ **moskvax**   One of the **sites** in the **path** of the famous April Fool's **kremvax post** in 1984.

■ **MOTAS**   (written only) *Member of the appropriate sex*. A way of referring to a potential partner without specifying that person's sex.

■ **motd**   (written only) *Message of the day*.

■ **Motion Picture Experts Group**   An ISO committee that proposed the **JPEG** audiovideo compression standard.

■ **MOTOS**   (written only) *Member of the opposite sex*.

■ **MOTSS**   (written only) *Member of the same sex*.

■ **motto!**   A follow-up post on a **news-group**, proposing the previous post as a

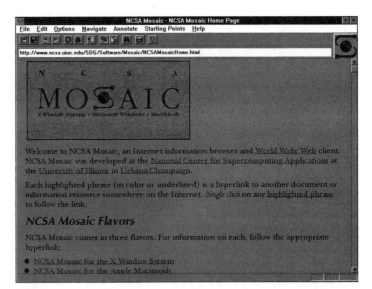

Mosaic

motto for the group or for **Usenet** as a whole, perhaps facetiously.

■ **mouse potato** A human being who spends inordinate chunks of his or her waking life glued to a computer screen, mouse in hand.

mouse potato

■ **Mozilla** A slang name for the **Netscape** Web browser.

■ **MPEG** A compressed file format for movies (audiovideo files).

■ **.mpg** A file **extension** that indicates MPEG compression.

■ **mput** The command in the **UNIX** ftp program for *multiple put*, to send a number of files at once.

■ **MRNet (Minnesota Regional Network)** [service provider] info@mr.net, (612) 342-2570.

■ **MS-DOS** An operating system for IBM PCs and compatibles, made by **Microsoft**.

■ **MSEN, Inc.** [service provider] info@msen.com, (313) 998-4562.

■ **MTU**

See **Maximum Transmission Unit**.

■ **MU*** An abbreviation for any one of a series of acronyms for *multiuser* role-playing game environments.

See also **MUD**.

■ **mud** (v) To explore a **MUD**.

■ **MUD** A *multiuser domain/dimension/dungeon*. A role-playing game environment that allows people all over the Net to play together in something like interactive text adventures. Other names for MUDs include *MOO, MUSE, Muck, Mush, Fugue, TinyFugue,* and *TinyMUD*.

MUD

MUDs are said to be highly addictive and it sometimes seems that only college students have enough time to explore them thoroughly.

They are now also used as conference spaces and educational aids.

For more information, see the **newsgroups** rec.games.mud.announce and alt.mud or the **FTP site** actlab.rtf.utexas.edu.

■ **multicast** (v) To send a **packet** simultaneously to multiple **sites**.

(adj) Said of a packet intended to be received by a number of **hosts**.

See also **broadcast**.

■ **multicast backbone**
See MBONE.

■ **Multics** A late '60s predecessor to UNIX.

■ **multimedia** A form of communication combining text with graphics, page layout, motion pictures, animation, sounds, and so on.

See also **hypermedia**.

■ **Multiple User Dimension**
See MUD.

■ **Multiple User Domain**
See MUD.

■ **Multiple User Dungeon**
See MUD.

■ **Multiple Virtual Storage (MVS)** IBM's standard **mainframe** operating system, similar to **VM** (Virtual Machine).

■ **multiplex** (adj) Using a single transmission medium to transmit over multiple **logical channels** at once, such as when an Internet

site maintains HTTP, FTP, SMTP, telnet, and other channels.

■ **Multipurpose Internet Mail Extensions (MIME)**
See MIME.

■ **multitasking** (n) The simultaneous execution of two or more programs by a single computer.

■ **MUSE** A *multiuser simulation environment* (for role-playing games).
See also MUD.

■ **MV Communications** [service provider] info@mv.com, (603) 429-2223.

■ **MVS**
See Multiple Virtual Storage.

■ **MX Record**
See Mail Exchange Record.

■ **MYOB** (written only, also *myob*) *Mind your own business.*

■ **my two cents** A tag appended to **Usenet** or **list posts**, indicating "this is just my opinion," or "I just wanted to get my two cents in."

my two cents

■ **n** The *next article* command in many UNIX newsreaders.

■ **nagware** Shareware that reminds the user, automatically and frequently, to register the software and pay for it.

■ **NAK** (rhymes with *pack*) A *negative acknowledgment* from a computer that a **packet** of data has not been received successfully, i.e., the **checksum** figure does not match that of the sent packet (ASCII 21).

■ **Name Binding Protocol (NBP)** AppleTalk's **transport layer protocol**. It resolves numeric AppleTalk addresses into names and vice versa.

■ **name server** 1. Also *domain name server*, an application that maintains a table of **domain names** and corresponding **IP addresses** in order to resolve the domain names of messages; 2. Also *CSO name server*, a **searchable white pages** listing of **real names** and associated **e-mail addresses**, usually reached via **gopher**.

■ **naming conventions** *See* **newsgroup name.**

■ **NAND** (rhymes with *hand*) [Boolean operator] *Not and.* A text **search** with NAND between two words will match any documents that fail to contain both words.

■ **Naples Free-Net** [service provider] hainswm@firnvx.firn.edu, (800) 466-8017. *See also* **free-net.**

■ **nastygram** 1. An **e-mail** chastisement from a **net.god** for violating **netiquette**; 2. A particularly vicious **flame**; 3. A **letterbomb.**

■ **National Center for Supercomputing Applications (NCSA)** Part of the National Science Foundation and the creator of **NCSA telnet** and **Mosaic.**

■ **National Information Infrastructure (NII)** The U.S. government's name for the Internet and other public networks. More information about the government's plans for the NII is available via **anonymous FTP** from ftp.ntia.doc.gov in the /pub directory in a file called NIIAGENDA.ASC.

■ **National Information Standards Organization (NISO)** A U.S. organization for standards in information, technology, and computing, most specifically as related to the Internet and **WAIS**, author of the revised WAIS standard.

■ **National Institute for Standards and Technology (NIST)** An organization of the U.S. government that promotes national standards of measurement, technology, computing, and networking (formerly the National Bureau of Standards).

A
B
C
D
E
F
G
H
I
J
K
L
M
N
O
P
Q
R
S
T
U
V
W
X
Y
Z

■ **National Public Telecommunications Network (NPTN)** A nonprofit network that promotes **free-net**s and public networking in general.

■ **National Research and Education Network (NREN)** The network established by the High-Performance Computing Act of 1991, intended to link government agencies, research organizations, and schools.

■ **National Science Foundation (NSF)** The U.S. government agency that funds and runs **NSFnet**, and consequently many university links to the Internet. Besides its involvement with the Net, NSF promotes science and research.

■ **natural language** The way real human beings communicate, as contrasted with computer languages, which are generally much more logical, literal, and inflexible.

■ **natural language query** A query written in **natural language** (for example, plain English) seeking information from a database.

■ **navigate** A computer jargon term meaning to get around a program, find commands, move through a document, or hunt around the Internet (see illustration, opposite).

■ **Navigator** CompuServe's graphical software for browsing its **online service**.

■ **Nazis** Mention them, or Hitler specifically, and you've officially ended a **thread** on **Usenet**.

See also **Godwin's Rule**.

■ **NBP**

See **Name Binding Protocol**.

■ **ncftp** A sophisticated **UNIX FTP** program (a cut above **ftp**) that helps to automate and streamline FTP operations.

■ **NCSA**

See **National Center for Supercomputing Applications**.

■ **NCSA telnet** A free **telnet client** for **Macintosh** or **Windows**, available via **anonymous FTP** from ftp.ncsa.uiuc.edu.

■ **NEARnet** [service provider] nearnet-join@nic.near.net, (617) 873-8730.

■ **Neosoft, Inc.** [service provider] info@neosoft.com, (800) GET-NEOS.

■ **net.** 1. The original **Usenet** hierarchical distinction, superseded by the **big seven** hierarchies (**comp.**, **news.**, **misc.**, **rec.**, **sci.**, **soc.**, and **talk.**) in the **Great Renaming**; 2. A prefix added to a lot of common words to suggest their counterparts on the Internet (such as **net.cop**, **net.god**, and so on). (See illustration, opposite page.)

navigate

■ **.net** An Internet **domain**, corresponding to constituent networks.

■ **Net** Also *net* and *'net,* often used as an abbreviation for the **Internet** or for **Usenet**, really a more general term for the lump sum of interconnected computers on the planet.

■ **net address** An Internet address.

■ **net.celebrity** Someone famous on the Net (usually meaning on **Usenet**).

net. 2

■ **net.citizen** A responsible member of an online community.

■ **Netcom Online Communication Service** [service provider] info@netcom.com, (408) 554-8649, (800) 501-8649.

■ **net.cop** A derogatory term for someone who tries to censor or control the **posts** of others on **Usenet**.

■ **NetCruiser** **Windows** software for **CSLIP** access to the Internet, distributed by Netcom Online Communication Services (it only connects via Netcom).

■ **netdead** (adj) Said of someone who has signed off **IRC** and can no longer be reached.

■ **Netfind** An Internet resource for finding e-mail addresses, reachable by **telnet** (the exact address depends on where you are).

■ **net.god** An apparently powerful being on the **Net**.

■ **nethack** A popular text-adventure dungeon game, similar to *Rogue*.

■ **nethead** 1. A Dead Head (fan of the Grateful Dead) who participates in the rec.music.gdead **newsgroup** (which is **gated** to the dead-flames **mailing list**) or any of the many Dead discussion groups on **online services**; 2. Any obsessed Internet user (a more recent definition of the term).

■ **net.heavy** A person who knows a lot about how the **Internet** and **Usenet** work and whose opinions carry a lot of weight.

■ **netillinois** [service provider] joel@bradley.edu.

A
B
C
D
E
F
G
H
I
J
K
L
M
N
O
P
Q
R
S
T
U
V
W
X
Y
Z

■ **netiquette** Accepted proper behavior on the **Net**, especially in regard to **e-mail** and **Usenet**. Violate netiquette at your peril. Although the Internet and Usenet are effectively anarchies, they still have strong social cultures, and most of the rules and regulations of the Net are enforced by peer pressure.

See also **shouting**.

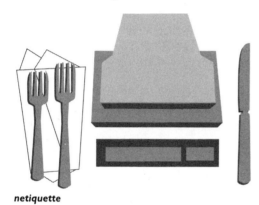

netiquette

■ **netizen** A net.citizen.

■ **net.kook** Any frequent **Usenet poster** whose **post**s reveal a strange and possibly obsessive personality. For more information, see the **newsgroup** alt.usenet.kooks.

■ **netlag** An excessive delay on **IRC** that causes messages to bunch up.

■ **net.legend** A net.celebrity, net.kook, or other famous **Internet/Usenet** figure, many of whom are discussed in the Net.Legends FAQ.

■ **Net.Legends FAQ** A FAQ document that praises and excoriates various **net. legend**s, available via **gopher** from dixie. aiss.uiuc.edu port 6969 (choose urban. legends, then Net.Legends FAQ and other

assorted FAQs, then Net.Legends.FAQ or any of the other related FAQs).

■ **NetManage Chameleon** TCP/IP software for **Windows** and **DOS**.

■ **netnews** Also *net news*, another name for **Usenet**.

■ **net.personality** A somewhat well-known person on the Net.

■ **net.police**

See **net.cop**.

■ **.netrc** A setup file for the **UNIX ftp** and **ncftp** programs.

■ **Netscape** The state-of-the-art **Web browser** (circa 1995) for **Microsoft Windows**, **Macintosh**, and **X Window**, which, on top of allowing point-and-click Internet access and integration of text, pictures, sound, and movies, also provides security features and the ability to interact with documents before they're fully loaded. It's available for free to individual users via **anonymous FTP** from ftp.mcom.com. (See figure, opposite page.)

■ **netter** Someone who explores the **Net**.

■ **network** A group of computers or other devices connected by a communications channel, to enable the sharing of files and resources among users. Networks typically provide for the sharing of printers and distribution of e-mail.

■ **network adapter card**

See **network interface card**.

■ **network address** 1. The unique name of a **node** on a network; 2. An e-mail **address**.

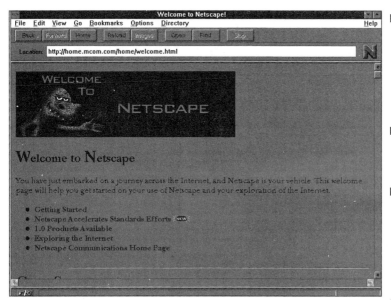

Netscape

■ **Network File System (NFS)** Not to be confused with *NSF* (the **National Science Foundation**), a **UNIX presentation layer protocol** developed by Sun Microsystems that makes it possible for a user to access files elsewhere on the network just as if they were on the user's own computer.

■ **Network Information Center (NIC)** An organization that provides information and help to users of a network, as the **InterNIC** does for the Internet.

See also **Defense Data Network Network Information Center.**

■ **network interface card** Also called a *LAN adapter*, a **card** installed into a PC to attach it to a **LAN**.

■ **network interface controller** *See* network interface card.

■ **network layer** The third layer of the **OSI Model**. (IP governs the network layer in the **TCP/IP protocol** suite.)

■ **network news** A synonym for **Usenet**.

■ **Network News Transfer Protocol (NNTP)** The **protocol** used to distribute **Usenet** newsgroups.

■ **network operating system (NOS)** A set of programs that enables networked computers to share files and devices.

■ **Network Operations Center (NOC)** An organization that oversees a network, monitoring its traffic and solving problems.

■ **network peripheral** A device, such as a printer, that is directly connected to a network and not to one of the computers or workstations.

■ **Network Time Protocol (NTP)** A protocol that synchronizes time information on the Internet.

■ **Network-USA** [service provider] all-info@netusa.net, (516) 543-0234.

■ **NevadaNet** [service provider] zitter@nevada.edu, (702) 784-6133.

■ **newbie** (n) A beginner on the Internet or especially **Usenet** (not as derogatory as **clueless newbie**).

- **newgroup**   A special kind of control message that creates a new **newsgroup**.

- **newgroup wars**   Competing **newgroup** and **rmgroup** messages repeatedly **posted** by people who alternately want and don't want a new **newsgroup** to be propagated.

- ***The New Hacker's Dictionary***   The printed-book version of the **jargon file**, published by MIT Press and well worth owning in book form.

    The contents of the jargon file are also available via the **Web** at http://www.ccil.org/jargon/jargon.html.

- **New Jersey Computer Connection**   [service provider] info@pluto.njcc.com, (609) 896-2799.

- **newline**   Any character or group of characters used to indicate the start of a new line in an **ASCII text file**. The newline characters vary from system to system. An **ASCII file** that is mistakenly transmitted as a **binary file** to an incompatible system can end with garbage characters such as ^M at the end of each line.

- **New Mexico Free-Net**   [service provider] lnewby@unm.edu, (505) 277-8148.

- **New Mexico Technet**   [service provider] reynolds@technet.nm.org, (505) 345-6555.

- **news**   Usenet articles, **posted** to **newsgroup**s.

- **news.**   A Usenet hierarchy devoted to Usenet policy, guidelines, and administrative issues.

- **newsfeed**   The **packet** of **news** articles passed along from one computer to the next on **Usenet**.

- **newsfroup**   A common typo for **newsgroup**, now accepted (facetiously) as an alternative spelling.

- **newsgroup**   A **Usenet** discussion group.

- **newsgroup creation**   In the **big seven** Usenet **newsgroup** hierarchies, new newsgroups can be created only after a formal RFD (**Request for Discussion**) and a subsequent CFV (**Call for Votes**).

    In the **alternative newsgroup hierarchies**, it is much easier to create a new newsgroup, which accounts for the proliferation of abandoned **silly group**s.

- **newsgroup name**   The hierarchical name of a **Usenet newsgroup**, starting with the first-level hierarchical distinction, followed by a **dot**, then one or more further qualifying names, none of which may be longer than 15 characters, each of which is separated by a dot.

    In proper newsgroup naming, hyphens or underscores rather than dots should be used to break up compound words. For example, alt.fan.jimi.hendrix is incorrect (and implies other jimis besides hendrix with their own fans), but alt.fan.jimi-hendrix is correct.

- **newshroup**   A common typo for **newsgroup** which, unlike **newsfroup**, has *not* been accepted as a humorous alternative spelling.

- **.newsrc**   A setup file for **newsreader**s on **UNIX** systems that keeps track of which

Usenet newsgroups the user is subscribed to and which **articles** have been read.

■ **newsreader** A program used to read Usenet **articles**, and usually also to save, respond to, and **post follow-up**s to articles, as well as to post new articles.

■ **news server** A program or computer that supplies a **newsfeed**.

■ **NewsWatcher** A newsreader for the Macintosh, available via **anonymous FTP** from sumex-aim.stanford.edu.

■ **newsweeding** A pun on *newsreading*, meaning the process of killing or ignoring uninteresting **threads** and zeroing in on the worthwhile content of a high-volume newsgroup.

■ **Nexis** An information service of Mead Data giving access to a **searchable** database of news and magazine articles and abstracts.

■ **Nextstep** An operating **system** for UNIX that offers a **graphical user interface**.
See also X Window.

■ **NeXT-WAIStation** Nextstep software that functions as both a **WAIS server** and as a **client**.

■ **NFS**
See Network File System (not to be confused with *NSF*, the **National Science Foundation**).

■ **nibble** Half a **byte** (generally four **bits**).

■ **NIC** 1. *See* Network Information Center; 2. [**service provider**] info@nic.com, (201) 934-1445.

■ **nick** A nickname used on IRC, not necessarily the same as your **username**.

■ **nickname** An alias or **address book** entry in some e-mail programs (such as **Eudora**).

■ **Nightmare File System** A derogatory term for **Network File System**.

■ **NII**
See National Information Infrastructure.

■ **NISO**
See National Information Standards Organization.

■ **NIST**
See National Institute for Standards and Technology.

■ **nixpub** A list of Internet **service providers**, posted regularly to comp.bbs.misc and alt.bbs, also available via **anonymous FTP** from vfl.paramax.com in the /pub/ pubnetc directory.

■ **nn** A UNIX newsreader (it stands for *no news*, as it tries to hide everything you don't want to see).

■ **NNTP**
See Network News Transfer Protocol.

■ **nntpd** A UNIX news server program.

■ **NOC**
See Network Operations Center.

■ **NO CARRIER** The message a **modem** displays when it detects no **carrier** signal from the phone line. (See illustration, next page.)

■ **Nodal Switching System (NSS)** The routing method of the **NSFnet** backbone.

A B C D E F G H I J K L M N O P Q R S T U V W X Y Z

NO CARRIER

■ **node** 1. In a network, any computer or other device (such as a printer); 2. Any computer on the Internet, a **host**.

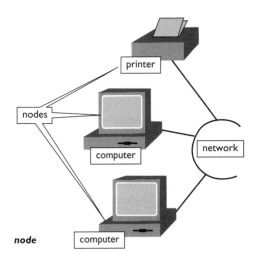

node

■ **nodename** The unique name of a device attached to a network.

■ **noninteractive** Automated, taking place all at once, without input from a user.
See also **batch**.

■ **non-return to zero (NRZ) encoding**
A data-transmission method that employs two voltage levels—negative and positive—to represent 0 and 1, as opposed to **Man-chester encoding**, which enables network interface cards to transmit digital signals using direct current, encoding data, and timing signals in the same data stream.

■ **Northern California Regional Computing Network** [service provider] pblythe@aol.com, (916) 891-1211.

■ **Northfield Free-Net** [service provider] andreacris@aol.com, (507) 645-9301.
See also **free-net**.

■ **North Shore Access** [service provider] info@northshore.ecosoft.com, (617) 593-3110.

■ **North Texas Free-Net** [service provider] kenlc@tenet.edu, (214) 320-8915.
See also **free-net**.

■ **NorthWest Net** [service provider] ehood@nwnet.net, (206) 562-3000.

■ **Northwest Nexus Inc.** [service provider] info@nwnexus.wa.com, (206) 455-3505.

■ **NOS**
See **network operating system**.

■ **NOT** [Boolean operator] *Not*. Used to reverse the logical relationship to one of the **search** elements. A text search for *x* AND NOT *y* will match only documents that contain *x* and do not contain *y*.

- **notwork** A network that isn't working.

- **NovaLink** [service provider] info@novalink.com, (800) 274-2814.

- **NPTN**

  See **National Public Telecommunications Network.**

- **NREN**

  See **National Research and Education Network.**

- **NRZ**

  See **non-return to zero.**

- **NSA line eater** A (probably) mythical National Security Agency program that would sift through the entire **Usenet newsfeed** (and perhaps all e-mail traffic as well) looking for telltale words (such as *glock, Uzi, TNT,* and so on) that would incriminate terrorists and anarchists. Some people deliberately put such words in their **sig blocks** to confuse the NSA line eater.

- **NSF**

  See **National Science Foundation.**

- **NSFnet** A major Internet **backbone**, operated by the **National Science Foundation.**

- **NSS**

  See **Nodal Switching System.**

- **NSTN** [Canadian **service provider**] parsons@hawk.nstn.ns.ca.

- **NTP**

  See **Network Time Protocol.**

- **Nuance Network Services** [service provider] staff@nuance.com, (205) 533-4296.

- **nuke** To **kill** a file or a process.

- **null device** A **logical** device that corresponds to no actual **physical** device, functioning as a sort of wastebasket.

  See also **bit bucket.**

- **numeric string** Any sequence of numbers taken as text rather than as a numeral.

- **Nuntius** A **newsreader** for the **Macintosh,** available via **anonymous FTP** from sumex-aim.stanford.edu.

- **NUPop** A **newsreader** for Windows, available via **anonymous FTP** from ftp.acns.nwu.edu.

- **nybble**

  See **nibble.**

- **nyetwork** A network that isn't working.

- **NYSERnet** [service provider] info@nysernet.org, (315) 443-4120.

- **Nyx, the Spirit of the Night** [service provider] aburt@nyx.cs.du.edu.

  See also **free-net.**

A
B
C
D
E
F
G
H
I
J
K
L
M
N
O
P
Q
R
S
T
U
V
W
X
Y
Z

tion that makes use of self-contained *objects* that can contain both programming code and data, and which function as modular program pieces.

■ **obligatory * content** Something added to a **mailing list** or Usenet post to make it relevant to the charter of the list or **newsgroup** (replacing the * with the subject of the group, as in *obligatory Amiga content* or *obligatory cat content*, and so on).

See also **Ob-**.

■ **Ocean State Free-Net** [service provider] howardbm@dsl.rhilinet.gov, (401) 277-2726.

See also **free-net**.

■ **OCLC**

See **Online Computer Library Center.**

■ **octet** Eight **bits**, especially on a system in which eight bits do not equal a **byte**.

■ **octothorpe** A number sign (#).

■ **odd parity** A method of verifying the correctness of transmitted data by summing each **byte**, adding a **parity bit** of 1 if necessary to make the sum odd, before sending the data, and then repeating the summation on the receiving end.

See also **parity**.

■ **offline** 1. Not currently connected to the **Net**; 2. Not responding to **network** requests; 3. Said of a person no longer involved in a **chat**.

See also **online**.

■ **offline mail reader** A program that connects to the **Net**, **download**s your e-mail,

■ **o** The *options* command (for setting user preferences) in many **UNIX** programs.

■ **oak.oakland.edu** A huge **FTP** archive at Oakland University.

■ **OARnet** [service provider] nic@oar.net, (614) 292-8100.

■ **Ob-** A prefix for an obligatory addendum to an off-topic **Usenet** or **list** post. Say you get into a political debate in the rec.music.dylan **newsgroup**. To keep your post technically relevant to the group, you might add:

```
ObDylan: Ah, but I was so much
older then/I'm younger than that
now.
```

See also **obligatory * content.**

■ **OBI**

See **Online Book Initiative.**

■ **object-oriented** Said of an operating system, programming language, or applica-

and then disconnects, allowing you to read, reply to, and send mail without being charged for **connect time**.

See also Eudora.

■ **offline newsreader** A newsreader that connects to the Net, **download**s all unread articles in all subscribed **newsgroup**s, and then disconnects, allowing you to read, reply to, and **post** articles without being charged for **connect time**.

■ **oic** *Oh, I see.*

■ **oldbie** A longtime user of the Net, coined by analogy to **newbie**.

You kids shore have it easy! Why, I remember, in *my* day we had to walk two miles *uphill* in snow against the wind to pick up our newsfeed and we had to specify the entire bang path. Why, I remember *one* time I had to mount a new volume when . . .

oldbie

■ **Oldie** A text editor available in the Delphi Information Service.

■ **Oklahoma Public Information Network** [service provider] fn-mail@okcforum.osrhe.edu, (405) 947-8868.

■ **Old Colorado City Communications** [service provider] dave@oldcolo.com, thefox@oldcolo.com, (719) 632-4848, (719) 593-7575, (719) 636-2040.

■ **Olympus—The Olympic Peninsula's Gateway to the Internet** [service provider] info@pt.olympus.net, (206) 385-0464.

■ **Omaha Free-Net** [service provider] lowe@unomaha.edu, (402) 554-2516.

See also **free-net**.

■ **Onet** [Canadian **service provider**] eugene@vm.utcs.utoronto.ca.

■ **127.0.0.1** The Internet *loopback address*, it is always the address of your **localhost**, the computer you are currently logged in to.

■ **online** 1. Currently connected to the Net; 2. Available for network requests; 3. Said of a person, participating in a **chat**.

See also **offline**.

■ **Online Book Initiative (OBI)** An organization that publishes uncopyrighted (or no longer copyrighted) books via the Internet, reachable via **anonymous FTP** at world.std.com.

See also Project Gutenberg.

■ **Online Career Center** A nonprofit organization that maintains a **searchable** database of employment information. It offers free access to job listings and résumés to both employers and job-seekers. For more information, **gopher** to gopher.msen.com or send e-mail to occ@msen.com.

■ **online community** Also *virtual community*, a group of people with shared interests who meet, communicate, and interact via a **network**, **BBS**, Internet discussion group, or any other form of electronic common space. Online communities have many of the properties of real-world communities.

online

■ **Online Computer Library Center (OCLC)** A nonprofit organization providing computer services (such as cataloging and interlibrary loans) for over ten thousand libraries and educational institutions. OCLC maintains the **FirstSearch Catalog**. For more information, send mail to listserv@ oclc.org

■ **online information service**

See online service.

■ **online service** A company that maintains a proprietary network and provides **e-mail**, **forums**, **chats**, games, databases of information, downloadable files, and information services (stocks, airlines, and so on), such as **America Online**, **CompuServe**, **Delphi**, **eWorld**, **GEnie**, **Prodigy**, **Micro-soft Network**, and so on.

Most online services have e-mail connections to the Internet (though some charge extra for that e-mail). More and more are adding other Internet facilities, such as **FTP**, **gopher**, and soon the **Web**, blurring the distinction further between online services and Internet **service providers**.

■ **open** (adj) Said of a **protocol**, using algorithms and technologies available to anyone (as contrasted with **proprietary**).

(v) To make a connection to a **remote host**.

See also **close**.

■ **OPEN (Olympic Public Electronic Network)** [service provider] lhaas@aol.com, (206) 417-9302.

■ **open protocol** A protocol that may be utilized by a variey of developers, not just the organization that formulated the protocol.

■ **Open Software Foundation (OSF)** An alliance of DEC, IBM, and Hewlett-Packard.

■ **Open Systems Interconnection (OSI)** An international organization sponsored by the **ISO** with a mission to create international computer communications standards, such as the **OSI Model**, specifically to facilitate internetworking among incompatible systems.

See also **Government OSI Profile**.

■ **operating environment**　A front end for an **operating system**, a set of tools and a consistent look and feel that allow the user to interact with the computer. For instance, **Microsoft Windows** is an operating environment that runs on top of the **MS-DOS** operating system.

■ **operating system**　The software that governs all communication with and use of a computer's system resources, such as memory, disk space, the attention of the processor, and peripheral devices (monitor, keyboard, mouse, printer, modem, and so on). It also mediates between applications and system resources. The operating system starts running before any other software and stays in memory the whole time a computer is on.

Popular operating systems include **DOS**, **Macintosh**, **OS/2**, **UNIX**, and **VMS**.

See also **operating environment**.

■ **option**　A command or selection available on a menu or list.

■ **OR**　[Boolean operator] *Or*. A text **search** with OR between two words matches any documents containing either word.

■ **Oracle**

See **Usenet Oracle**.

■ **Orange County Free-Net**　[service provider] palmer@world.std.com, (714) 762-8551.

See also **free-net**.

■ **.org**　An Internet **domain** corresponding to (nonprofit) organizations.

■ **ORION**　[service provider] annie@ozarks.sgcl.lib.mo.us, (417) 837-5050 ext. 15.

■ **Orlando Free-Net**　[service provider] bruce@goliath.pbac.edu, (407) 833-9777.

See also **free-net**.

■ **OS**

See **operating system**.

■ **OS/2**　An IBM **operating system** for PCs and compatibles.

■ **OSF**

See **Open Software Foundation**.

■ **OSF/1**　A **port** of **UNIX** that runs on VAXen.

■ **OSI**　*Open Systems Interconnection*, an international organization sponsored by the **ISO** with a mission to create international computer communications standards, such as the OSI Model, specifically to facilitate internetworking among incompatible systems.

■ **OSI Model**　The seven-layer networking reference model (sometimes called the

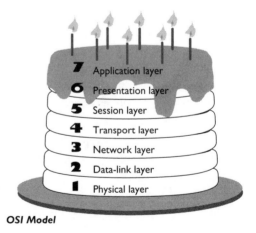

OSI Model

seven-layer cake) defined by the ISO's OSI to facilitate the internetworking of incompatible computers and networks.

The organization of the seven layers, together known as a **protocol stack**, represents the dependence of each layer on the next lower layer in the stack.

From lowest to highest:

Layer number	Layer name	Defines protocols for
1	Physical layer	Interface hardware, cabling, communications medium
2	Data link layer	Transmission of data frames from node to node
3	Network layer	Data routing, addressing, and verification
4	Transport layer	Structure of mesages, delivery, some error checking
5	Session layer	Connecting, maintaining communications, security, logging, tracking

Layer number	Layer name	Defines protocols for
6	Presentation layer	Encoding, conversion, file format, data presentation
7	Application layer	Interaction between the network and applications

■ **otoh** (written only, also *OTOH*) *On the other hand*.

■ **otth** (written only, also *OTTH*) *On the third hand*.

■ **Outernet** A collective name for all the networks, **BBS**s, and **online service**s that have e-mail **gateway**s with the Internet but no full connection.

■ **overhead** (n) The accumulation of **protocol** information wrapped around data transmitted over networks.

■ **Owensboro Bluegrass Free-Net** [service provider] donna@ndlc.occ.uky.edu, (502) 686-4530.

See also **free-net**.

A
B
C
D
E
F
G
H
I
J
K
L
M
N
O
P
Q
R
S
T
U
V
W
X
Y
Z

- **p** The *previous* command in many **UNIX** newsreaders.

- **PACCOM** [service provider] torben@hawaii.edu, (808) 956 5896.

- **packet** Any unit of **data** (the size varies) sent across a **network**. Besides the data, a packet also includes the addresses of the sender and the recipient, as well as error-control information. On the Internet, a packet is the same thing as a **datagram**. A large piece of data will be split into several packets, each of which may take an

independent route to the destination, where they will be reassembled. (See illustration below.)

See also frame, segment.

- **Packet Internet Groper**
  See PING.

- **Packetized Ensemble Protocol (PEP)**
  A **proprietary** feature of Telebit brand **modems** that allows two modems to be connected directly.

- **packet sniffer** 1. A person who tries to "listen in" on Internet traffic in search of information to steal; 2. The program that such a person employs to "sniff out" interesting **packets**.

- **packet-switched network** A network made up of interconnected circuits that route **packets** over a variety of alternative

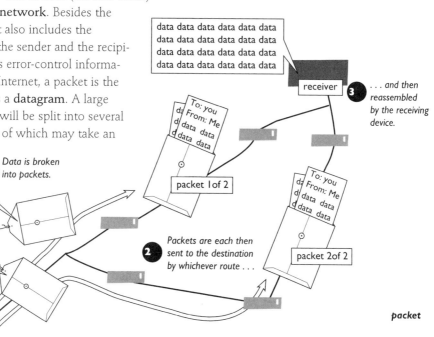

data data data data data data
data data data data data data
data data data data data data
data data data data data data

receiver ❸ *. . . and then reassembled by the receiving device.*

❶ *Data is broken into packets.*

data data data
data data data
data data data
data data data
data data data
data data data
data data data
data data data

To: you
From: Me
data data
data data

packet 1 of 2

❷ *Packets are each then sent to the destination by whichever route . . .*

To: you
From: Me
data data
data data

packet 2 of 2

sender

packet

packet sniffer

paths, as opposed to a **circuit-switched network**, in which packets are routed over **dedicated lines**. (See illustration below.)

See also packet switching, public data network.

■ **packet switching**   A method of transmitting data in which **packet**s for many unconnected operations are routed simultaneously over a communications channel (often a telephone line) to make best use of the

line. Related packets are reassembled at the destination.

See also **packet-switched network**.

■ **packet switch node (PSN)**   The computer that handles the routing of **packet**s in a **packet-switched network**.

■ **page**   (v) To display a document one screenful at a time in a **character-based interface**.

(n) A document published on the **Web**.

■ **paging program**   A program (sometimes called a *pager*) that displays documents one screenful at a time, such as the **UNIX** utility **more**.

■ **Palm Beach Free-Net**   [service provider] currye@mail.seflin.lib.fl.us, (305) 357-7318.

See also **free-net**.

■ **Panix Public Access Unix**   [service provider] alexis@panix.com, jsb@panix.com, (212) 877-4854, (212) 691-1526, (718) 965-3768.

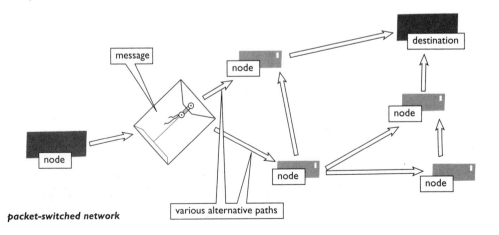

packet-switched network

■ **PAP**

See Printer Access Protocol.

■ **paper-net** The U.S. Postal Service.
See also snail mail.

■ **parallel** (adj) Said of a connection in which **bit**s are transmitted simultaneously.
See also serial.

■ **parallel port** A port in the back of a PC that can connect via a cable to a **parallel device**.
See also serial port.

■ **paren** (n) A parenthesis.

■ **parent directory** 1. In a **hierarchical file system**, the **directory** for which the current directory is a **subdirectory**, symbolized in UNIX, DOS, and OS/2 by two dots (..); 2. Any directory which contains other directories.
See also child directory.

■ **parity** An error-checking method in data transmission in which an extra **bit** is added to each **byte** (between the **data bit** and the **stop bit**) to round off bit-total values to even or odd numbers. The **parity bit** must match at both ends of the transmission. (See illustration.)

Parity is therefore one of the settings you have to specify on your **modem** to make a connection. It's usually set to None or Even, but it depends on the modem you're calling.

See also even parity, odd parity.

■ **parity bit** A redundant **bit** added to a **byte** in data transmission as part of an error-checking technique.
See also even parity, odd parity, parity.

■ **parity error** An error caused by mismatched **parity bit**s in a **byte** of transmitted data.
See also parity.

■ **parse** (v) To interpret an instruction by breaking it down and analyzing its parts.

■ **Pascal** A beginner's programming language, often used as a stepping stone to **C**.

■ **passive star** A network design with a central **hub** that connects all the **branches** but does not retransmit signals that pass through it (see illustration, next page).
See also active star.

■ **password** A secret code used to restrict access to an **account**, **channel**, file, and so on to only authorized users who know the password.

A bad password is one that is a real word or is otherwise easily guessable (a birth date, a pet's name, and so on). A good password

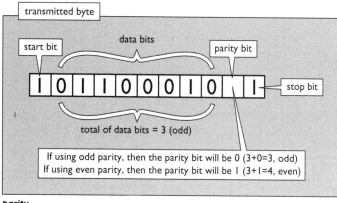

parity

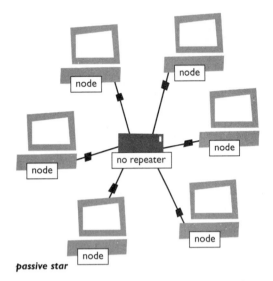

passive star

contains upper- and lowercase letters and numerals, and the longer it is, the better.

■ **passwd** The UNIX command to change an account's **password**.

■ **patch** (n) A quick-and-dirty correction that fixes a **bug**, or at least works around it. (v) To fix a problem with a temporary work-around or **kluge**.

■ **path** 1. A **bang path**, the route an e-mail message takes between its sender and receiver; 2. The channel through which a signal passes; 3. A completely specified location of a directory or file, starting from the **root** directory.

■ **PC** A *personal computer*, generally a **micro-computer**, usually either an **IBM** PC or compatible, a **Macintosh**, or perhaps an Amiga.

■ **PC-compatible** Said of a computer that emulates the functionality of an **IBM PC**.

■ **PC Eudora** A Windows mail program (a **port** of Eudora for the Macintosh) that

uses **Post Office Protocol** (POP) and can function as an **offline mail reader**. It is available via **anonymous FTP** from ftp.qualcomm.com.

■ **PC Gopher for DOS** A gopher client for the **IBM PC** or compatible running any flavor of **DOS**, available via **anonymous FTP** from sunsite.unc.edu.

■ **PC Pursuit** A SprintNet service that allows users to connect directly to another computer (as opposed to an **online service**).

■ **PC/TCP Plus for DOS** DOS software that enables an **IBM PC** or compatible to connect via **modem** to a computer connected to the Internet for **FTP** and **telnet**.

■ **PC-Xware** Windows software that includes TCP/IP, NFS, FTP, and **server** access for **X Window** applications, developed by Network Computing Devices, Inc.

■ **PDIAL** *Public Dial-Up Internet Access List*, Peter Kaminski's excellent list of Internet service providers, complete with cost information, posted regularly to alt.internet. access.wanted and alt.bbs.lists, and available via **anonymous FTP** from rtfm.mit.edu

PC

in the /pub/usenet/news.answers directory, with the file name pdial.

■ **PDN**

See public data network.

■ **PDP-11** A series of DEC computers now largely superseded by **VAXen**. PDP stands for *programmed data processor*. The PDP-11 series was preceded by PDP-10, according to **hacker** lore the first real timesharing machine.

■ **PeaceNet** A BBS for nonprofit organizations, religious organizations, and people concerned with peace and justice. For more information, **anonymous** FTP to igc.org in the /pub directory.

■ **peer** A network **device** that communicates directly with other devices on the network.

■ **peer-to-peer** (adj) A network architecture in which each computer on the network can communicate directly with other **nodes** and function as both a **client** and a **server** (see illustration).

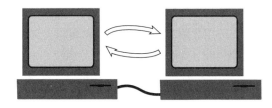

Each computer on a peer-to-peer network can function as a file server for the other.

peer-to-peer

■ **Pegasus Mail** Also known as *p-mail*, a freeware e-mail program for IBM PCs and compatibles and **Macintosh**es, available via FTP from risc.ua.edu.

■ **PEINet** [Canadian **service provider**] sales@peinet.pe.ca, (902) 566-0450.

■ **PEM**

See privacy-enhanced mail.

■ **Pennyrile Area Free-Net** [service provider] mroseberry@delphi.com, (502) 886-2913.

See also free-net.

■ **PENpages** A database and information service covering every imaginable aspect of rural life in general and agriculture in particular, administrated by Pennsylvania State University. It is updated daily and the latest additions are always available on the main menu.

To connect, **telnet** to psupen.psu.edu and log in as your two-letter state abbreviation (no password).

■ **Pentium** A 64-bit **microprocessor**, Intel's successor to the 80486 chip (named Pentium after the courts decided that Intel could not defend as a trademark the number 586 or 80586).

The discovery of an error in the much-vaunted chip has spun off a long series of jokes about rounding errors (for example, "Q: How many Pentiums does it take to screw in a lightbulb? A: 1.9999965786.").

■ **peon** An ordinary user with no special privileges.

See also newbie.

■ **PEP**

See Packetized Ensemble Protocol.

■ **Performance Systems International**

See PSI.

■ **period**

See dot.

■ **peripheral** (adj) Said of a device that is not essential to the computer or physically a part of it (as opposed to the processor or hard-disk drive), such as a printer or modem.

(n) A peripheral device.

■ **Philadelphia Free-Net** [service provider] torgj@delphi.com, (215) 688-2694.

See also free-net.

■ **phreak** (v) To **crack** (break into) a network or phone system.

(n) One who enjoys cracking secure networks or phone systems.

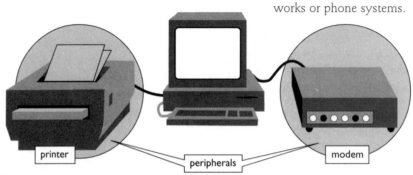

peripheral (n)

■ **Perl** A programming language (it stands for *practical extraction and report language*) distributed over **Usenet**, favored by **UNIX** system administrators.

■ **permissions** Settings associated with an **account** on a network or multiuser system that define a level of **access** (to certain system resources) permitted to the user of the account.

■ **PGP** A shareware public-key encryption program (it stands for *pretty good privacy*), developed by Phillip Zimmerman. For more information see the **Web** page at http://www.mantis.co.uk/pgp/pgp.html.

■ **phage** (n) A program that modifies other programs or databases in unauthorized ways.

See also **virus**, **worm**.

■ **physical** Said of hardware and mechanical connections, as opposed to **logical**.

■ **physical layer** Layer 1 (the bottom layer) of the **OSI Model**; it defines **protocols** for connecting cables and other hardware.

■ **pico** A full-screen, **modeless text editor** for **UNIX** machines based on the built-in editor in the **pine** e-mail program.

■ **pile-on** (n) A **flame war** in which many participants take turns attacking a single victim, creating long **posts** of polymorphous abuse.

■ **pine** A UNIX e-mail program whose name is a **recursive acronym** (pine stands for *pine is not elm*). Pine has a built-in full-screen **modeless editor**, MIME support, and the ability to **attach** files.

- **.pinerc** (*dot-pine-are-see*) A setup file for pine.

- **ping** (v) 1. To check the presence of a **host** with **PING**; 2. To send **e-mail** to an entire **mailing list**, requesting a response, in order to check which addresses are still valid.

  (n) The **UNIX** command that uses the PING **protocol**.

- **PING** Said to stand for *Packet Internet Groper*, a **protocol** for sending a signal to see whether another network **host** or other device is **online** and responding. (It's probably actually named for the sound made by submarine sonar/depth equipment.)

- **Pioneer Neighborhood (Pioneer Global)** [service provider] info@pn.com, (617) 646-4800.

- **pipe** (v) To send the output of a process or dump the contents of a file to a device (such as a printer), program (such as one that will process the data), or another file.

  (n) The | character (also called a *vertical bar*), used in the piping process.

- **Pipeline** [service provider] info@pipeline.com, staff@pipeline.com, (212) 267-3636.

- **Pipeline for Windows** Windows front end software for a connection to a **service** provider, developed by **Pipeline**.

- **.pit** The file **extension** for **Macintosh** PackIt files. (PackIt has largely been superseded as a Macintosh **compression** standard by **StuffIt**.)

- **pita** (written only, also *PITA*) *Pain in the arse*.

- **Pittsburgh Free-Net** [service provider] iddings@clp2.clpgh.org, (412) 622-6502. *See also* **free-net**.

- **pixel** A single dot on a monitor or in a bit-mapped image (from *picture element*).

- **.pkg** The file **extension** for an AppleLink Package file.

- **pkunzip** The **uncompression** program for pkzipped files.

- **pkzip** A DOS file **compression** program.

- **plain ASCII** Also called *flat ASCII*, said of an **ASCII** text file (a document with no word-processor formatting).

- **.plan** (*dot plan*) A **text** file that is displayed when your **username** is **finger**ed. Originally intended to alert people to your whereabouts or immediate plans, .plan files have evolved into personalized files sometimes filled with information or absurdities. My current .plan is shown at the top of the next page.

  See also **.project**.

- **Planet Access Networks** [service provider] info@planet.net, (201) 691-4704.

- **plan file** *See* **.plan**.

- **platform** A computer or **operating system** type.

- **plokta** (written only, also *PLOKTA*, v) *Press lots of keys to abort*. Many **newbie** posts

```
Released December 1:
    Enterzone, a quarterly hyperzine on the World Wide Web
    <http://enterzone.berkeley.edu/enterzone.html>
Current Project:
    Internet Dictionary (Sybex)
Available Now:
    A Guided Tour of the Internet (Sybex)
    WordPerfect 6 Roadmap (Sybex)
    Word for Windows Quick & Easy (Sybex)
Last Story:
    No Bird but An Invisible Thing (hypertext version)
    <http://enterzone.berkeley.edu/homies/nobird/nobird.html>
```

end with a pathetic series of attempts to quit while still in **insert mode**, like so:

```
This is my first post so please
don't flame me.
—blff

:wq


ZZ

quit
:wq

help
?
bye
```

See also **any key**.

- ***plonk*** A follow-up post that means "I just put you in my **kill file**." (It's supposed to be the sound of the **bozo** falling into the kill file.)

- **p-mail** 1. **Pegasus Mail**; 2. Physical mail, as opposed to **e-mail**.

- **point at** To start a **client** program, such as a **Web browser**, by supplying it with an address, as in "Point your Web browser at http://enterzone.berkeley.edu/enterzone. html to see the latest episode of Enterzone."

- **point of presence (POP)** A local phone number connected to a **modem** connected to the **network** of a **service provider**, to enable users to log in to the network without paying long distance charges.

- **Point-to-Point Protocol (PPP)** A TCP/IP protocol, similar to **SLIP**, for transmitting **IP datagram**s over **serial** lines such as phone lines. With PPP, PC users can connect to the Internet and still function in their native environment (instead of having to deal with a character-based **UNIX** environment).

- **poll** (v) 1. To check a **port** to see whether a **device** is connected and available for network or communications activity; 2. To connect to another system to check for new mail or news.

■ **Ponca City/Pioneer Free-Net**
[service provider] philber106@aol.com,
(405) 767-3461.

See also free-net.

■ **POP**

See point of presence or Post Office
Protocol.

■ **pop machine**

See Coke machine.

■ **port** (n) 1. A socket on the back of a computer for connecting cables and hence modems, printers, etc.; 2. On Internet hosts, a channel dedicated to a specific program, so that a multiplexing host can run telnet sessions on one port, FTP connections on

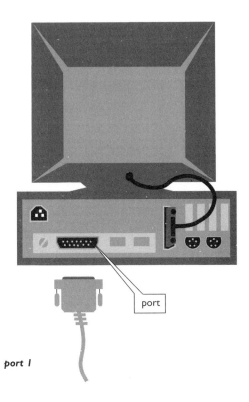

port 1

another, logins on another, etc.; 3. The interface between a router and a network; 4. A version of a program that was originally designed for a different platform.

(v) To translate software designed for one platform so that it will run on another.

See also Internet Assigned Numbers Authority.

■ **Portal Communications, Inc.**
[service provider] cs@cup.portal.com,
info@portal.com, (408) 973-9111.

■ **post** (v) 1. To send a message to a mailing list or an article to a newsgroup; 2. To publish information in any medium on the Internet. (The word *post* comes from the bulletin-board metaphor, in which scraps of paper are posted to the board to be read by anyone who comes by, as opposed to the British usage, which means to send mail.)

(n) A message sent to a mailing list or newsgroup. (See illustration, next page.)

■ **postcardware** Shareware that's almost free, except the programmer requests that satisfied users send a postcard (so she can see how far the software has spread).

■ **poster** One who posts.

■ **postmaster** A person who oversees a network's e-mail connection to the Internet. Questions about users at a host or problems with e-mail to or from that host can often be addressed to postmaster@*hostname.domain*.

■ **Post Office Protocol (POP)** A protocol that specifies how a personal computer can connect to a mail server on the Internet and download e-mail.

A
B
C
D
E
F
G
H
I
J
K
L
M
N
O
P
Q
R
S
T
U
V
W
X
Y
Z

■ **PostScript**   *post*
A proprietary "page-description" computer language developed by Adobe Systems. It describes pages (text, graphics, layout) in mathematical terms. PostScript files generally have a .ps or .eps extension.

■ **Pot. Kettle. Black.**
A shorthand **newsgroup** or **mailing list follow-up**, criticizing the previous **poster** for exhibiting the same foibles she was faulting another for. (It's short for the aphorism "That's like the pot calling the kettle black.")

Pot. Kettle. Black

■ **pour**   (v) To **pipe** the output from a process or file to a device or other file.

■ **power cycling**   Turning the **hardware** off, waiting, and then turning it on again.

■ **PPP**   *Point-to-Point Protocol*, a TCP/IP protocol similar to **SLIP** for transmitting **IP** data-grams over **serial** lines such as phone lines. With PPP, PC users can connect to the Internet and still function in their native environment (instead of having to deal with a character-based **UNIX** environment).

■ **Prairienet Freenet**   [service provider]
abishop@uiuc.edu, jayg@uiuc.edu, (217) 244-1962, (217) 244-3299.

See also **free-net**.

■ **PREPnet**   [service provider]
prepnet@cmu.edu, (412) 268-7870.

■ **presentation layer**   Layer 6 of the **OSI Model**, it defines how data is formatted, encoded, converted, and presented.

■ **Pretty Good Privacy**
See **PGP**.

■ **prime time**   The period of heaviest usage of a network, usually 9–to–5 during the work week.

■ *Principia Discordia* An underground tract that elucidates the worship of Eris, ancient goddess of discord.

See also Discordian Society.

■ **printed circuit** A computer chip with microcircuits literally printed (via a photographic process) onto it.

■ **Printer Access Protocol (PAP)** The AppleTalk protocol that defines how a workstation and a printer communicate.

■ **privacy** Because the Internet is not inherently secure, users are cautioned to e-mail and post only information that they don't mind being public, or take steps to increase the privacy of their communication, either via encryption, through anonymity, or by using other communications channels entirely.

■ **privacy-enhanced mail (PEM)** E-mail–handling systems that incorporate encryption techniques to secure privacy and verification of message integrity.

■ **private key** In public-key encryption, the secret key the user reveals to no one and uses to sign outgoing messages and to decrypt incoming messages that were encrypted with the public key.

■ **private virtual circuit (PVC)** Software circuits that maintain a private line between hosts.

■ **privatization** On the Internet, generally refers to the U.S. government's process of placing maintenance of backbone networks in the hands of private organizations. So far this has not significantly changed the pricing structure for individual users.

■ **privileges** Also called *access privileges*, a set of system resource and directory actions that a user is permitted to perform.

See also go root.

■ **process** A program or part of a program being executed in a multitasking operating system. More generally, one task of many that a computer is doing.

■ **ProComm Plus** A popular communications package for IBM PCs and compatibles, sold by Datastorm Technologies, Inc.

■ **Prodigy Information Service** America's largest online service, adding full Web access; (800) PRODIGY [776-3449].

■ **.profile** A startup file in some flavors of UNIX.

■ **programmer** A person who writes computer programs.

See also hacker.

■ **programming** The process of writing programs.

■ **.project** (*dot project*) On some systems, a file similar to a .plan that is displayed when a user is fingered, intended to discuss the project the user is currently working on.

■ **project file**

See .project.

■ **Project Gutenberg** An organization that publishes uncopyrighted books on the Internet, reachable via anonymous FTP at mrcnext.cso.uiuc.edu.

See also Online Book Initiative.

■ **Prometheus Information Network Group, Inc.** [service provider] info@ping.com, (800) PING-TEL.

A
B
C
D
E
F
G
H
I
J
K
L
M
N
O
P
Q
R
S
T
U
V
W
X
Y
Z

■ **prompt** (n) Also *command-line prompt*, a string of text that a **character-based operating system** displays on the screen to tell a user that it is ready to accept input (such as a command or the name of a program to run).

■ **propagation** The process of dissemination for **packet**s in general, and **Usenet newsfeed**s in particular, as they are passed from computer to computer. Propagation delays (see illustration) are responsible for the sometimes confusing situation that occurs when you read a **follow-up** to a **post** that hasn't yet appeared at your site.

■ **proprietary** Said of a technology, architecture, or set of **protocol**s whose design is the property of the company that developed it.

See also **open**.

■ **Prospero** A distributed directory system, file system, and index service (and the pro-

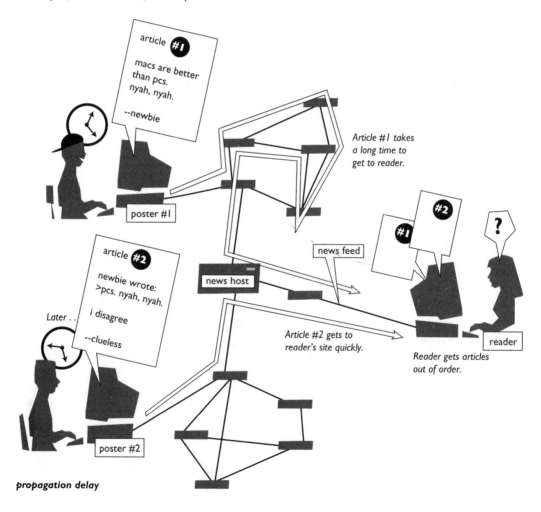

propagation delay

tocol that underlies it) that allows users to access both local and remote directories in the same way. For more information, connect via **anonymous FTP** to prospero.isi. edu and go to the /pub/prospero directory.

■ **protocol** An agreed-upon set of rules that allows otherwise incompatible machines or software to communicate. Protocols can govern a wide range of the aspects of communications, from the order in which **bits** are transmitted to the rules for opening and maintaining a connection to the format of an electronic mail message.

■ **protocol family**

See protocol stack.

■ **protocol layer** One portion of a set of protocols that handles one aspect of the transmission of data.

See also OSI Model.

■ **protocol stack** A set of **protocol layer**s that work together to provide reliable communication between a computer and a network or another computer, also called a *protocol family* or *protocol suite*. The **TCP/IP** protocol stack includes such protocols as TCP, IP, FTP, SMTP, **telnet**, and so on.

See also OSI Model.

■ **protocol suite**

See protocol stack.

■ **.ps** The file **extension** for PostScript files.

■ **pseudo** (n) A new identity assumed on **Usenet** in order that the user might act (provocatively or otherwise) without those actions being associated with the user's real (or better-known) name.

■ **PSI (PSILink/Performance Systems International, Inc.)** [service provider] info@psi.com, all-info@psi.com, psilink-info@psi.com, (800) 827-7482, (703) 620-6651.

■ **PSILink**

See PSI.

■ **PSN**

See packet switch node.

■ **/pub** A UNIX directory often found on FTP hosts, where public information is stored and made available.

■ **pubic directory** Slang for an FTP *public directory*.

See also /pub.

■ **public data network (PDN)** A type of commercial **packet-switched network** offering wide-area services to customers, with sophisticated error-checking, buffering, and handling of **protocols**. Tymnet, SprintNet, and the CompuServe Packet Network are all PDNs.

■ **Public Dial-Up Internet Access List (PDIAL)** Peter Kaminski's excellent list of Internet service providers, complete with cost information, posted regularly to alt. internet.access.wanted and alt.bbs.lists, and available via **anonymous FTP** from rtfm. mit.edu in the /pub/usenet/news. answers directory, with the file name pdial.

■ **public directory**

See /pub.

■ **public domain** (adj) Available for free to the public, uncopyrighted, as are much

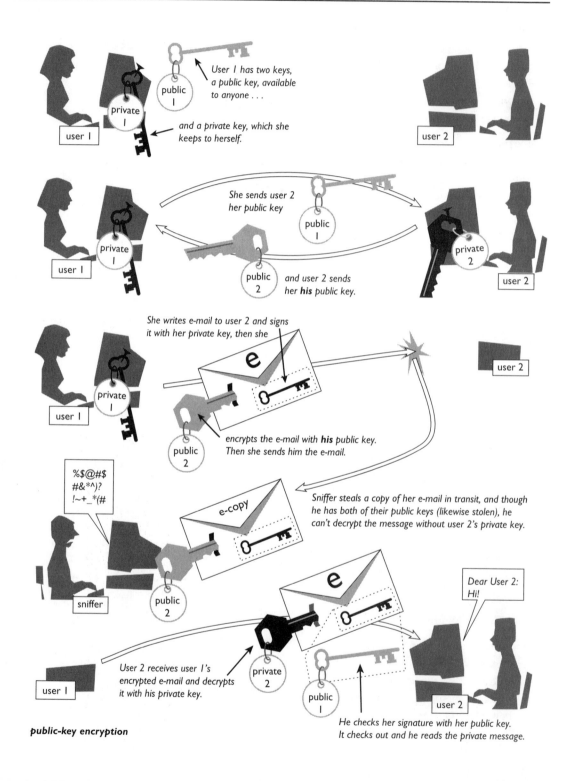

public-key encryption

of the information, system software, and applications available on the Internet.

See also copyleft, freeware, shareware.

■ **public key** In public-key encryption, the **key** a user distributes freely and which correspondents use to **encrypt** messages to the user and **decrypt** the user's signature (encrypted with the user's **private key**) on messages from the user.

■ **public-key encryption** A form of **key encryption** which uses two **keys**, a **public key** (for **encrypt**ing messages) and a **private key** (for **decrypt**ing messages) to enable users to verify each other's messages without having to securely exchange secret keys. (See illustration, opposite page.)

■ **public libraries** Many public libraries have made their card catalogs available and

searchable via the Internet, often from **telnet** addresses. The easiest way to search many libraries is with **Hytelnet**.

■ **Public Telecomputing Network** [service provider] pionke@interaccess.com, (312) 464-5138.

■ **publishing** Posting on the Net (to **newsgroups**, the **Web**, **gopher**, etc.) is considered equivalent to publishing, though the paradigm is different—the reader comes to you and you do not distribute the information.

■ **PUCnet Computer Connections** [service provider] info@PUCnet.com, pwilson@PUCnet.com, (403) 448-1901.

■ **put** (v) To copy a file from your **host** computer to a **remote** site, particularly via **FTP** (see illustration below).

(n) The FTP command to put a file.

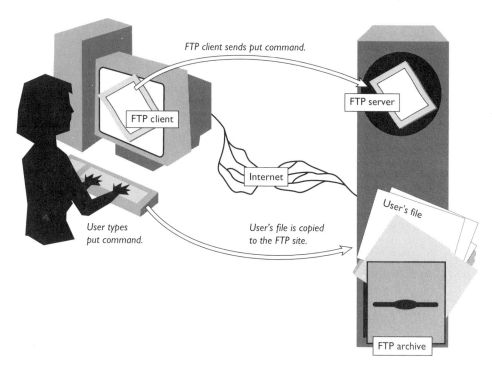

FTP client sends put command.

FTP server

FTP client

Internet

User's file

User types put command.

User's file is copied to the FTP site.

FTP archive

■ **'puter**   (*pewter* or *pooter*) A computer, usually a personal computer.

■ **PVC**

See private virtual circuit.

■ **pwd**   The UNIX command (short for *print working directory*) that displays the current working **directory** (the directory the user is "in").

change the quotations in their **sig block** daily (or more often).

■ **query** (n) 1. A **search** request submitted to a database to find a particular record (piece of information) or all records that meet certain criteria, such as an **archie** query; 2. A **question mark**.

■ **question mark** ? 1. A **wildcard** character in **UNIX** (and hence in many Internet applications), it stands for any single character; 2. A **help** command in some character-based applications.

See also **star**.

■ **questionnaires** Usenet newsgroups are often bombarded by purveyors of questionnaires hoping to exploit a ready-made audience. That the responders are self-selecting doesn't seem to bother the questioneers, but to regular readers of the newsgroups, these **post**s and the ubiquitous surveys get tiresome awfully fast.

■ **queue** (*cue*, n) A list of items (such as print jobs or messages) waiting to be sent from one **device** to another.

■ **QuickTime** An **Apple** technology that debuted with **Macintosh** System 7. It compresses, stores, and plays back files combining text, sound, animation, and video. Many QuickTime clips are distributed via the **Internet** and the **Web**.

■ **quit** To stop running an application and (usually) return to the **operating system**.

■ **quotation of the day**
See qotd.

■ **quoting** Including a relevant portion of a preceding **article** when **posting** a **follow-up**.

■ **q** The **quit** command in many **UNIX** programs. (Often a capital *Q* will mean *quick quit* and will allow you to quit without any questions.)

■ **qotd** (written only, also *QOTD*) *Quotation of the day*. Some systems display a quotation when you **log in**. Some **Usenet** posters

```
ATDT5551213
CONNECT 19200
Login: xian
Password: ******

QOTD
See here how everything leads up
to this day, and it's just like any other
day that's ever been—sun going up and
then the sun here going down, shine
through my window, and my friends
they come around.
—Robert Hunter

You have new mail.
%
```

qotd

Most **newsreader**s precede quoted text with a symbol, such as >, and try to indicate who said what, though multiple embedded quotations often require that the latest author untangle the attributions.

It is bad **netiquette** to quote no text (unless the follow-up makes it absolutely clear what it is responding to), and it's both bad netiquette and an unmistakable marker of a **clueless newbie** to quote an entire article merely to add "I agree" or "Right on, d00d!!" at the end.

■ **QWERTY** (n) The standard typewriter and computer-keyboard layout, so named for the first six characters of the first alphabetical row.

QWERTY

■ **r** 1. The **reply** command in many **UNIX** mail programs; 2. The *reply by e-mail* command in many UNIX **newsreaders**.

■ **The Rabbit Network Inc.** [service provider] info@rabbit.net, (800) 456-0094.

■ **radio**
See Internet Talk Radio.

■ **RAIN (Regional Access Information Network)** [service provider] rain@rain.org, (818) 889-8610.

■ **RainDrop Laboratories** [service provider] via the **Web**: http://www.rdrop.com/.

■ **RAM** (*ram*) *Random access memory*, **memory** that any application or process can **read** or **write** to. It's frequently confused with storage, because both resources are often measured in **megabytes**.

■ **random access memory**
See RAM.

■ **ranking** The order in which a **WAIS** program displays the results of a database search—from most likely to least likely.
See also **relevance feedback**.

■ **RARE**
See **Reseaux Associés pour la Recherche Européenne**.

■ **RARP**
See **Reverse Address Resolution Protocol**.

■ **rb** The **Ymodem** command for receiving (**uploading**) a file.
See also **rx, rz, sb**.

■ **.*rc**
See **rc file**.

■ **rc file** A **UNIX** text file with a file name of the form *.*rc*, containing command line instructions or other startup information for an application or for the operating system itself. Examples include **.newsrc**, **.pinerc**, and so on.

■ **rcp** The UNIX *remote copy* command.

■ **read** To copy data from a **disk** into memory.
See also **write**.

■ **README file** An information file describing the contents of an **FTP** directory or the files associated with an application.

■ **readme.txt** Typical name for a README file.

■ **read notification** A feature of some e-mail programs that lets you know when the recipient of your e-mail has received and opened the message.

A B C D E F G H I J K L M N O P Q R S T U V W X Y Z

README file

■ **read-only** (adj) Said of a file that can be read but not altered.

■ **read-only memory**
See ROM.

■ **read-write** (adj) Said of a file that can be both **read** and written to (altered).
See also **write**.

■ **real life** The **offline** world, as in the question "What do you do in real life?"

■ **real name** Also called a *full name*, a user's full name as it appears on e-mail messages and **Usenet posts**, as opposed to their **username** (the real name can also be a pseudonym). On **UNIX** systems, the user's real name is a variable that can be set with the **chfn** command. Many **Windows** and **Macintosh** Internet applications allow the user to enter or change a real name on the fly.

■ **Real Soon Now** Also *RSN*, similar to *as soon as possible* but with a subtext that it ain't really gonna happen any time soon.

■ **real time** Also *realtime*, the time used for **synchronous** communication, in which both participants must be available (as in a telephone conversation). Also, taking place at the present time, live, not delayed or recorded. (See illustration, opposite page.)

■ **Real/Time Communications**
[service provider] info@realtime.net, hosts@wixer.bga.com, (512) 451-0046.

■ **reboot** To restart a **crashed** operating system, either through a designated key combination (a **warm boot**), or by turning it off and on again (**power cycling**).

■ **rec.** A Usenet hierarchy devoted to recreation.

■ **receipt notification** A proof-of-delivery feature provided by some e-mail programs (similar to the idea of registered mail in the real world).

■ **record** (n) A set of related data from a database.

■ **recursive acronym** An acronym that contains the acronym itself in its spelled out

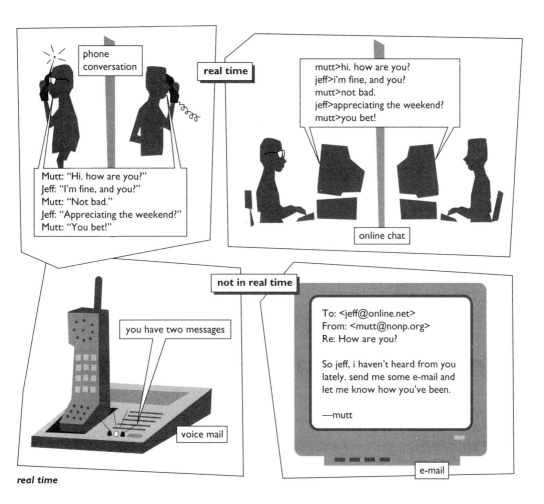

phone conversation

real time

mutt>hi. how are you?
jeff>i'm fine, and you?
mutt>not bad.
jeff>appreciating the weekend?
mutt>you bet!

Mutt: "Hi. how are you?"
Jeff: "I'm fine, and you?"
Mutt: "Not bad."
Jeff: "Appreciating the weekend?"
Mutt: "You bet!"

online chat

not in real time

you have two messages

voice mail

To: <jeff@online.net>
From: <mutt@nonp.org>
Re: How are you?

So jeff, i haven't heard from you lately. send me some e-mail and let me know how you've been.

—mutt

e-mail

real time

form, such as **GNU**, which stands for *GNU's not UNIX*, and **pine**, which stands for *pine is not elm*.

- **redirection** Sending output from one device or file to another device or file.
See also **pipe**.

- **redundant path** A secondary path that a **router** can assign to a **packet** when the normal route is not available (see illustration, next page).

- **refresh** To redraw the screen, usually either to reflect changes to the data or to restore the screen when something has marred its intended appearance.

- **Regional Access Information Network**
See RAIN.

- **register** (v) To sign up and pay for **shareware**.
(n) A designated area of **memory**.

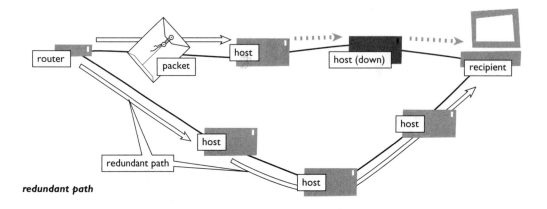

redundant path

■ **registered jack (RJ)** Any of a series of specialized jacks used for connecting wires, such as RJ-11 and RJ-45.

■ **rehi** (*ree-high*) *Hi again*, typed on IRC when you rejoin a **channel**.

■ **relevance feedback** A system used by WAIS applications to rank documents retrieved in a **search** in order of relevance to the search criteria. Documents are ranked based on the number of times that **key words** from the **query** appear in them.
See also **ranking**.

■ **reliable** Said of networks with **dedicated** connections.

■ **religious issues** Neverending debates (such as those that go on in some of the **talk.** newsgroups) on subjects such as abortion, gun control, or **IBM PC** vs. **Mac.**

■ **remailer** A program that receives **e-mail** and then resends it, with different information attached.
See also **anonymous remailer**.

■ **remote** Said of a **host** or other network resource that is located on a computer or

network elsewhere, as opposed to a **local** host or resource.

■ **remote access** The process of accessing another computer's resources, such as files or printers. **Dial-up accounts** and **telnet** are both forms of remote access.

■ **remote echo**
See **echo** (definition 3).

■ **remote login** To connect to a **remote** computer over a network, usually done on the Internet with **telnet** or **rlogin**.

■ **remove** To **kill** or erase a file or directory.
See also **rm**.

■ **rename** To change the name (or **path**) of a file or directory.

■ **repeater** A **device** that connects two stretches of cable and boosts the power of the signal it passes, to reduce **line noise** and the risk of errors.

■ **reply** (v) To respond to an e-mail message or **Usenet post**.

(n) 1. A message sent in response to a previous message or post; 2. An e-mail command that takes the **return path** from the current message and makes that address the recipient of a new message, possibly quoting the previous message as well.

- **repost** (n) An article **posted** again in full. (Many **newsgroup**s expect that reposts be labeled as such in their subject lines.)

  (v) To **post** the same information again.

- **Request for Comments**

  See **RFC**.

- **Request for Discussion (RFD)** The first stage in the formal process of **Usenet newsgroup** creation.

  See also **Call for Votes**.

- **-request** A suffix appended to the **user-name** of a human-administered **mailing list** to form the username of the administrative address for the list. (So a human-administered mailing list called atoz@netcom.com would have an administrative address called atoz-request@netcom.com associated with it.) It is a **Bad Thing** to **post** administrative requests (generally to sub-scribe or unsubscribe) to the actual mailing list rather than to the -request address.

- **Research Libraries Information Network (RLIN)** An online catalog of catalogs with information from most major research libraries in the United States, reachable by **telnet** at rlg.stanford.edu (it's not free). For information, send e-mail to bl.ric@rlg.standord.edu or call (800) 537-RLIN.

- **Reseaux Associés pour la Recherche Européenne (RARE)** A European group of research networks. For more information, connect via **anonymous FTP** to ftp.rare.nl.

- **Reseaux IP Européenne (RIPE)** A group of European **TCP/IP** networks.

- **resolution** 1. Conversion of a **physical** address into a **logical** address (*address resolution*); 2. The degree of detail, sharpness, or fineness of an image.

- **resolve** (v) To convert a **physical** address to a **logical** address or vice versa.

- **return from the dead** (v) To be recon-nected to the Internet after a hiatus.

- **Return key**

  See **Enter key**.

- **return path** An address in the **header** of an e-mail **program** that tells the recipi-ent's **mail program** where to send a reply message.

- **Reverse Address Resolution Protocol (RARP)** A **TCP/IP** protocol for convert-ing **logical** addresses to **physical** addresses.

- **RFC** *Request for Comments*, one of a set of documents that contain Internet **protocol**s, **standard**s, and information, and together more or less define the Internet, in an open way. The standards contained in them are followed carefully by software developers (both commercial and **freeware**). The name Request for Comments can be confusing, since the contents are settled, but they arrived from free and open discussion on the **Net**.

  RFCs can be found via **anonymous FTP** at the ftp.internic.net site, among others.

  See also **FYI**.

- **RFD**

  See **Request for Discussion**.

■ **rib site**   A computer with a high-speed link to a **backbone site** that distributes traffic to smaller networks.

See also **leaf site**.

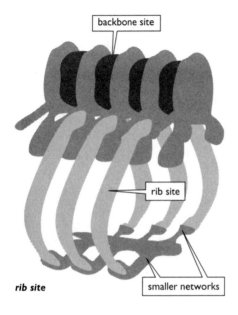

rib site

■ **Richland Free-Net**   [service provider] earmrcpl@class.org, (419) 521-3111/3110.

See also **free-net**.

■ **rights**   Another name for **privileges**.

■ **Right Thing**   Something which is absolutely the right thing to do.

See also **Bad Thing**, **Good Thing**, **Wrong Thing**.

■ **ring topology**   A network architecture in which the **nodes** are arranged in a circle (see illustration, opposite).

See also **bus topology**, **star topology**.

■ **RINGO**   An experimental service at MIT that allows you to rate a list of musicians and bands and receive back some

suggestions about other music you might like. To participate, send e-mail to ringo@media.mit.edu.

■ **Rio Grande Free-Net**   [service provider] donf@laguna.epcc.edu, (915) 775-6077.

See also **free-net**.

■ **RIP**

See **routing information protocol**.

■ **RIPE**

See **Reseaux IP Européenne**.

■ **RISCnet**   [service provider] info@nic.risc.net, (401) 885-6855.

■ **RISQ**   [Canadian **service provider**] cirisq@risq.net, (514) 398-8990.

■ **RJ**   A registered jack.

■ **RJ-11**   A typical phone jack. (See illustration, opposite page.)

■ **RJ-45**   A modular jack that can hold up to four pairs of wires, used most often to

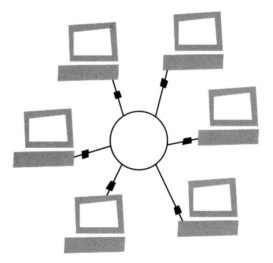

ring topology

connect unshielded **twisted-pair** wiring in LANs. An RJ-45 looks like a phone jack (RJ-11) except bigger.

- **RL** (written only) Real life.

- **RLIN** (*ar-lin*)

  See Research Libraries Information Network.

- **rlogin** A protocol (and program) for remote **login** from one **UNIX** machine to another. It automatically supplies the **username** and **password** given when the user first logged in.

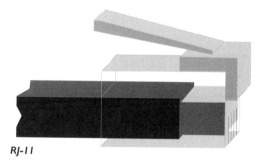

RJ-11

- **rm** The **UNIX** *remove* command, for deleting a file. (Be very careful not to type *rm *** and press Enter by mistake—there's no "undelete" in UNIX!)

- **rmdir** The **UNIX** *remove directory* command, for deleting a directory.

- **rmgroup** A special kind of control message that removes a **newsgroup**.

- **rn** The most common **UNIX** newsreader. It's not a **threaded newsreader**.

  See also **nn, tin, trn.**

- **robocancel** (v) To automatically cancel articles. A controversial (because it's a form of censorship) method for dealing with **spam**mers and **roboposter**s.

- **robopost** (v) To **post** automatically, usually done by a **'bot** that is programmed to post reams of articles and responses to **Usenet**.

- **roboposter** 1. A **'bot** that automatically **post**s and **repost**s huge numbers of articles to **Usenet**; 2. The **programmer** behind the roboposting 'bot.

  A reputed roboposter using the name of Serdar Argic singlehandedly rendered soc.history (and a number of other **newsgroup**s) unreadable without a **kill file** to screen him out. His howling through the wires (ranting Holocaust revisionism about the Turks and the "x-Soviet" Armenians) came to an unexpected but welcome halt in the spring of 1994.

- **robot** A user on **IRC** or in a **MUD** (or, less commonly, on **Usenet**) that is actually a program. Some perform useful functions while others are merely annoying.

- **robust** Said of software that doesn't **crash** often and recovers well when it does.

- **Rochester Free-Net** [service provider] jerry@rochgte.fidonet.org, (716) 594-0943.

  See also **free-net.**

- **rofl** (written only, also *ROFL*) *Rolling on the floor laughing.*

- **Rogue** A widely circulated text-adventure **role-playing game**, with a dungeon/swords-and-sorcery motif.

- **role-playing game** A game or activity, such as a **MUD**, in which participants take

A
B
C
D
E
F
G
H
I
J
K
L
M
N
O
P
Q
R
S
T
U
V
W
X
Y
Z

rofl

on fictional identities and strive to remain in character.

- **ROM** (rhymes with *prom*) *Read-only memory*. Fixed **memory** that can't be altered.

- **root** (n) 1. In a **hierchical file system**, the first **directory**, to which all other directories are subdirectories; 2. On **UNIX** machines, a **superuser** account with unlimited **permissions**.

  See also **go root**.

- **rot13** (*rot-thirteen*) A simple **cipher** in which each letter is replaced with the one 13 letters away from it in the alphabet, traditionally used to hide **spoilers** and off-color jokes from sensitive eyes (see illustration, opposite). (Because the alphabet has 26 letters, the same rotation will both encode and decode.)

- **rotfl** (written only, also *ROTFL*) *Rolling on the floor laughing.*

- **route** (n) The **path** a **packet** takes from sender to destination.

  (v) To send a packet along a path.

- **router** A **device** that physically connects two networks or a network to the Internet, converting addresses and sending on only the messages that need to pass to the other network.

  See also **bridge, brouter**.

- **routing information protocol (RIP)** A **TCP/IP protocol** that specifies how **router**s exchange information.

- **routing table** A list used by a **router** to determine the best route for a **packet**.

- **RS-232C** A 25-pin connector, such as the one used to connect a computer to an external **modem**.

- **RSN**

  See **Real Soon Now**.

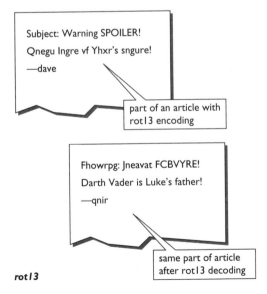

rot13

- **RTBM** (written only, also *rtbm*) *Read the bloody manual!*

  See also RTFM.

- **RTFAQ** (written only, also *rtfaq*) *Read the FAQ!* Typical reply to a **newbie** who **posts** a frequently asked question.

- **RTFM** (written only, also *rtfm*) *Read the fucking manual!* An impatient reply to someone asking questions about a program that could be answered by reading the documentation (or the online **man pages**).

- **rtfm.mit.edu** A huge FTP archive, with FAQs from many **Usenet newsgroup**s, RFCs, FYIs, and more.

- **RTM** (written only, also *rtm*) *Read the manual!* A nicer form of RTFM.

- **RTMP**

  See **routing table maintenance protocol**.

- **rx** The **Xmodem** command for receiving (**upload**ing) a file.

  See also **rb**, **rz**, **sx**.

- **rz** The **Zmodem** command for receiving (**upload**ing) a file.

  See also **rb**, **rx**, **sz**.

A
B
C
D
E
F
G
H
I
J
K
L
M
N
O
P
Q
R
S
T
U
V
W
X
Y
Z

■ **s** The **save** command in many **UNIX** applications.

■ **SAA**

See Systems Application Architecture.

■ **Sacramento Free-Net** [service provider] sacrapar@class.org, (916) 484-6789.

See also free-net.

■ **samizdat** (*sam-is-dot*) Also *samizdata*, from the Russian word for self-published underground pamphlets, a word used to describe the flow of unofficial information on the Internet, particularly **e-zine**s.

■ **San Antonio Free-Net** [service provider] mlotas@espsun.space.swri.edu, (210) 561-9815.

See also free-net.

■ **Sandpoint Free-Net** [service provider] mcmun911@crow.csru.uidaho.edu, (208) 263-6105.

See also free-net.

■ **Santa Barbara RAIN** [service provider] rain1.018558e-312ngrhub@hub.ucsb.edu, (805) 967-7246.

■ **Santa Fe Metaverse** [service provider] (505) 989-7117.

■ **SatelNET Communications** [service provider] admin@satelnet.org, (305) 434-8738.

■ **save** Literally, to copy a file or some data from **memory** (**RAM**) to a disk (or other storage medium). More loosely, to preserve the work you're doing by storing it on a disk.

■ **Savvy** [service provider] info@savvy.com, (800) 275-7455.

■ **sb** The **Ymodem** command for sending (**download**ing) a file.

See also **rb**, **sx**, **sz**.

■ **sci.** A **Usenet hierarchy** devoted to science.

■ **screen dump** A copy of the contents of a screen, saved to a file or sent to a printer.

■ **screen name** An **America Online** term for a user's **real name** or one of several allowable pseudonyms.

■ **screen-oriented** Said of applications that permit the user to move the cursor around the screen.

See also **line-oriented**.

■ **script** A sequence of commands to be executed by an **application** or **operating system**, often saved as a **text file**.

See also **macro**.

A
B
C
D
E
F
G
H
I
J
K
L
M
N
O
P
Q
R
S
T
U
V
W
X
Y
Z

■ **scroll**   (v) To browse through a document, moving the text up the screen as if on a continuous parchment. Usually suggests being able to move as little as a line at a time, as opposed to the display of a **paging program,** which always moves through a document one screenful at a time.

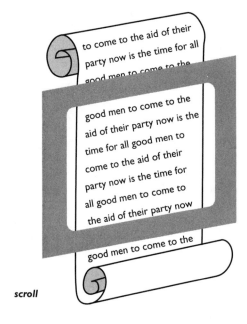

scroll

■ **scroll-back**   The ability to **scroll** to an earlier part of a document, which in a terminal-emulation program requires that it be saved in a **buffer.**

See also **back.**

■ **Scruz-Net**   [service provider] info@ scruz.net, (800) 319-5555, (408) 457-5050, (408) 457-1020 FAX.

■ **SCSI**   (*scuzzy*) Stands for *Small Computer Systems Interface,* a standard for connecting personal computers to certain **peripheral** devices, including CD-ROM drives and external hard drives.

■ **ScumOS**   (*scum-oss* or *scum-oh-ess*) A derogatory name for **SunOS.**

■ **scuzzy**
See **SCSI.**

■ **SDD**
See **software description database.**

■ **SDLC**
See **Synchronous Data Link Control.**

■ **.sea**   A file **extension** that indicates a **Macintosh self-extracting archive.**

■ **search**   (v) To seek information from a database, document, or other source, usually by specifying **key word**s to match.

(n) The process of seeking specific information from a source.

(adj) Said of programs, interfaces, or tools that facilitate the process of seeking specific information.

■ **searchable**   (adj) Said of indexes, databases, and documents that are formatted to facilitate **search**es by standard Internet search tools, such as **WAIS, gopher,** and Web clients.

■ **search criterion**   A set of **keywords** separated by **Boolean operator**s (such as AND, OR, and NOT) specified in a **query** in order to find matching documents or entries in a database, such as an **archie** or WAIS server.

■ **search key**
See **key word.**

■ **Seattle Community Network**   [service provider] randy@cpsr.org, (206) 865-3424.

■ **Seattle Online** [service provider] bruceki@online.com, (206) 328-2412.

■ **secondary service provider** An organization that provides a direct Internet connection to a regional set of networks.

■ **security** The Internet is not inherently secure. For example, **e-mail** messages are in some ways more like postcards than like letters sealed in envelopes. Your mail generally passes through many **site**s on the way to its destination, and **postmaster**s and other **superuser**s can read your mail if they want, although it would be unethical for them to do so.

If you are interested in making your e-mail more private or secure, look into **encryption** software, such as **PGP**. New **Web** products such as **Netscape** are exploring methods of making private transactions over the Internet as well.

■ **seed** In a **tape tree**, the original master tape from which the first set of copies is made.

■ **See you on the Net!** A farewell customarily uttered to net.friends whom you've happened to run into in **real life**.

■ **SEFLIN Free-Net** [service provider] currye@mail.seflin.lib.fl.us, (305) 357-7318. *See also* **free-net**.

■ **segment** 1. A length of cable in a network; 2. A unit of data packaged by **TCP** for **IP**.

■ **select articles** (v) In a **newsreader**, to choose which **article**s to read (by their titles or authors).

■ **self-extracting archive** An executable file, containing one or more **compressed** files, that will **extract** the files it contains when run.

■ **SENDIT** [service provider] sackman@ sendit.nodak.edu, (701) 237-8109.

■ **SEORF** [service provider] bawn@ oucsace.cs.ohiou.edu, (614) 662-3211.

■ **sequenced packet exchange (SPX)** A Novell NetWare **transport layer** protocol that coordinates mesages between **workstation**s.

■ **serial** Said of a connection, such as a phone line, in which **bit**s are transmitted one at a time. *See also* **parallel**.

■ **Serial Line Internet Protocol (SLIP)** A **TCP/IP** protocol for transmitting **IP** datagrams over **serial** lines, such as phone lines. With SLIP, personal computer users can connect to the Internet and still function in their native environment (instead of having to deal with a character-based **UNIX** environment).

■ **serial port** A port in the back of a **PC** that can connect via a cable to a **serial** device, such as a **modem** or printer. *See also* **parallel port**.

■ **server** A network application or computer that supplies information or other resources to **client** applications that connect to it. In conventional networking, server usually refers to a computer; for Internet **client/ server** applications, server usually refers to a program.

A
B
C
D
E
F
G
H
I
J
K
L
M
N
O
P
Q
R
S
T
U
V
W
X
Y
Z

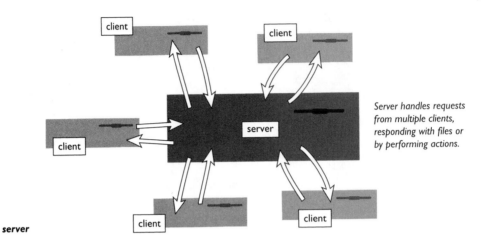

server

Server handles requests from multiple clients, responding with files or by performing actions.

Many Internet features are provided by servers: **file server**s, **mail** servers, **WAIS** servers, **Web** servers, **FTP** servers, **archie** servers, **name server**s, **finger** servers, and so on.

■ **service provider** A company that provides direct access to the Internet.

See also **free-net**, **online service**.

■ **SESQUINET** [service provider] farrell@rice.edu, (713) 527-4988.

■ **session** A period of connection and exchange of communications between **host**s (see illustration, opposite).

■ **session layer** Layer 5 of the **OSI Model**, it specifies how computers make and maintain connections.

■ **setext** A sophisticated text-formatting program for **UNIX**.

■ **SGML**

See **standard generalized markup language**.

■ **shareware** Software available for a free trial that must be registered and paid for if you decide to use it. Payment may also buy you manuals, support, and updates. Much shareware is distributed via the Internet. A large **FTP** archive for **Macintosh** software can be found at sumex.aim.stanford.edu; another large FTP site for **IBM PC** and compatible software can be found at

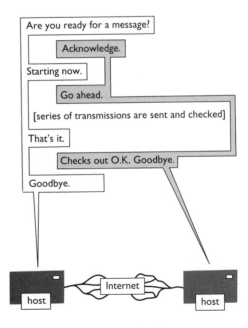

session

wuarchive.wustl.edu in the /systems/ibmpc directory.

See also **freeware.**

■ **shar file** Also called a *sharchive*, a **UNIX archive file** that contains one or more **compress**ed files. It can be uncompressed in a UNIX **shell** without any special software.

■ **Shawnee Free-Net** [service provider] ad592@freenet.hsc.colorado.edu, (618) 549-1139.

See also **free-net.**

■ **shell** 1. An **operating environment**, that is, a program through which a user communicates with the **operating system**. There are many **flavor**s of **UNIX** shells, such as Bourne, Korn, Bourne again (bash), C shell, and so on; 2. A command in many applications that allows you to enter **shell command**s without quitting the program.

■ **shell account** An Internet account that provides access to a **UNIX shell**, usually via a **modem** and a **terminal-emulation** program.

■ **shell command** An operating-system command entered at a command-line prompt or from within an application.

■ **shell out** (v) To temporarily escape an application and get access to a **shell** without quitting the program.

■ **Shergold, Craig** If you get the chain mail telling you to send this poor kid a get well card, don't! He is the famous "dying boy" (no longer dying and no longer a little boy) who, according to a perennially circulating **meme**, is hoping to become the *Guinness Book of World Records* champion for postcards received. Due to the persistence of this story (it was true once, over 10 years ago), the hospital he stayed in still gets postcards.

■ **shielded cable** A cable protected from electromagnetic interference by wire mesh and plastic, such as a **coaxial cable**. Shielded cable will not interfere with other electronic devices and is secure from wire tapping.

See also **shielded twisted-pair, unshielded cable, unshielded twisted-pair.**

■ **shielded twisted-pair (STP)** A cable shielded with foil and a copper braid surrounding the wire in twisted pairs, suitable for high-speed transmission over long distances, often used in **token ring** networks (see illustration, below).

See also **shielded cable, unshielded cable, unshielded twisted-pair.**

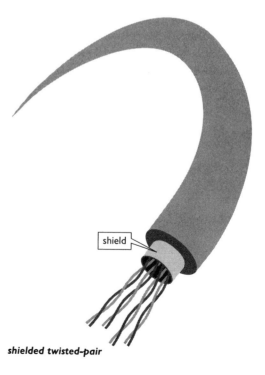

shield

shielded twisted–pair

■ **shitogram** A particularly nasty flame.

■ **shouting** On the Internet, TYPING IN ALL CAPS is frequently interpreted as shouting, and is one of the many signs of a newbie.

> HI! I'M NEW HERE. IS THIS THE RIGHT PLACE TO ASK FREQUENTLY ASKED QUESTIONS? BECAUSE I'VE BEEN WONDERING, WHAT DOES FAQ STAND FOR?
> —NEWBIE

> There's no need to shout. We can all hear you just fine. As for what does faq stand for, I suggest you rtfaq.
> —e.e.

shouting

■ **shovelware** A whole **CD-ROM** of free-ware and shareware, easily obtainable from the **Net** and thrown together without rhyme or reason.

■ **Shub-Internet** A mythical god or demon thought to be responsible for all slowdowns on the **Net**. It lives under the Pentagon and is worshipped by some **MUD** people. Its name is spoken aloud at great peril.

■ **Sibylline, Inc.** [service provider] info@sibylline.com, (501) 521-4660.

■ **sig** *See* sig block.

■ **.sig** *See* sig block.

■ **SIG**

See Special Interest Group.

■ **sig block** Also *sig, .sig, signature, .signature, signature block, or signature file*, a **text file** containing a user's name and, optionally, e-mail address, other identifying information, aphorisms, **ASCII graphic**s, etc., automatically attached to the ends of e-mail messages and **Usenet post**s. A **UNIX** sig block is a file called .signature in the user's home directory.

It is generally considered a breach of **netiquette** to have a sig block over four lines long. Sig blocks are the bumper stickers of the information highway.

■ **signal** (n) An electronic impulse passing over a medium such as a wire, carrying data from one device to another; 2. More loosely, any useful information.

See also **noise**, **signal-to-noise ratio**.

free junk from the net

CD-ROM

shovelware

- **signal-to-noise ratio** 1. Literally, an electrical engineering measurement of the quality of a communication medium; 2. On the Internet, colloquially used as a metaphor for the proportion of useful information to junk on a **list** or in a **newsgroup**.

- **signature**

  See sig block.

- **.signature**

  See sig block.

- **signature block**

  See sig block.

- **signature file**

  See sig block.

- **sig quote** A quotation contained in a **sig block**, not unlike a yearbook quotation and frequently about as interesting.

- **sig virus** A meme in **sig block**s that became very popular around late 1991 to early 1992, usually some variation on "Hi! I'm a sig virus. Copy me into your signature file and join the fun."

- **silicon** The mineral that computer chips (and sand) are made from.

- **Silicon Valley Public Access Link** [service provider] msiegel@svpal.org, (415) 968-2598.

- **silly group** A newsgroup created simply for the sake of amusement, either because the name itself is silly or because the topic to be discussed in it is silly, many of which can be found in the alt.silly-group.* **hierarchy**. Some silly groups have a *gag.gag.gag* ending, for instance, alt.tv.dinosaurs.barney. die.die.die.

- **Simple Mail Transfer Protocol (SMTP)** The TCP/IP protocol that specifies how computers exchange electronic mail. It works with **Post Office Protocol**, and is one of the reasons that Internet e-mail functions so well.

- **Simple Network Management Protocol (SNMP)** A TCP/IP protocol that specifies how **nodes** are managed on a **network**, using **agents** to monitor network traffic and maintain a **management information base**.

- **Simple Wide Area Information Server (SWAIS)** A WAIS interface for VT100 terminals that shows **sources** in numbered lists.

- **simplex** Transmission of a **signal** in one direction at a time.

  See also **duplex, full duplex, half duplex.**

- **.sit** The file **extension** of a Macintosh StuffIt file.

- **site** An Internet **host** that allows some kind of **remote access**, such as **FTP, telnet, gopher**, and so on.

- **site name** Also *sitename*, the portion of an Internet address that precedes the (**sub-domain**, if any, and the) **domain**. In the address mang@garnet.blob.com, *garnet* is the site name.

- **64K line** A 64 kps telephone circuit, also called a **DS0** line. A 64K line is called a **clear channel** when its entire 64 kps **bandwidth** is available for transmission.

- **slack** (n) 1. Unused storage space on a disk; 2. According to the teachings of the **Church of the SubGenius**, the prerequisite

A
B
C
D
E
F
G
H
I
J
K
L
M
N
O
P
Q
R
S
T
U
V
W
X
Y
Z

of all human happiness. For more information, see the **newsgroup** alt.slack.

- **slash**   /, in UNIX (and hence in **gopher** addresses and URLs), the separator character between **directory** levels.

- **SLIP**   *Serial Line Internet Protocol*, a **TCP/IP protocol** for transmitting **IP datagram**s over **serial** lines, such as phone lines. With SLIP, personal computer users can connect to the Internet and still function in their native environment (instead of having to deal with a character-based **UNIX** environment).

- **SLIP emulator**   A UNIX program, such as **TIA**, that runs in a **shell account** and mimics the behavior of a **SLIP** connection, enabling a shell user to run Internet applications on a personal computer.

- **SLONET**   [service provider] pwagner@oboe.calpoly.edu, (805) 544-7328.

- **slot**   A rack inside a computer where an expansion **card** can be put.

- **Small Computer Systems Interface** *See* SCSI.

- **smart terminal**   A terminal that can handle some of the display processing, taking some of the load off the computer it's connected to (an obsolete term in the PC world).
  See also **dumb terminal.**

- **SMDS** *See* **Switched Multimegabit Data Service.**

- **smiley**   A sideways smiley face, also called an *emoticon,* used to indicate an emotion.

Here are some examples of smileys:

:-)   ;)   %^$

smiley

- **SMTP** *See* **Simple Mail Transport Protocol.**

- **smurf**   (n) A sickly-sweet **newsgroup** participant (from the icky-cute little blue elf characters from Saturday morning television rot).

- **SNA** *See* **Systems Network Architecture.**

- **SNAFU**   *Situation normal—all fucked up*, an old U.S. Army term used frequently on the **Net**.
  See also **FUBAR.**

- **snail**   (n) A snail mail address, especially labeled as such in a **sig block**.
  (v) To send **snail mail.**

- **snail mail**   Internet slang for U.S. Postal Service mail, so called for its relative slowness compared to electronic mail.

- **snarf**   (v) To **fetch** a set of files across a network, as with **FTP**.

snail mail

■ **sneakernet** The kind of network in which you copy the file to a diskette, walk the diskette over to another computer (that's the sneaker part), and then copy the file onto the new computer. The lowest-tech LAN.

sneakernet

■ **SNMP**

See Simple Network Management Protocol.

■ **'Snooze** A derogatory term for Usenet News, commenting on the low signal-to-noise ratio.

■ **SNR**

See signal-to-noise ratio.

■ **S/N ratio**

See signal-to-noise ratio.

■ **SO** *(ess-oh) Significant other*, a genderless term for partner, spouse, lover, etc. common on Usenet.

■ **soc.** The Usenet hierarchy devoted to society (and usually sectarian groups in it).

■ **socket** A subdivision of a network node reserved for a single application or process. *See also* Winsock.

■ **socket client** An application or process that reserves a socket for a specific purpose.

■ **socket number** A unique number assigned to a socket by a network.

■ **soda machine**

See Coke machine.

■ **soda remailer** An anonymous remailer. For information, send mail to remailer@ soda.csua.berkeley.edu with remailer-info as your subject.

See also **anon.penet.fi**.

■ **soft boot** (v) To reboot only part of a system without restarting the whole thing.

■ **software** 1. A program—either an application or operating system—that a computer can execute, as opposed to hardware (the computer itself); 2. A suite of related programs.

■ **software description database (SDD)** A list of file names and directories accessible via archie.

A
B
C
D
E
F
G
H
I
J
K
L
M
N
O
P
Q
R
S
T
U
V
W
X
Y
Z

■ **solidus**   A slash (/).

■ **sorcerer's apprentice mode**   What happens when a program or process spins out of control, spawning more and more processes from itself until it eventually crashes its system, or worse, slows down or crashes parts of the Internet.

See also **ARMM**, **despew**.

■ **source**   A remote database storing files available to **WAIS searches**.

■ **source code**   The original, uncompiled program instructions that make up a piece of **software**.

■ **South Coast Computing Services, Inc.** [service provider] info@sccsi.com, (713) 661-3301

■ **Southern Tier Free-Net** [service provider] cubicsr@vnet.ibm.com, (607) 752-1201

See also **free-net**.

■ **SPACEWAR**   The original spaceship combat game, first created on **DEC PDP** machines, then **ported** to **UNIX**, and eventually inspiring one of the first video games.

■ **spam**   (v) To **post** (or **robopost**) huge amounts of material to **Usenet**, or to post one **article** to huge numbers of inappropriate **group**s. (The term comes from the commercial meat product Spam and the Monty Python routine in which rowdy Vikings in a diner chant "Spam, Spam, Spam, Spam Spam, Spam, Spam, Spam, wonderful Spam, marvelous Spam," and so on, *ad nauseam*.)

Cross-posting, even to an inappropriately large number of groups, is not the same thing as spamming, because any decent newsreader will ignore the same crossposted article after it has displayed it once, no matter in what newsgroup it appears.

■ **Special Interest Group (SIG)**   1. An e-mail discussion group; 2. One of several technical discussion groups sponsored by ACM (the **Assocation for Computing Machinery**).

■ **spelling flame**   The lowest type of **flame**, a criticism of the spelling of your opponent, a cheap shot, given the crude **editor**s available to many users, and evidence that you have nothing of substance to add to the argument.

■ **spew**   To **post** excessively.

See also **despew**.

■ **Spirit of the Night**

See **Nyx**.

■ **splat**   (n) An asterisk (*).

■ **spoiler**   A **post** that reveals a plot twist or the solution to a puzzle or riddle. It is good **netiquette** to label such a post with the word *spoiler* in the subject line and/or to encode the post with **rot13**.

spoiler

■ **SprintLink** [service provider] mkiser@icm1.icp.net, (800) 817-7755.

■ **SprintNet**   A global **public data network** providing local dial-up access from six hundred locations. SprintNet is a **packet-switched network** using **X.25** protocols. It used to be called *Telenet* (not to be confused with **telnet**).

■ **SPX**

See **sequenced packet exchange**.

■ **SQL** (*sequel*) *See* **Structured Query Language**.

■ **squick** (v) To exceed someone's threshold for violent or tasteless imagery.

■ **stack**

See **protocol stack**.

■ **standard** (n) A description of the expeced performance of a device or system.

See also **protocol**.

■ **standard disclaimer** A disclaimer attached to the end of a **Usenet** or **mailing list post**, usually to the effect that the user is not speaking in an official capacity for the user's employer or access provider.

```
>thus my 10 years of research culminate
>in these findings.

I agree!
  --jojo
--
jojo@yoyodyne.com
Joey Joe-Joe "Junior" Shabadoo

The opinions in this message are those
of Joey Joe-Joe Jr.'s and not those of
Yoyodyne, Inc., unless explicitly stated.
```

standard disclaimer

■ **standard generalized markup language (SGML)** A set of formatting tags designed to show the logical relationships between text elements. The language of Web documents, HTML (hypertext markup language), is a subset of SGML.

■ **star** *, 1. A **wildcard** character in **UNIX** (and hence in many Internet applications), it stands for any number of characters; 2. In e-mail and especially on **Usenet**, where plain **ASCII** text is the norm, writers place a * before and after words to emphasize them: "I'm *really* sorry about posting your phone number."

See also **question mark**.

■ **star-dot-star** *.*, the DOS wildcard for any file name. (In **UNIX**, just * will suffice.)

■ **StarNet Communications, Inc.** [**service provider**] info@winternet.com, (612) 941-9177.

■ **start bit** A **bit**, set to 0, preceding the transmission of a **byte**, to tell the receiving computer that the following bits are a **character**.

See also **stop bit**.

■ **star topology** A network architecture in which all the **node**s are connected to a central **hub** computer and not to each other.

See also **bus topology**, **ring topology**.

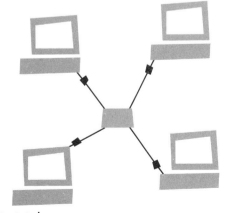

star topology

■ **Star Trek** A 1960s science fiction TV program that spun off a series of movies and three (and counting) further TV series, the subject of seven or eight **Usenet newsgroups** (if you include alt.sexy.bald. captains, which might as easily be construed as a *Love Boat* newsgroup).

■ **startup** (adj) Said of a process or set of instructions that take place when a system or application is started up, usually in order to set user preferences.

■ **STD** An **RFC** that has been adopted as an Internet standard. (*STD* stands for *standard*.) STDs are numbered consecutively.

■ **stop bit** A bit, set to 1, following the transmission of a **byte**, to tell the receiving computer that the character is complete. Also, the number of stop bits is one of the things you have to set to use your **modem** (usally 1 or 2; it depends on the modem you're calling).

See also **start bit**.

■ **stop word** A word so common that it is useless to **search** for (such as *and*, *address*, *record*, and so on). Most **searchable databases** have lists of stop words and **filter** them out during searches. (Also called *buzz words*.)

See also **WAIS**.

■ **store-and-forward** (n) 1. A method of transmitting messages in which they reside at intermediate **nodes** before being sent to their eventual destination in order to wait for a more cost-effective transmission time or to wait until the receiving network is available; 2. The usual method of e-mail distribution, in which e-mail is stored on a server until the user connects to check her mail, at which point it is forwarded to the user.

■ **STP**

See **shielded twisted-pair**.

■ **string** A sequence of **characters** (letters, numbers, or symbols) to be input or output as data.

■ **stroke** A slash (/).

■ **Structured Query Language (SQL)** An **ANSI** and **ISO** standard language used to search relational databases.

■ **stub network** A network that transmits data only among **localhosts** (see illustration on opposite page).

See also **transmit network**.

■ **StuffIt** An extremely popular Macintosh **compression** program that was originally distributed as **shareware**. It is now a commercial product, but StuffIt Expander, which can **uncompress** StuffIt and other compressed files, is **freeware**, available from the sumex-aim.stanford.edu **FTP site**.

■ **Sturgeon's Law** "90% of everything is crap," attributed to science-fiction author Theodore Sturgeon (though he reportedly used the word *crud* in the original).

■ **subdirectory** In a hierarchical file system, a **directory** that is the child of another directory.

■ **subdomain** A named portion of an Internet **domain**, usually a network, university, or company. In editor@ enterzone.berkeley.edu, *berkeley* is the subdomain.

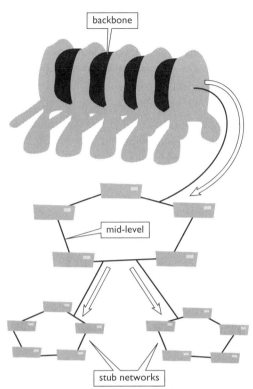

*get their access from mid-level networks,
don't provide access to other networks*

stub network

- **Subject says it all.** What some people write as the contents of a **post** or e-mail message for which the entire question or comment is contained in the Subject line.

- **subnet** A subdivision of a network.

- **subnet address** The portion of an IP address that identifies a **subnet**.

- **subnet mask**
  See subnet address.

- **subnet number**
  See subnet address.

- **subscribe** To join a **mailing list** or start reading a **newsgroup**.

- **substring search** An **archie** option that specifies that the text to be searched for may be contained within a longer file name and need not match the file name exactly.

- **Sugar Land Unix** [service provider] info@NeoSoft.com, (713) 438-4964.

- **suite** 1. A group of related **protocol**s; 2. A group of related programs that make up a **software** package.

- **summarize** To collect the results of a survey or voting process via e-mail and then **post** the results to a **newsgroup** to prevent all the votes or opinions from being posted individually to the Net.

- **Suncoast Free-Net** [service provider] mullam@firnvx.firn.edu, (813) 273-3714.

- **Sun Microsystems** A computer company that makes **workstation**s.

- **SunOS** (*sun-oss* or *sun-oh-ess*) A **flavor** of **UNIX** for Sun Microsystems **workstation**s.

- **supercomputer** The most powerful type of computer. Supercomputers cost tens of millions of dollars and are used for very complex calculations and modeling.
  See also microcomputer, minicomputer.

- **SuperTCP/NFS for Windows** Windows TCP/IP software, developed by Frontier Technologies Corp.

- **superuser** A special user account with unlimited **permissions**.
  See also root.

A
B
C
D
E
F
G
H
I
J
K
L
M
N
O
P
Q
R
S
T
U
V
W
X
Y
Z

■ **SURAnet** [service provider]
info@sura.net, (301) 982-4600.

■ **surf** (v) To **browse**, following tangents
(trendy slang). You can surf **Usenet** or
gopherspace, but the **Web** is best suited for
surfing, since **hypertext link**s allow you to
follow digressions more or less infinitely.

1960s

1980s

1990s

surf

■ **SWAIS**

See Simple Wide Area Information
System.

■ **SWIF-NET** [service provider]
gulery@minuet.siue.edu, (618) 397-0968.

■ **switch** (n) A command-line instruction
that modifies a command, often preceded
by a **slash** in **UNIX** and **DOS**.

(v) To send **packet**s along whatever route is
best without attempting to send related
packets via the same routes.

■ **switched access** A network connection
that disappears when not needed, such as
the type used for **SLIP** or **PPP** connections.

■ **switched connection**

See **switched access**.

■ **Switched Multimegabit Data Service
(SMDS)** A new high-speed technology for
data networks, developed by Bell Labs.

■ **sx** The **Xmodem** command for sending
(**download**ing) a file.

See also **rx**, **sb**, **sz**.

■ **synchronous** (adj) Said of communication that happens for both participants
at the same time (see illustration on opposite page). **IRC** is a synchronous form of
communication, while e-mail is **asynchronous**.

■ **Synchronous Data Link Control
(SDLC)** A data link layer protocol used
on IBM **SNA** networks.

■ **synchronous transmission** A transmission method that uses a clock signal to
synchronize the sending and receiving computers in order to regulate the data flow,

instead of using **start bits** and **stop bits**, as in **asynchronous transmission**. Data is then sent at a fixed rate.

■ **syntax** Rules for properly formed commands.

■ **sysadmin**

See system administrator.

■ **sysape** A pejorative term for *sysop* (a system operator).

■ **sysop** (*siss-op*)

See system operator.

■ **system** 1. A program that supervises a computer and coordinates all its functions, also called an **operating system**; 2. An entire computer taken together with all its devices; 3. A large program.

■ **system administrator** Someone who runs or maintains a **network**.

■ **system file** A file reserved for use by the system and not ordinarily **kill**able by a user (at least not without a warning).

■ **system operator** Someone who runs or maintains a **BBS**.

■ **Systems Application Architecture (SAA)** A set of **standard**s that specify interfaces (user interface, programming interface, and communications) for IBM software.

■ **Systems Network Architecture (SNA)** A set of communications **protocol**s for networks running on IBM **mainframe** computers, incompatible with the **OSI Model**.

■ **Systems Solutions** [service provider] sharris@marlin.ssnet.com, (302) 378-1386, (800) 331-1386.

■ **sz** The **Ymodem** command for sending (**download**ing) a file.

See also rz, sb, sx.

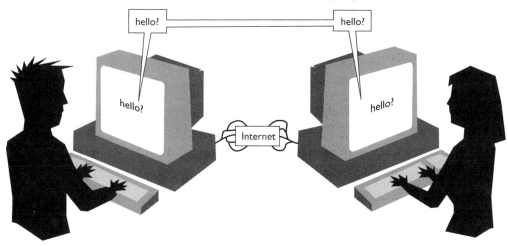

synchronous

■ **table of services** A service provider's internal list of Internet services (such as **FTP**, **finger**, **IRC**, and so on) offered to users.

■ **TAC**

See **Terminal Access Controller**.

■ **talk** (n) 1. One-to-one **synchronous chat**ting over the **Net**; 2. The **UNIX** command for initiating or accepting a talk request (the form of the command is talk *username@address*).

■ **talk.** A **Usenet hierarchy** devoted to discussion, argument, and debate.

■ **talk mode** A **UNIX** feature in which two or more users can participate in an online conversation in real time.

See also **chat**, **IRC**, **talk**.

■ **talk radio**

See **Internet Talk Radio**.

■ **Tallahassee Free-Net** [service provider] levitz@cs.fsu.edu, (904) 644-1796.

See also **free-net**.

■ **TANSTAAFL** (written only, also *tanstaafl*) *There ain't no such thing as a free lunch*, often pointed to as a general principal of the universe, probably taken from economist Milton Friedman's book *There's No Such Thing as Free Lunch*.

■ **tape tree** A distributing mechanism for audio cassette tapes employed in some of the music-related **newsgroup**s and **mailing list**s (see the rec.music.* **Usenet** hierarchy), in which a **seed** tape is copied by a **root** participant for a number of **branch**es, each of which, in turn, dub copies for their children on the tree, until copies of the tapes reach **leaf** participants, who have parents but no children in the tree structure.

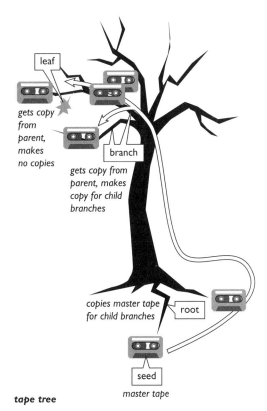

tape tree

■ **tar** (n) A **UNIX** program (*tape ar*chiver) that concatenates a number of files into a single file (without **compress**ing them).

(v) To create an **archive file** with the tar program.

See also **untar**.

■ **.tar** A file **extension** indicating that the file is a **tar**red file, an **archive** consisting of several concatenated files.

■ **tar file** A file containing several files, concatenated with the **UNIX** tar program.

■ **Tarrant County Free-Net** [**service provider**] jcoles@pubcon.com, (817) 763-8437.

See also **free-net**.

■ **.tar.Z** A file **extension** indicating that the file is **tar**red *and* compressed with the **UNIX** **compress** program.

■ **T-carrier** A series of long-distance, digital, point-to-point communications circuits numbered **T1**, **T2**, **T3**, **T4** (see illustration, opposite).

■ **TCP** *Transmission Control Protocol*, part of the TCP/IP stack. It functions on the **transport layer** (layer 4) of the **OSI Model**, establishing and verifying the data connection.

■ **TCP Connect/II** A suite of Macintosh software comprising Internet tools such as **e-mail**, a **Usenet newsreader**, **FTP**, and **telnet**, developed by InterCon Systems Incorporated.

■ **TCP/IP** A **protocol stack**, designed to connect different networks, on which the Internet is based (see illustration on opposite page). The suite includes protocols for **remote login** (telnet), file transfer (**FTP**),

e-mail (**SMTP**), and so on. TCP/IP can work with any hardware or operating system.

TCP/IP was developed by **DARPA** in the late 1970s as a set of robust internetworking protocols that could survive the partial destruction of constituent networks (as might occur in a nuclear war).

See also **IP**, **TCP**.

■ **TCP/IP stack** *See* **TCP/IP**.

■ **TECO** A once popular **text editor** with a powerful built-in programming language, now largely supplanted by **emacs**.

■ **teledildonics** A trendy term for online sex, alluding to the mechanical "interface" devices that might evolve in the near future.

■ **Telenet** The original name of **SprintNet** (often confused with **telnet**).

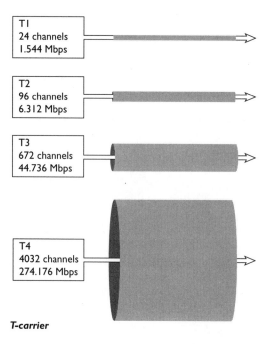

T1
24 channels
1.544 Mbps

T2
96 channels
6.312 Mbps

T3
672 channels
44.736 Mbps

T4
4032 channels
274.176 Mbps

T-carrier

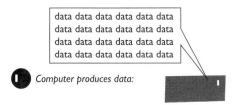

❶ *Computer produces data:*

data data data data data data
data data data data data data
data data data data data data
data data data data data data

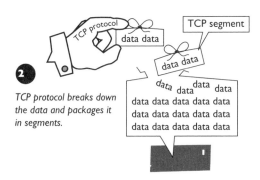

TCP protocol

data data

TCP segment

data data

data data data data
data data data data data
data data data data data
data data data data data
data data data data data

❷ *TCP protocol breaks down the data and packages it in segments.*

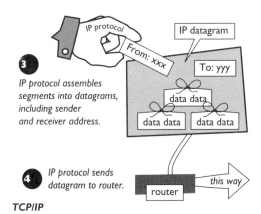

IP protocol

IP datagram

From: xxx

To: yyy

data data

data data   data data

❸ *IP protocol assembles segments into datagrams, including sender and receiver address.*

❹ *IP protocol sends datagram to router.*

router   this way

TCP/IP

■ **Teleport** [service provider] info@ teleport.com, (503) 223-4245.

■ **Telerama Public Access Internet** [service provider] info@telerama.lm.com, info@telerama.pgh.pa.us, (412) 481-3505.

■ **telex** An international communications system made up of linked terminals that can send and receive data. Some **online services** offer telex access.

■ **telnet** 1. A terminal-emulation protocol (defined in **RFC** 854) for **remote login** over the Internet, part of the **TCP/IP** suite; 2. The **UNIX** program that uses that protocol.

(v) To log in to a remote computer via the telnet protocol.

■ **10BaseF** The **Ethernet** specification (802.3 standard) for **fiber-optic cable.** (*10* for the 10 Mbps **bandwidth,** *base* for baseband, and *F* for fiber-optic.)

■ **10Base5** The **Ethernet** specification (802.3 standard) using "thick" **coaxial cable,** also known as *thicknet.* (*10* for 10 Mbps **bandwidth,** *base* for **baseband,** and *5* for 500-meter-long cable segments.)

■ **10BaseT** The **Ethernet** specification (802.3 standard) using two pairs of **unshielded twisted-pair** (UTP) wire. (*10* for 10 Mbps **bandwidth,** *base* for baseband, and *T* for **twisted-pair cable.**)

See also **coaxial** cable.

■ **10Base2** The **Ethernet** specification (802.3 standard) using "thin" **coaxial cable** (⅜") also known as *thinnet,* or *cheapernet.* (*10* for 10 Mbps **bandwidth,** *base* for **baseband,** and *2* for 200-meter-long cable segments.)

■ **Tennessee Valley Free-Net** [service provider] (205) 544-3849.

See also **free-net.**

■ **term** A **DOS** program that enables a personal computer to function as a **UNIX** terminal-emulation program over a **dial-up** connection.

A B C D E F G H I J K L M N O P Q R S **T** U V W X Y Z

■ **terminal** A keyboard-and-monitor combination, one of many, connected to a computer. The terminal passes the user input from the keyboard to the computer and displays the computer's output on the monitor (screen). (See illustration below.) Large, multiuser computers such as **mainframe**s have traditionally been accessed via terminals, as have **UNIX** machines.

See also **dumb terminal, smart terminal, terminal-emulation program.**

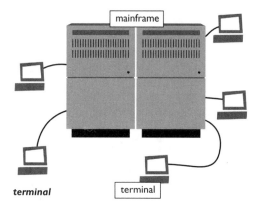

terminal   *terminal*

■ **Terminal Access Controller (TAC)**
A device that provides and maintains a dial-up terminal connection to the Internet.

■ **terminal emulation** Behaving like a specific type of **terminal** (such as a DEC VT100 or VT52 or an IBM 3270), passing keyboard input to a computer and displaying computer output on the screen (possibly in a window).

■ **terminal-emulation program** Software a personal computer uses to imitate a specific type of terminal (such as a VT100, ANSI, or TTY terminal) and connect to a host.

■ **terminal/host computing** The model of computing used by **dumb terminal**s and **host** computers, in which the **terminal** is only a messenger and the host does all of the processing.

See also **client/server.**

■ **terminal server** A device that enables several **modem**s (usually assembled on a modem bank) or **terminal**s to connect to a **host** on one **channel** by sending a combined signal.

■ **terminal window** A window in a **graphical user interface** in which a **terminal-emulation program** displays an emulated terminal screen connected by network to a remote computer.

■ **terminator** A device connected to the end of a **LAN** cable to prevent signals from being transmitted.

■ ***.test** Any of the **newsgroup**s with names such as misc.test, alt.test, rec.test, and so on, designated for **test post**s. If you **post** to a *.test newsgroup, **daemon**s all over the Internet send you e-mail acknowledgments when your post reaches their site. It is a breach of **netiquette** to post test messages to any newsgroup other than *.test newsgroups.

One trap often set for **newbie**s is a post with its **follow-up line** set to a *.test newsgroup. Anyone who responds to the post without noticing and removing the *.test group will suffer a mailbox flooded by well-meaning daemons.

■ **test post** A post with no meaningful content, posted to a **newsgroup** (preferably a *.test newsgroup) so that the user can determine if her newsreader software and Internet connection are working properly.

■ **T_EX** *(tekh)* Also written *TeX*, a free, very powerful, macro-based typesetting/text-formatting system for **UNIX**.

See also **troff**.

■ **Texas Metronet** [service provider] info@metronet.com, (214) 705-2900, (817) 543-8756.

■ **text editor** An application for editing text files, usually less fully featured than a word processor. The Notepad accessory in **Windows** is a text editor, as are the **UNIX** programs **vi**, **pico**, **emacs**, **ee**, and **joe**, among others.

■ **text file** Also *ASCII file* or *ASCII text file*, a file containing only **ASCII** characters. This means no formatting—no bold or italics, no headers, footers, margin adjustments, non-breaking hyphens, and so on.

See also **binary file**.

■ **text file transfer** A form of file transfer, both with **FTP** and with **upload**ing/**download**ing programs (**kermit**, **zmodem**, etc.) used to transfer files containing only **ASCII** characters. (**Newline** characters are automatically converted for the operating system being transferred to.)

See also **binary file transfer**.

■ **text transfer** 1. A text file transfer; 2. A transfer of text directly from a **local** file to a **remote** computer, as if typed directly from the keyboard, or from the output of a remote program running on a remote **host** computer to the terminal window and/or to a text file on the local computer.

■ **Tezcatlipoca Inc.** [service provider] info@tezcat.com, (312) 850-0181.

■ **T4** A long-distance, digital, point-to-point communications circuit developed by AT&T that transmits a signal at 274.176 Mbps, with up to 168 **T1** channels (4,032 channels of 64 Kbps), handling both voice and data.

■ **TFTP** *Trivial File Transfer Protocol*, a simplified version of **FTP** that does not include password protection.

■ **thanks in advance** Often abbreviated *TIA* or more whimsically as aTdHvAaNnKcSe, a common sign-off for requests made in **Usenet** or elsewhere on the Internet.

■ **The Internet Adapter (TIA)** A UNIX program that enables a **dial-up shell account** to emulate a **SLIP** connection, allowing the user to run Internet software native to his desktop environment without the full costs (or full functionality, either) of real SLIP. TIA is available from Cyberspace Development at http://marketplace.com/.

■ **THEnet** [Texas (and part of Mexico) service provider] info@nic.the.net, (512) 471-2444.

■ **theology**

See **religious issues**.

■ **thickwire**

See **10base5**.

■ **Thinnet**

See **10base2**.

■ **thinwire**

See **10base2**.

■ **Thomas** U.S. Congressional archives on the **Web**, administered by the Library of Congress, named for Thomas Jefferson, at http://thomas.loc.gov/. (See figure.)

Thomas

■ **thread** (n) 1. A series of messages related to the same topic in a discussion group, such as an original **post** and related **follow-ups**. It is appropriate to read an entire thread before contributing to it to avoid repeating something that may already have been contributed one or more times; 2. A process that is part of a larger process or program.

See also threaded newsreader.

■ **threaded newsreader** A newsreader that organizes **posts** according to **thread** and

allows you to read your way up or down a thread, such as **trn**, **tin**, and **Newswatcher**.

■ **3270** An IBM **terminal** type.

See also **tn3270**.

■ **throughput** A measure of the rate of data transmitted, expressed as **bits per second**.

■ ***thwap*** A virtual slap, as on **IRC**, indicating that you've just smacked the recipient for writing something stupid or inappropriate.

■ **TIA** 1. An abbreviation for **thanks in advance**; 2. The Internet Adapter, a SLIP-emulation program for **UNIX**.

■ **TidBITS** A weekly news-letter about the Internet and **Macintosh** computers, dis-tributed via e-mail by Adam Engst. For more information, contact info@tidbits.com.

■ **tidy** Cool, stylish, and con-fident, from the idea of well-structured, well-organized, and easy-to-read programming **code**.

■ **tilde** The ~ character, used to issue com-mands in the **UNIX mail** program.

■ **tilde escape** A command in the **UNIX mail** program that starts with a **tilde** character (~) and performs a function, rather than inserting text into the mail.

■ **Time to Live (TTL)** An IP packet **header** field that tells how long the packet should be held before it's purged.

■ **time out** (v) To fail, as a network process, because the remote server or computer has not responded in time, to close a connection after waiting too long for acknowledgment.

See also **hash**.

■ **timeout** (n) The occasion when a **remote** computer **time**s **out**.

■ **tin** A threaded **newsreader** for UNIX.

■ **TinyFugue**

See MUD.

■ **Tiny MUD**

See MUD.

■ **TLA** (written only) *Three-letter acronym*, many of which persist throughout the Internet.

See also ETLA.

■ **TMN (The Meta Network)** [service provider] info@tmn.com, (703) 243-6622.

■ **tn3270** A program similar to **telnet** that emulates a **3270** terminal connected to an IBM **mainframe**.

■ **toaster** A mildly pejorative name for a Macintosh or PC.

toaster

■ **toggle** (n) A **logical** or **physical switch** (or even a single **bit**) that can be set to two positions, usually on and off. A light switch is a toggle.

(v) To change a switch or bit from one state to the other (from 0 to 1 or back again).

toggle

■ **token ring** A (typically IBM) type of network architecture in which **node**s are connected in a closed circle. The nodes continually pass a token (a special message) around the circle. To transmit data, a node has to wait until it's "it." Then the data rides along with the token and gets off at the right stop. (See illustration on next page.)

See also **Carrier Sense Multiple Access with Collision Detection**, **Ethernet**.

■ **TokenTalk** An Apple product that enables **AppleTalk protocol**s to work on a **token ring** network.

■ **Toledo Free-Net** [service provider] rad@uoft02.utoledo.edu, (419) 537-3686.

See also **free-net**.

A
B
C
D
E
F
G
H
I
J
K
L
M
N
O
P
Q
R
S
T
U
V
W
X
Y
Z

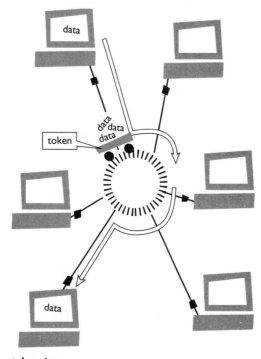

token ring

- **T1** A long-distance, digital, point-to-point communications circuit, developed by AT&T, that transmits a **DS1** signal at 1.544 Mbps, with 24 (voice) channels of 64 Kbps. If the circuit uses fewer than 24 channels, it's called *FT1* or *fractional T1*. T1 is also called *High-Cap*, *T-span*, and *T-carrier*.

- **tool** A utility program, a useful program that performs a set function.

- **topic drift** As **threads** wear on in discussion groups, they frequently stray from the original topic as listed in the Subject **header**. Some **posters** take the initiative of changing the Subject line to spawn new threads.

  This same phenomenon is noticed in e-mail conversations, in which the original header,

perhaps preceded by *Re: Re: Re:* outlasts its relevance.

- **topic group** Any electronic common space for people who share an interest.

  See also **BBS, echo, forum, newsgroup, mailing list, Special Interest Group.**

- **topology** Any type of **physical network** layout, organizing the devices and the cables connecting them. Most **LANs** have **bus topology, star topology,** or **ring topology.**

- **toy** A computer or system less powerful than the one used by the speaker, not necessarily derogatory. (Toys can be fun.)

- **TP**

  See **twisted-pair cable.**

- **traditional newsgroup hierarchy** The seven **newsgroup** hierarchies in **Usenet** news proper: **comp., misc., news., rec., sci., soc.,** and **talk** (see illustration, opposite page). New newsgroups in any of the traditional hierarchies can only be created after a formal process, including a **request for discussion** and a **call for votes.**

  See also **alternative newsgroup hierarchy.**

- **traffic** 1. **Mailing list** or **newsgroup** posts, taken as a whole; 2. Network activity, measured in **bits per second, kilobits per second,** or **megabits per second.**

- **trailer** Information following the data in a **packet**, signifying the end of the data and possibly including error-checking information.

  See also **header.**

- **transceiver** A device that both transmits

and receives signals, exchanging frames between a **node** and a **network**

■ **Transmission Control Protocol (TCP)** Part of the **TCP/IP** stack. It functions on the **transport layer** (layer 4) of the **OSI Model**, establishing and verifying the data connection.

■ **Transmission Control Protocol/ Internet Protocol**

See TCP/IP.

■ **transmit network** A network that communicates with at least two other networks and transmits data among networks as well as among **local nodes**.

See also **backbone**, **stub network**.

■ **transport layer** Layer 4 of the **OSI Model**, controlling delivery and verification of messages.

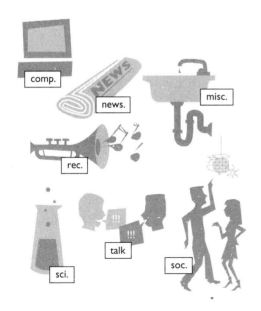

traditional newsgroup hierarchy

■ **tree administrator** In a **tape tree**, the person who designs the tree and administers the process, not necessarily the person who provides the **seed** (usually not, in fact).

■ **tree-killer** A printer.

■ **Triangle Free-Net** [service provider] hallman@gibbs.oit.unc.edu, (919) 962-9107.

See also **free-net**.

■ **Tri-Cities Free-Net** [service provider] tcfn@delphi.com, (509) 586-6481.

See also **free-net**.

■ **Tristate Online** [service provider] sysadmin@cbos.uc.edu, (513) 397-1396.

■ **Trivial File Transfer Protocol**

See TFTP.

■ **trn** A threaded newsreader for UNIX, based on **rn**.

■ **troff** A UNIX text processor that can produce output for typesetting equipment, superseded largely by T$_{E}$X.

■ **Trojan horse** An attack program, hidden inside a seemingly benign program, that enables the program's creator to gain access to the user's system (see illustration, next page).

See also **virus**, **worm**.

■ **troll** (v) 1. To deliberately **post** egregiously false information to a **newsgroup** in hopes of tricking dense know-it-alls into correcting you; 2. From the fishing term, to explore information sources or communication methods on the **Net**, looking for something specific, as in the *New Yorker* cartoon in which a boss tells his

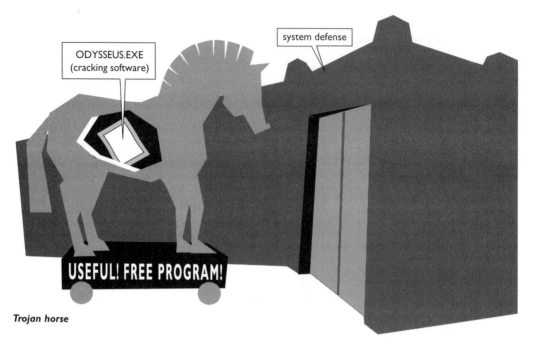

Trojan horse

employee: "I hear you've been trolling for babes on the Internet."

(n) A deliberately false post.

See also YHBT. YHL. HAND.

■ **Trumpet newsreader** Windows **newsreader** software that works with NNTP, available by **anonymous FTP** from biochemistry.cwru.edu.

■ **Trumpet for Windows** Windows Internet software featuring a **newsreader** and a **mail program**, available by **anonymous FTP** from biochemistry.cwru.edu.

troll 1

■ **T-span**

See T1.

■ **T3** A long-distance, digital, point-to-point communications circuit, developed by AT&T, that transmits a signal at 44.746 Mbps, with up to 28 **T1** channels (762 voice channels of 64 Kbps), running over a **leased line**, usually **fiber-optic cable**.

■ **TTL**

See Time to Live.

■ **T2** A long-distance, digital, point-to-point communications circuit, developed by

AT&T, that transmits a signal at 6.3 Mbps, with up to four **T1** channels (92 channels of 64 Kbps). T2 is used within telephone company networks, not commercially.

■ **tunafish test** A series of **posts** in 1994 to a *.test newsgroup via the **anon.penet.fi anonymous remailer** service that may have compromised the identities of some of the remailer's users.

■ **Tundra Services (University of Alaska Southeast)** [service provider] JNJMB@acad1.alaska.edu, (907) 465-6453.

■ **tunneling** Encapsulating a **datagram** of one **protocol** within that of a different protocol to transport the enclosed data

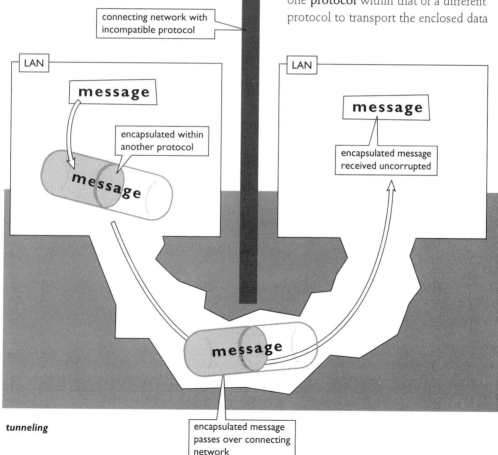

connecting network with incompatible protocol

LAN

message

encapsulated within another protocol

message

LAN

message

encapsulated message received uncorrupted

message

tunneling

encapsulated message passes over connecting network

across an intervening **backbone** that does not support the former protocol.

■ **tuple** (*toople*) A pair of related values in a **routing table** (the network number and the number of **hop**s to that network).

■ **TurboGopher** 1. A **gopher client** for the **Macintosh**, available via **anonymous FTP** from sumex-aim.stanford.edu; 2. An improved version of the original **gopher** software developed at the University of Minnesota.

■ **Tuscaloosa Free-Net** [service provider] rdoctor@ua1vm.ua.edu, (205) 348-2398.

See also **free-net**.

■ **tweak** 1. To make small changes in order to get something just exactly perfect; 2. To tease someone in a minor way.

■ **twiddle** (n) A tilde (~).

■ **twilight zone** An imaginary place where only **IRC channel op**s may go.

■ **Twin Cities Free-Net** [service provider] fritchie@stolaf.edu, (507) 646-3407.

See also **free-net**.

■ **twisted-pair**

See **twisted-pair cable**.

■ **twisted-pair cable** Cable comprising four or more copper wires, twisted in pairs (one grounded, one carrying a signal) to reduce interference, usually one pair for sending, one for receiving. There are two types of twisted-pair cable: **shielded twisted-pair** (STP) and **un-shielded twisted-pair** (UTP). (See illustration, opposite.)

See also **coaxial cable**.

■ **twisted-pair wire**

See **twisted-pair cable**.

■ **.txt** A file **extension** indicating a **text file**.

■ **Tymnet** A global **public data network**, offering local **dial-up** access in one hundred countries, including access to some online services and Internet **service providers**.

■ **TZ-Link** [service provider] info@j51.com, (914) 353-5443.

See also **free-net**.

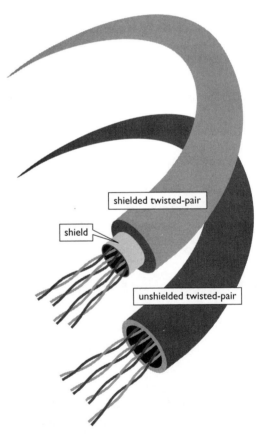

shielded twisted-pair

shield

unshielded twisted-pair

twisted-pair cable

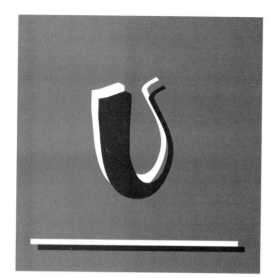

- **UART** (*you-art*)

  See Universal Asynchronous Receiver/Transmitter.

- **UDP**

  See User Datagram Protocol.

- **UKnet** [United Kingdom **Service** Provider] postmaster@uknet.ac.uk.

- **UL**

  See urban legend.

- **Ultrix** A port of UNIX that runs on VAXen.

- **UN*X** A generic term for the various **flavors** and **ports** of UNIX, used also to refer to UNIX without including the ™ notice erroneously thought to be required by AT&T.

- **unbalanced line** A cable containing electrically unequal wires, such as a **coaxial** cable.

  See also balanced line, balun.

- **uncompress** (v) To unsquish a **compress**ed file.

  (n) A UNIX **uncompression** program.

- **uncompression** A method of unsquishing a **compress**ed file.

- **UnCover** A search service provided by CARL with access to over ten thousand journals.

- **undelete** To restore a deleted file. This is not possible on **UNIX** systems.

- **underline**

  See underscore.

- **undernet** A network of IRC **servers** formed as an alternative to EFnet, the "mainstream" IRC net. Undernet IRC servers always have **domain name**s of the form *city.state*.undernet.org or *city.country*.undernet.org.

- **underscore** In e-mail and **Usenet posts**, only plain text may appear, so to suggest underlining and italics, users often precede and follow text with the underscore character (_), like so: "The origin of fnord is explained in _Illuminati!_"

- **undirected information** Information intended for the public at at large, such as **Usenet** or **mailing list posts**.

  See also directed information.

- **Unicode** A standard 16-bit character code (as compared with **ASCII**, which is a 7-bit character code) with 65,536 possible characters, as well as the ability to encode color and graphics. A possible eventual successor to ASCII.

A B C D E F G H I J K L M N O P Q R S T **U** V W X Y Z

- **uniform resource locator (URL)** A Web address. It consists of a **protocol**, a **host name**, a **port** (optional), a **directory** (optional), and a file name (optional). In the URL http://enterzone.berkeley.edu/enterzone.html, the protocol is **HTTP**, the host name is enterzone.berkeley.edu, and the file name is enterzone.html. URLs can be used to address other Internet resources besides **Web page**s, such as **FTP sites**, **gopher server**s, **telnet** addresses, and so on.

- **Universal Asynchronous Receiver/Transmitter (UART)** A device that combines the transmitting and receiving functions of **asynchronous** communications over a **serial** line.

- **Universal Time Coordinate (UTC)** Greenwich mean time, used to synchronize computers on the Internet.

- **University of Alaska Southeast, Tundra Services** [service provider] JNJMB@acad1.alaska.edu, (907) 465-6453.

- **University of Maryland Info Database** A huge information resource intended to demonstrate the breadth of potential information on the Net. **Telnet** to info.umd.edu and log in as *info*.

- **UNIX** (*you-nix*) An 32-bit, multiuser, multitasking **operating system** common to workstations and dominant (but getting gradually less so) on the Internet. It was originally developed at Bell Labs in 1969 by Ken Thompson, and is now owned by Novell, although it has spawned many **port**s and clones.

  Dealing with UNIX is a frustrating barrier to most Internet **newbie**s, what with its arbitrary command abbreviations, rigorous syntax, case-sensitivity, lack of an undelete feature, and so on. Fortunately, alternative routes to the Internet that require no knowledge of UNIX (or very little) are sprouting up every day.

- **UNIX box** A computer running the **UNIX** operating system.

- **unix2dos** A program that converts **UNIX** text files to **DOS** format, by changing the line breaks.

  See also **dos2unix**.

- **UNIX to UNIX Copy Program** *See* UUCP.

- **UNIX weenie** 1. A programmer who has to use **UNIX** but would prefer not to; 2. Someone who admits to liking UNIX.

- **UNIX wizard** A helpful **UNIX** expert, such as those who answer questions in the comp.unix.wizards **newsgroup**.

UNIX wizard

■ **unmoderated** Said of lists and newsgroups whose **post**s are not vetted by a moderator.

■ **unread** (adj) Said of **newsgroup** articles that the user has not yet read or has marked as such. Unread articles will show up again the next time the user returns to the newsgroup.

■ **unselect articles** (v) To remove the selection tag from **Usenet** articles selected for reading.

■ **unshielded cable** Cable that's not protected from electromagnetic or radio-frequency interference by a foil shield.

■ **unshielded twisted-pair (UTP)**
A cable containing unshielded wire in twisted pairs.
See also **shielded twisted-pair**, **10baseT**.

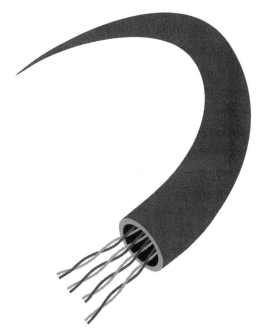

unshielded twisted-pair

■ **unsubscribe** 1. To remove one's name from a **mailing list**; 2. To remove the name of a **newsgroup** from the list of subscribed groups.

■ **untar** (v) To separate a **tar**red file into its component parts.

■ **up** (adj) Working, functioning just fine, turned on.
See also **boot**.

■ **upload** To transfer a file over a **modem** from a desktop computer to a **remote** computer.

■ **upstream** Where your **newsfeed** comes from.

■ **urban legend** Also *UL*, a story passed around and usually attributed to a *FOAF* (a friend of a friend), frequently (but not always) based on a kernel of falsehood. The **newsgroup** alt.folklore.urban (and its less noisy cousin alt.folklore.suburban) is the home of UL debunkers.

■ **URL** (*you-are-ell* or *earl*) *Uniform resource locator*, a **Web** address. It consists of a **protocol**, a **host name**, a **port** (optional), a **directory** (optional), and a file name (optional). In the URL http://enterzone.berkeley.edu/enterzone.html, the protocol is **HTTP**, the host name is enterzone.berkeley.edu, and the file name is enterzone.html. URLs can be used to address other Internet resources besides **Web page**s, such as **FTP site**s, **gopher** servers, **telnet** addresses, and so on.

■ **U.S. Department of Defense (DoD)**
The original funder of **ARPA** and hence **ARPAnet**, the predecessor to the Internet.

A
B
C
D
E
F
G
H
I
J
K
L
M
N
O
P
Q
R
S
T
U
V
W
X
Y
Z

■ **Usenet** 1. From *User Network* and often written *USENET*, the collection of computers and networks that share news articles. Usenet is *not* the Internet (though it overlaps pretty well). It's sometimes called the world's largest electronic bulletin board. 2. The **newsgroup**s in the traditional newsgroup hierarchies.

See also **traditional newsgroup hierarchy**.

■ **Usenet cabal** An imaginary set of **net.god**s who establish the policy for Usenet.

■ **Usenet News** The traffic of **posted** articles in the **Usenet newsgroup**s.

■ **Usenet newsgroup** A newsgroup in one of the seven traditional newsgroup hierarchies. Newsgroup names go from the general to the specific: rec.music.makers.bass (pronounced *rec-dot-music-dot-makers-dot-base*) is the newsgroup for musicians who play the bass.

See also **traditional newsgroup hierarchy**.

■ **Usenet Oracle** A cooperative project of mostly humorous questions and oracular responses. Anyone can submit questions or answers. To find out more about the Oracle, send mail to oracle@cs.indiana.edu with the word *help* in the Subject line, or read the rec.humor.oracle **newsgroup**.

■ **user** Anyone logged on to a computer system or network.

■ **user agent** One way to refer to a **mail** program.

■ **User Datagram Protocol (UDP)** A connectionless transport **protocol** in the TCP/IP suite. UDP is used for **Simple** Network Management Protocol, database lookups, and other functions instead of **TCP**, because it does not add overhead to the transmission.

■ **user-friendly** Said of computers, systems, and applications that are easy to understand and learn and that function as expected once some basic principles are understood.

user-friendly

■ **username** A **login**, the name a user logs in with. Also, the first part of an Internet e-mail address (up to the @).

Choose your username well. In many ways it is more important (on the Net) than your real name. It's the name people see most often.

■ **USnail** (*you-ess-snail*) *See* **snail mail**.

■ **/usr** A directory on many UNIX machines containing users' home directories.

■ **UTC**

See **Universal Time Coordinate**.

■ **utility** A program that performs some useful function, often something that helps monitor or **tweak** an **operating system**.

■ **UTP**

See unshielded twisted-pair.

■ **.uu** A file extension that indicates a uuencoded file.

■ **UUCP** From *Unix to Unix Copy Program,* a protocol and a program for copying files, news, and mail from one UNIX box to another during intermittent dial-up connections.

See also UUCPNET.

■ **UUCPNET** An international store-and-forward network of UNIX machines (and others) that use the UUCP protocol to exchange mail and news, which is where Usenet originated.

See also bang path.

■ **.uud** A file extension that indicates a uuencoded file.

■ **uudecode** (*you-you-decode,* n) A UNIX program that converts uuencoded files back into their binary form.

(v) To turn a uuencoded file back into its normal form.

■ **.uue** A file extension that indicates a uuencoded file.

■ **uuencode** (*you-you-encode,* n) A UNIX program that converts binary files into an ASCII format suitable for inclusion in an e-mail message (and one-third again as long as the original).

(v) To convert a binary file into a text form that can be sent as part of an e-mail message.

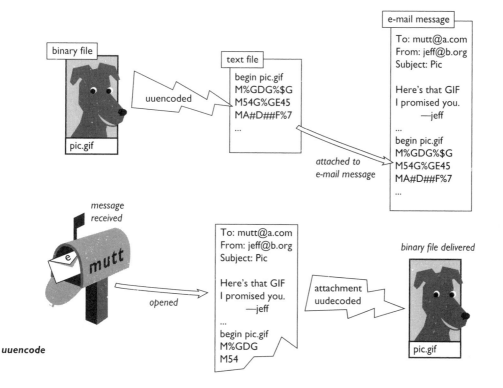

uuencode

- **UUNET Canada, Inc.** [Canadian service provider] info@uunet.ca, (416) 368-6621.

- **UUNET Technologies, Inc.** [service provider] info@uunet.uu.net, (800) 488-6383, (703) 204-8000.

- **UUnorth** [service provider] uunorth@ uunorth.north.net, (416) 225-8649.

- **uupc** A Macintosh program that can transfer files using the **UUCP** protocol.

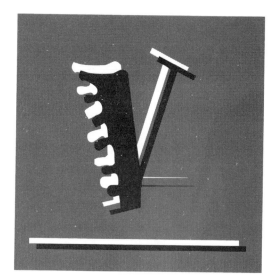

vacation A UNIX program that sets up a return message to be sent to anyone who sends you e-mail, telling them that you're on vacation.

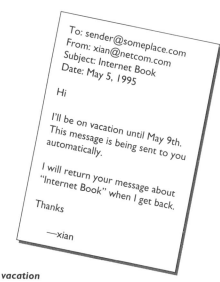

To: sender@someplace.com
From: xian@netcom.com
Subject: Internet Book
Date: May 5, 1995

Hi

I'll be on vacation until May 9th. This message is being sent to you automatically.

I will return your message about "Internet Book" when I get back.

Thanks

—xian

vacation

vanilla (adj) Plain, unmodified, fresh out of the box, said of applications, systems, and hardware.

vanilla

VaPEN—Richmond [service provider] hcothern@vdoe386.vak12ed.edu, (804) 225-2921.

vaporware Software that a developer has been promising for a long time (possibly as a marketing strategy) but which is nowhere in sight.

vaporware

■ **VAX** A DEC minicomputer (the name comes from *Virtual Address Extension*) with 32-bit architecture, a successor to the PDP-11 series, favored by **hacker**s.

■ **VAXen** A whimsical plural of **VAX**.

■ **verbose** A mode of certain programs, such as **ftp**, in which they return as much information as possible and narrate their processes for the user's benefit. (See illustration, opposite.)

See also **brief**.

■ **VERnet** [service provider] jaj@virginia.edu, (804) 924-0616.

■ **Veronica** A searchable index of **gopher** menus (it supposedly stands for *Very Easy Rodent-Oriented Netwide Index to Computerized*

Archives, but more likely is named after the Archie Comics character Veronica—note the other applications **archie** and **Jughead**). The results are themselves presented to you as a gopher menu.

■ **vertical bar**

See **pipe**.

■ **v.42** A **modem** standard defined by CCITT, describing **error control**.

■ **v.42bis** A **modem** standard defined by CCITT, describing data **compression**.

■ **vi** A common but difficult to learn **UNIX text editor** with two modes, edit and insert. (To start inserting text, press *i*; to stop inserting, quit, and save, press Escape, then *ZZ*.)

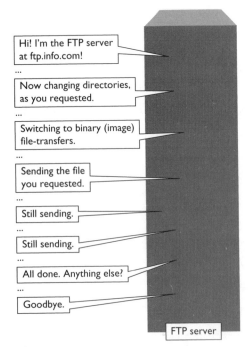

verbose

■ **viewer** 1. An application used to view image files, such as **GIF**s and **JPEG**s; 2. By extension, any auxiliary application that enables the user to open, see, or play a file in a special format.

■ **Village of Cambridge** [service provider] service@village.com, (617) 494-5226.

■ **vine** A variation on the **tape tree** concept used for digital tapes (for which there is no generational loss of quality from one copy to the next), in which the source tape is passed along to each participant in the vine, copied, and then passed again.

■ **Viola** Also called *ViolaWWW*, a **Web browser** for the **X Window** operating environment.

■ **virtual** Said of something that exists only in software, not **physically**.

■ **virtual circuit** A technology used in **packet-switched networks**, in which users share communication paths that appear to each as a dedicated end-to-end connection.

■ **virtual community** Also *online community*, an electronic community of people who share some discussion groups or **chat** rooms and behave socially much like people in a small village who know all their neighbors. The **Well** is often cited as a virtual community.

■ **Virtual Machine**
See **VM**.

■ **Virtual Memory System**
See **VMS**.

■ **virtual reality** An overused term for computer-simulated three-dimensional

virtual reality

This is so cool! I'm in a room . . . it looks like an office . . . I'm working . . . There's lots of work in the IN box . . .

environments with which the user can interact, often by wearing equipment such as gloves and goggles. By analogy, role-playing environments such as **MUD**s are sometimes considered examples of virtual reality.

■ **virtual terminal**
See **terminal-emulation program**.

■ **virus** A program that deliberately does damage to the computer it's on, often hidden inside an apparently benign program.
See also **Trojan horse**, **worm**.

■ **VM** An IBM **mainframe** operating system (it stands for *Virtual Machine*), similar to **MVS**.

■ **VMS** An operating system used on **VAXen** (it stands for *Virtual Memory System*).

- **vmsnet.** An alternative **hierarchy** in the Usenet mold dedicated to discussion of the **VMS** operating system.

- **vn** A now rare **UNIX newsreader** (it stands for *visual newsreader*), on which the **Windows** newsreader **WinVN** is loosely based.

- **Vnet Internet Access Internet Access, Inc.** [service provider] info@char.vnet.net, (704) 374-0779.

- **voice** (v) To call someone on the telephone.

- **voice-net** A facetious name for the telephone system, as often cited with phone numbers in **sig blocks**.

- **volume** A generic name for a storage medium or portion thereof, such as a disk, diskette, or network file server.

- **Vote ACK** Also called a *Mass ACK*, a **Usenet post** listing the e-mail address of each person who votes for and against a proposed **newsgroup**.

- **VR**

  See **virtual reality**.

- **VT52** A **DEC terminal** type, less commonly emulated than the **VT100**.

- **v.32** A **modem** standard defined by CCITT, describing 9600-bps modems.

- **v.32bis** A **modem** standard defined by CCITT, describing 14400-bps modems.

- **VT100** A **terminal** type, originally designed by **DEC** for **VAXen**, that has become the standard terminal. If you dial up a **UNIX shell**, then your communications program probably emulates a VT100.

voice-net

■ **WAIS** (ways) *Wide Area Information Server*, a **client/server** database-search system with access to over four hundred sources. WAIS uses the **Z39.50** standard for data **search**es. A WAIS search is made with a **natural language query**, and successful **match**es are ranked according to **relevance feedback**. WAIS searches ignore **buzz words** (also called *stop words*), extremely common words that might be found in any database or document. There are many different **client** programs for WAIS, with many different appearances. WAIS was developed by Thinking Machines Corp., Apple Computer, and Dow Jones.

■ **WAIS-for-Mac** Macintosh WAIS client software made by WAIS Incorporated, available via **anonymous FTP** from ftp.wais.com.

■ **WAIS Manager for Windows** Windows WAIS **client** software available via **anonymous FTP** from sunsite.unc.edu.

■ **WAN** *Wide area network*, a long-distance computer **network** using dedicated phone lines and/or satellites to interconnect **LAN**s across large geographical distances up to thousands of miles apart.

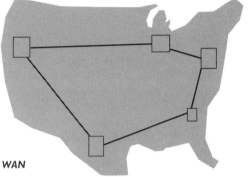

WAN

■ **wanna** Short for *wannafuck*, an unsolicited sexual inquiry, usually from a man to a woman (or someone with a possibly female name or **username**, especially someone who participates in sex-related **newsgroup**s).

■ **warez** (*wares*) An old **BBS** term for pirated game software, still heard mostly in **B1FF**speak.

■ **warlord** (v) To **post** someone else's large, ugly, or stupid **sig block** to the alt.fan. warlord **newsgroup** and then cut it down to size (from the **username** of a **newbie** with a **BUAG** medieval sword in his sig).

■ **warm boot** (v) To **reboot** a computer without turning it off.
See also **cold boot**.

■ **Washington University Services** A **gateway** to many Internet services,

A B C D E F G H I J K L M N O P Q R S T U V **W** X Y Z

libraries, and other information resources. To use it, **telnet** to wugate.wustl.edu and log in as services.

- **waste bandwidth** (v) To misuse system resources (even having too long a **sig block** is sometimes enough to bring out accusations of wasting **bandwidth**).

- **weather** There are many weather information servers on the Internet. For weather information, **telnet** to madlab.sprl.umich. edu, port 3000; or wind.atmos.uah.edu, port 3000.

- **Web** The most commonly used name for the *World Wide Web*, an interlinked collection of **hypertext** documents (**Web pages**) residing on **Web server**s and other documents, menus, and databases, available via **URLs** (uniform resource locators). Web documents are marked for formatting and linking with **HTML** (hypertext markup language), and Web servers use **HTTP** (hypertext transport protocol) to deliver Web pages.

  The Web was invented as an online documentation resource by physicists at the **CERN European Particle Physics Laboratory** in Switzerland.

- **Web address** A URL, consisting of a protocol, a **host name**, a **path**, and a file name. In the address of my **home page**, http://enterzone.berkeley.edu/homies/xian. html, the protocol is **HTTP**, the host name is enterzone.berkeley.edu, the path is /homies/ and the file name is xian.html.

- **Web browser** Client software for the World Wide Web, such as **www**, **lynx**, **Mosaic**, or **Netscape**. A Web browser displays **HTML** and other documents, and allows the user to follow **hypertext link**s.

- **Web page** An HTML document on the World Wide Web, usually containing **hypertext link**s to other documents on the Web, often on other **Web server**s entirely. Surfing the Web consists of following links from page to page.

- **Web server** An application that stores **Web page**s and associated files, databases, and **script**s, and serves up the pages to **Web browser**s, using **HTTP**.

- **weenie** 1. A luser; 2. A **hacker** deeply involved in a particular **operating system** (such as a **UNIX weenie**).

- **Weenix** A derogatory name for **UNIX**. *See also* **UNIX weenie**.

- **The WELL (Whole Earth 'Lectronic Link)** [service provider] info@well.sf. ca.us, (415) 332-4335.

- **well-connected** Said of a network with dependable e-mail links and a relatively full **newsfeed**.

- **West Texas Free-Net** [service provider] timelwell@delphi.com, (915) 655-7161.

  See also **free-net**.

- **Westnet** [service provider] pburns@yuma.acns.colostate.edu.

- **wetware** Also *liveware*, slang for human beings, seen as part of a greater computer system including **software** and **hardware**.

- **whatis** An **archie** command that looks for key **word**s in a software-description database containing file names and associated descriptions, used to find key words to search for.

■ **wheel** (n) A privileged user, someone with unrestricted access to some particular system resource.

See also **root, superuser**.

■ **whitehouse.gov** The **domain** of the executive branch of the U.S. government. The White House **Web server** is at http://www.whitehouse.gov/ (see figure). Send e-mail to the president at president@whitehouse.gov or the vice president at vice.president@whitehouse.gov.

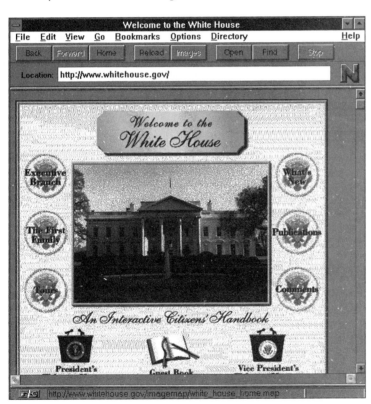

whitehouse.gov

■ **white pages** Informal name for databases of Internet e-mail addresses or other information. For example, **telnet** to wp.psi.net and log in as *fred*.

See also **Knowbot, Netfind, whois**.

■ **whois** One of many online databases of Internet e-mail addresses and other identifying information about users, **admin**s, **domain**s, and so on; 2. The **UNIX** command that draws on the whois resource.

■ **Whole Earth 'Lectronic Link**
See **The WELL**.

■ **who owns the Internet**? A perpetual question on the **Net**. The answer is no one in particular. All the hardware that composes the Net is owned by various people; the Internet itself, taken as an electronic space, belongs to its users.

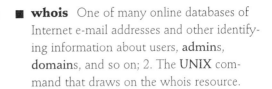

■ **WIBNI** (written only, also *wibni*) *Wouldn't it be nice if.*

■ **Wide Area Information Server**
See **WAIS**.

■ **wide area network**
See **WAN**.

■ **wildcard** A special character used to represent either any single character or any number of characters. Usual wildcard characters are ? (for single characters) and * (for any number of characters).

■ **WIMP** (adj) From *Window, Icon, Menu, Pointing device*, said of a **graphical user interface** such as **Macintosh**, **Windows**, or **X Window** (possibly pejorative).

■ **WinCIM** *CompuServe Information Manager for Windows.*

■ **Windows** Short for *Microsoft Windows*, a multitasking **operating environment** that runs on top of **MS-DOS** and provides **IBM** PCs and compatibles with a **GUI** (graphical user interface) not unlike that of the **Macintosh**, including icons, dialog boxes, menus, and a mouse pointer.

See also Windows 95, Windoze.

■ **Windows 95** The upcoming version of Windows (formerly known as *Chicago*). It is rumored to include **TCP/IP** support as well as direct access to **Microsoft Network**, which itself will include full access to the Internet (including the **Web**).

■ **Windows NT** A 32-bit **operating system** based on the **Windows** operating environment with built-in networking capabilities and no remaining traces of **DOS**.

■ **Windows socket** The conventional method of configuring the **Windows** operating environment for **TCP/IP** networking.

See also socket, Winsock.

■ **Windows for Workgroups** A version of **Windows** with built-in **peer-to-peer** networking capabilities.

■ **Windoze** A derogatory term for **Windows**, referring to its legendary slowness.

■ **WinGopher** A gopher client for Windows.

■ **winkey** A winking smiley:

    ;-)

■ **Winqvt/Net** Combined mail, news, telnet, and FTP software for **Windows**.

Available via **anonymous FTP** from wuarchive.wustl.edu.

■ **Winsock** A type of **Windows** application that sets up a **socket** and works with **TCP/IP protocol**s to establish an Internet connection.

■ **WinTrump**

See Trumpet for Windows.

■ **WinVN** A newsreader for Windows based on the **UNIX vn** newsreader that communicates with **Network News Transfer Protocol**-based news servers, available via **anonymous FTP** from titan.ksc.nasa.gov.

■ **WinWAIS** A Windows **WAIS client** program, available via **anonymous FTP** from ridgisd.er.usgs.gov.

■ **WinWeb** A **Web browser** for Windows, created by EINET, and available via **anonymous FTP** from ftp.einet.net in the /einet/pc/winweb directory.

See also MacWeb.

■ **WinZip** A Windows **compression** file that can handle **pkzip** and other compression formats.

■ **Wired**

See HotWired.

■ **WiscNet** [Wisconsin **service provider**] dorl@macc.wisc.edu.

■ **wizard** Someone who really understands how a piece of hardware or software works and is willing to help **newbies**; 2. By extension, any expert, as in the alt.sex.wizards newsgroup.

See also UNIX wizard.

■ **Wizvax Communication**
[service provider] info@wizvax.com,
(518) 271-0049.

■ **word wrap** The property most word
processors but not all **text editor**s have of
automatically starting new lines to fit into a
window or onto a page.

■ **workaround** A temporary **patch** for a
bug that avoids but does not fix the underlying problem.

■ **workgroup** A group of users, often on a
LAN, working on the same project.

■ **working directory** The current **directory,** the directory you're "in" right now.

■ **workstation** A computer on a network,
usually of a type somewhere in the range
between **microcomputer**s and **minicomputer**s.

■ **world** The default distribution choice for
newsgroup posts. Post distribution can also
be limited to geographical areas (by their
two-letter abbreviations) or to *local.*

■ **The World—Public
Access UNIX**
[service provider]
office@world.std.com,
(617) 739-0202.

■ **WorldWide Access**
[service provider] info@
wwa.com, (708) 367-1870.

■ **World Wide Web** Also
called the *Web, WWW, W3,*
and *w³,* an interlinked collection of **hypertext** documents
(Web pages) residing on
Web servers and other

documents, menus, and databases, available
via **URL**s (uniform resource locators). Web
documents are marked for formatting and
linking with **HTML** (hypertext markup language), and Web servers use **HTTP** (hypertext transport protocol) to deliver Web
pages. (See illustration below.)

The Web was invented as an online documentation resource by physicists at the
**CERN European Particle Physics Labora-
tory** in Switzerland.

■ **worm** A program that duplicates itself
repeatedly, potentially worming its way
through an entire network.

See also **Great Worm, Trojan horse,** virus.

■ **Worth County-Sylvester Ga. Free-
Net** [service provider] guske@
freenet.fsu.edu, (912) 776-8625.

See also **free-net.**

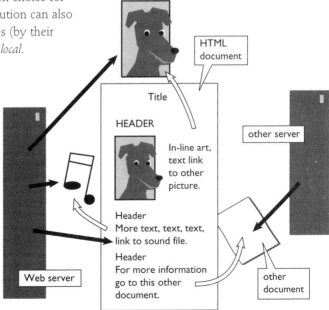

World Wide Web

■ **:wq** The *save and quit* command in **vi**, often seen at the end of **newbies' posts** when they fail to switch back from insert mode to edit mode before typing the command.

■ **write** To save, to copy the contents of **memory** onto a storage medium such as a disk.

See also **read**.

■ **Wrong Thing** An action that's clearly incorrect, not the **Right Thing**.

See also **Bad Thing**, **Good Thing**.

■ **wrt** (written only, also *WRT*) *With respect to.*

■ **WS_FTP** A Windows FTP client program made by John A. Junod, available via **anonymous FTP** from 129.29.64.246 in the /pub/msdos directory (see figure).

■ **WSArchie** A Windows archie client.

■ **WSIRC** A Windows IRC client.

■ **w³** (Also *W3*.)

See **World Wide Web**.

■ **wumpus** A game, originally written in BASIC, in which the user hunts a monster called the Wumpus, in a sort of maze of rooms containing various hazards. Depending on how near the Wumpus is, the user can hear, smell, or see it, and the user has "crooked" arrows with which to shoot through up to three connected rooms.

See also **nethack**, **Rogue**.

■ **wustl archives** A huge FTP archive at wuarchive.wustl.edu.

■ **WVnet** [West Virginia **service provider**] cc011041@wvnvms.wvnet.edu, (304) 293-5192.

■ **www** The original text-based UNIX Web browser, developed at CERN European Particle Physics Laboratory (see figure on opposite page). To try out www (if it's not installed on your system), **telnet** to info.cern.ch.

■ **WWW** Abbreviation for **World Wide Web**.

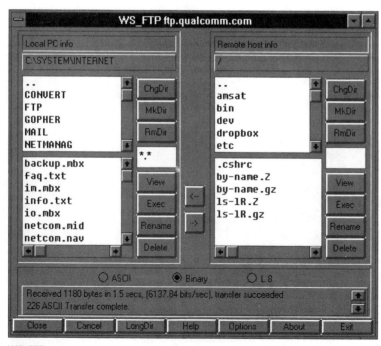

WS_FTP

```
                                    Welcome to the World-Wide Web
                   THE WORLD-WIDE WEB

This is just one of many access points to the web, the universe of
information available over networks. To follow references, just type the
number then hit the return (enter) key.

The features you have by connecting to this telnet server are very primitive
compared to the features you have when you run a W3 "client" program on your
own computer.  If you possibly can, please pick up a client for your
platform to reduce the load on this service and experience the web in its
full splendor.

For more information, select by number:

    A list of available W3 client programs[1]

    Everything about the W3 project[2]

    Places to start exploring[3]

Have fun!
1-3, <RETURN> for more, Quit, or Help: █
```

www

■ **WWW Browser for the Macintosh**
A Macintosh Web browser available via
anonymous FTP from info.cern.ch.

■ **www.whitehouse.gov**　The White
House Web server.

■ **WYSIAYG** (*whizzy-egg*) *What you see is all you get,* a pejorative phrase for the limitations and unhackability of some **GUI** software.

■ **WYSIWYG**
(*whizzy-wig*) *What you see is what you get,* a description of display technology (as in GUIs) that closely matches printed output on the screen, or claims to.

■ **Wyvern Technologies, Inc.**
[service provider] system@wyvern.com,
(804) 622-4289.

A
B
C
D
E
F
G
H
I
J
K
L
M
N
O
P
Q
R
S
T
U
V
W
X
Y
Z

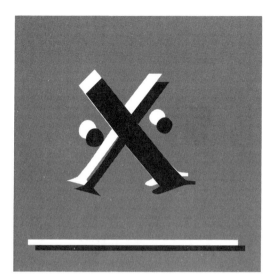

- **x** The **exit** command in many **UNIX** programs.

- **.x** The **extension** for SuperDisk **self-extracting archive** files and More DiskSpace **compress**ed files.

- **X**

  See X Window.

- **X Consortium** A group of hardware developers that oversees the **X Window** standard.

- **Xerox Network System (XNS)** A suite of communications **protocol**s, similar to TCP/IP, developed by Xerox Corporation and later used by Novell and other network developers.

- **Xerox PARC** Xerox's legendary Palo Alto Research Center, where the modern **GUI** (which combines the use of a mouse, windows, and icons) was invented, not to mention laser printers and **LAN**s.

- **X.500** A CCITT- and ISO-recommended standard for electronic directory services, using a distributed database of **X.400** information, including **username**s, postal addresses, telephone numbers, fax numbers, and so on.

  See also **Knowbot**.

- **X.400** A CCITT and ISO standard for international **e-mail** handling. X.400 is different from Internet e-mail standards, but mail can be transferred from one system to the other via **gateway**s.

- **XGopher** X Window gopher client software, available via **anonymous FTP** from boombox.micro.umn.edu.

- **Xibo** The evil anti-Kibo. This unfortunate devil has many fewer adherents than his nemesis.

- **XLibrary for the Macintosh** Macintosh software for designing **SLIP front end**s to network services, available via **anonymous FTP** from sumex-aim.stanford.edu.

- **Xmodem** A file-transfer **protocol** supported by just about every communications program. Xmodem sends 128-byte **block**s and is used for **upload**ing and **download**ing to and from **dial-up** Internet accounts and **BBS**s.

  See also **Kermit, Ymodem, Zmodem**.

- **Xmodem-CRC** An extension of Xmodem using more stringent error-checking (called a *cyclical redundancy check*).

- **Xmodem 1K**

  See **Ymodem**.

■ **XNet Information Systems** [service provider] info@xnet.com, (708) 983-6064.

■ **XNS**

See Xerox Network System.

■ **XOFF** Ctrl-S (ASCII 19), a character that pauses data transmission.

■ **XON** Ctrl-Q (ASCII 17), a character that resumes data transmission.

■ **XON/XOFF** A form of **flow control,** using **ASCII** characters 17 and 19 to control the flow of data over an **asynchronous** connection, usually one of the choices for configuring a **modem** to connect to a **dial-up** service.

See also **handshaking, hardware flow control.**

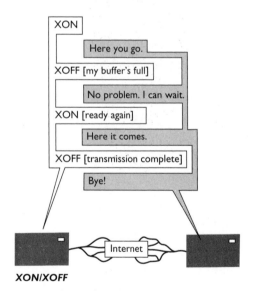

XON/XOFF

■ **XOR** [Boolean operator] *Exclusive or.* A text **search** with XOR between two words matches any documents containing one word or the other, but not both.

■ **XRemote** X Window software for connecting to a network over phone lines.

■ **XT**

See **crosstalk.**

■ **X.25** A CCITT-recommended standard for connecting computers to public **packet-switched networks** that specifies transmission and error-correction **protocols,** now largely superseded by **frame relay.**

■ **XWAIS** X Window WAIS client software available via **anonymous FTP** from sunsite.unc.edu.

■ **X Window** Also called *X,* an **open,** nonproprietary **graphical user interface** often used with **UNIX.** It was developed at MIT and is independent of the **hardware** or **operating system** it runs on. It's easy to find Internet **client** software for X Window. There are implementations of X called Motif and OpenLook.

- **YA-** (written only, also *ya-*) *Yet another...*

- **YAA** (written only, also *yaa*) *Yet another acronym.*

- **YABA** (written only, also *yaba*) *Yet another bloody acronym.*

- **YAFIYGI** (*yaffy-yiggy*, also written *yafiygi*) *You asked for it, you got it,* applied to certain forms of word-processing and desktop publishing applications in which the user gets no preview of the eventual appearance of the document (the opposite of **WYSIWYG**).

- **Yanoff's Internet Services List** A thorough and frequently updated list of Internet services, maintained by Scott Yanoff of the University of Wisconsin. It's available via **anonymous FTP** from csd4.csd.uwm.edu in the /pub directory, with the file name inet.services.txt. It's also **post**ed regularly to alt.bbs.internet.

- **YAUN** (*yawn*, also written *yaun*) *Yet another UNIX nerd.*

YAUN

- **yellow pages** 1. An informal name for the database of machine names and addresses of the **InterNIC** Registration Service; 2. An informal name for the security and file-access database of a **UNIX** system.

A
B
C
D
E
F
G
H
I
J
K
L
M
N
O
P
Q
R
S
T
U
V
W
X
Y
Z

■ **YHBT** (written only) *You have been trolled.*

■ **YHBT. YHL. HAND.** (written only) *You have been trolled. You have lost. Have a nice day.*

■ **YHL** (written only) *You have lost.*

■ **YMMV** (written only, also *ymmv*) *Your mileage may vary* (used metaphorically).

YMMV

■ **Ymodem** Also called *Xmodem 1K*, a file-transfer **protocol** supported by many communications programs. Ymodem sends 1024-byte **blocks**, is faster than **Xmodem**, and can send multiple files.

See also **Kermit**, **Zmodem**.

■ **You misspelled...** A form of silly **follow-up post** favored by kibologists (followers of **kibology**), in which the original **poster** is accused of spelling some entirely different word from the one obviously intended, but perhaps what the poster meant or should have meant.

See also **troll**.

■ **Youngstown Free-Net** [service provider] lou@yfn.ysu.edu, (216) 742-3075.

See also **free-net**.

■ **YP**

See **yellow pages**.

■ **YR** (written only, also *yr*) *Yeah, right.*

■ **.z** A file **extension** indicating a file that has been **compress**ed with **GNU** Zip.

■ **.Z** A file **extension** indicating a file that has been **compress**ed with the **UNIX** com-press program.

■ *Zen and the Art of the Internet*
Brendan Kehoe's excellent Internet primer, available as a paper book from Prentice Hall and online from many **FTP** and **gopher** sites (try an **archie** or **Veronica** search), including via **anonymous FTP** from ftp.cs.widener.edu in the directory pub/zen.

■ **'zine** Also *zine*, a **fanzine** or other under-ground publication, possibly produced on company time or using office equipment. Most 'zines are still produced on paper and mailed to subscribers, but many are archived on the Internet, and there are also some **e-zine**s, electronic 'zines distributed by **e-mail**, by **gopher**, or on the **Web**.
See also **e-text**.

■ **zip** (v) To **compress** a file with **pkzip** or another program.
(n) A **compression** program.

■ **.zip** A file **extension** indicating that the file has been **compress**ed with the pro-grams **pkzip**, **zip**, or **WinZip**.

■ **ZIP**
See Zone Information Protocol.

■ **zip codes** U.S. postal zip codes as of 1991 can be found via **anonymous FTP** from oes.orst.edu in the /pub/almanac/misc directory with the file name zipcode.txt.Z.

■ **zip file** A **compress**ed file.

■ **zip up** (v) To **compress** a file with **pkzip** or another program.

■ **ZIT**
See Zone Information Table.

■ **Zmodem** A batch file-transfer **protocol** supported by some communications pro-grams. Zmodem is faster than **Ymodem** and **Xmodem** and recovers from disconnec-tions more gracefully.
See also **Kermit**.

■ **zone** (n) A **logical** (as opposed to physical) group of users on a **LAN**, such as an AppleTalk network, within a larger group of interconnected networks.

■ **Zone Information Protocol (ZIP)** The protocol AppleTalk **router**s use to exchange **zone name**s and network numbers.

■ **Zone Information Table (ZIT)** A list of **zone name**s and corresponding network numbers used by AppleTalk **router**s.

A
B
C
D
E
F
G
H
I
J
K
L
M
N
O
P
Q
R
S
T
U
V
W
X
Y
Z

■ **zone list** A list of AppleTalk zones in the Chooser.

■ **zone name** 1. The text name of a zone, corresponding to a network number; 2. The name of an AppleTalk network zone.

■ **.zoo** A file extension indicating a file compressed with the zoo210 program.

■ **zoo210** A UNIX file compression program.

■ **Zork** A text adventure first written in the late '70s and distributed with BSD UNIX, also ported as *Dungeon*. Now sold in a commercial form as the *Zork Trilogy*.

■ **zorkmid** A unit of currency used in many computer games, originally from **Zork**.

■ **Zterm** A Macintosh communications and **terminal emulation** application.

■ **Z39.50** The ANSI information-retrieval service definition and **protocol** specification for library applications, a format by which all Internet database information could potentially be made available.

■ **ZZ** A *quit and save* command in **vi**.

Zork

GET A FREE CATALOG JUST FOR EXPRESSING YOUR OPINION.

Help us improve our books and get a *FREE* full-color catalog in the bargain. Please complete this form, pull out this page and send it in today. The address is on the reverse side.

Name _____   Company _____

Address _____   City _____ State ____ Zip _____

Phone (____) _____

1. How would you rate the overall quality of this book?

- ❏ Excellent
- ❏ Very Good
- ❏ Good
- ❏ Fair
- ❏ Below Average
- ❏ Poor

2. What were the things you liked most about the book? (Check all that apply)

- ❏ Pace
- ❏ Format
- ❏ Writing Style
- ❏ Examples
- ❏ Table of Contents
- ❏ Index
- ❏ Price
- ❏ Illustrations
- ❏ Type Style
- ❏ Cover
- ❏ Depth of Coverage
- ❏ Fast Track Notes

3. What were the things you liked *least* about the book? (Check all that apply)

- ❏ Pace
- ❏ Format
- ❏ Writing Style
- ❏ Examples
- ❏ Table of Contents
- ❏ Index
- ❏ Price
- ❏ Illustrations
- ❏ Type Style
- ❏ Cover
- ❏ Depth of Coverage
- ❏ Fast Track Notes

4. Where did you buy this book?

- ❏ Bookstore chain
- ❏ Small independent bookstore
- ❏ Computer store
- ❏ Wholesale club
- ❏ College bookstore
- ❏ Technical bookstore
- ❏ Other _____

5. How did you decide to buy this particular book?

- ❏ Recommended by friend
- ❏ Recommended by store personnel
- ❏ Author's reputation
- ❏ Sybex's reputation
- ❏ Read book review in _____
- ❏ Other _____

6. How did you pay for this book?

- ❏ Used own funds
- ❏ Reimbursed by company
- ❏ Received book as a gift

7. What is your level of experience with the subject covered in this book?

- ❏ Beginner
- ❏ Intermediate
- ❏ Advanced

8. How long have you been using a computer?

years _____

months _____

9. Where do you most often use your computer?

- ❏ Home
- ❏ Work

- ❏ Both
- ❏ Other _____

10. What kind of computer equipment do you have? (Check all that apply)

- ❏ PC Compatible Desktop Computer
- ❏ PC Compatible Laptop Computer
- ❏ Apple/Mac Computer
- ❏ Apple/Mac Laptop Computer
- ❏ CD ROM
- ❏ Fax Modem
- ❏ Data Modem
- ❏ Scanner
- ❏ Sound Card
- ❏ Other _____

11. What other kinds of software packages do you ordinarily use?

- ❏ Accounting
- ❏ Databases
- ❏ Networks
- ❏ Apple/Mac
- ❏ Desktop Publishing
- ❏ Spreadsheets
- ❏ CAD
- ❏ Games
- ❏ Word Processing
- ❏ Communications
- ❏ Money Management
- ❏ Other _____

12. What operating systems do you ordinarily use?

- ❏ DOS
- ❏ OS/2
- ❏ Windows
- ❏ Apple/Mac
- ❏ Windows NT
- ❏ Other _____

13. On what computer-related subject(s) would you like to see more books?

_____

_____

_____

_____

14. Do you have any other comments about this book? (Please feel free to use a separate piece of paper if you need more room)

_____

_____

_____

_____

- - - - - - - - - - - PLEASE FOLD, SEAL, AND MAIL TO SYBEX - - - - - - - - - - - -

SYBEX INC.
Department M
2021 Challenger Drive
Alameda, CA
94501

Let us hear from you.

 **T** alk to SYBEX authors, editors and fellow forum members.

G et tips, hints and advice online.

D ownload magazine articles, book art, and shareware.

Join the SYBEX Forum on CompuServe®

If you're already a CompuServe user, just type **GO SYBEX** to join the SYBEX Forum. If not, try CompuServe for free by calling 1-800-848-8199 and ask for Representative 560. You'll get one free month of basic service and a $15 credit for CompuServe extended services—a $23.95 value. Your personal ID number and password will be activated when you sign up.

Join us online today. Type **GO SYBEX** on CompuServe.
If you're not a CompuServe member, call Representative 560
at **1-800-848-8199** .

SYBEX

(outside U.S./Canada call 614-457-0802)

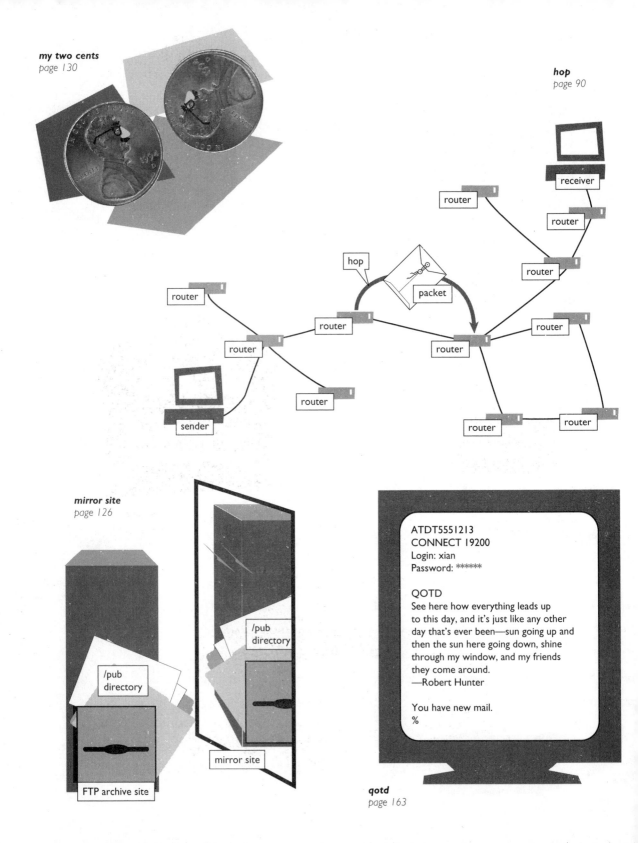

receiver

router

router

router

hop

packet

router

router

router

router

router

router

sender

router

/pub directory

/pub directory

mirror site

FTP archive site

ATDT5551213
CONNECT 19200
Login: xian
Password: *****

QOTD
See here how everything leads up
to this day, and it's just like any other
day that's ever been—sun going up and
then the sun here going down, shine
through my window, and my friends
they come around.
—Robert Hunter

You have new mail.
%